Fodor's Toronto

Toronto

Allan Gould

Y0-CAV-169

Fodor's Travel Publications, Inc.
New York • Toronto • London • Sydney • Auckland

ISBN 0–679–02350–X

Fodor's Toronto

Editor: Jillian L. Magalaner
Editorial Contributors: Mary Adachi, Caroline Liou, Marcy Pritchard
Creative Director: Fabrizio La Rocca
Cartographer: David Lindroth
Illustrator: Karl Tanner
Cover Photograph: Bob Krist
Design: Vignelli Associates

About the Author

Allan Gould has written 18 books, including an earlier guide to his chosen city, *The Toronto Book*, as well as critically acclaimed biographies of Canadian businesspeople *(The New Entrepreneurs: 75 Canadian Success Stories)* and an award-winning study of the Stratford Festival, coauthored with its founder, Tom Patterson *(First Stage: The Making of the Stratford Festival)*. Gould has taught theater history and the humanities at York University, the University of Toronto, and the Ontario College of Art. He writes for many Canadian magazines and has both written and performed political satire and biographical sketches for radio and TV. He has lived in Toronto with his wife, son, and daughter since 1968.

Special Sales

Fodor's Travel Publications are available at special discounts for bulk purchases (100 copies or more) for sales promotions or premiums. Special editions, including personalized covers, excerpts of existing guides, and corporate imprints, can be created in large quantities for special needs. For more information write to Special Marketing, Fodor's Travel Publications, 201 East 50th St., New York, NY 10022. Inquiries from Canada should be sent to Random House of Canada, Ltd., Marketing Department, 1265 Aerowood Dr., Mississauga, Ontario L4W 1B9. Inquiries from the United Kingdom should be sent to Fodor's Travel Publications, 20 Vauxhall Bridge Rd., London, England SW1V 2SA.

Contents

Foreword

The publishers thank Steve Johnson of the Metropolitan Toronto Convention and Visitors Association for all his help in gathering information for this book. The author thanks James Marck of *Now* magazine for his generous help with nightclubs, bars, jazz, and other nightlife entries; Larry Leblanc for his radio insights; Annette Poizner for her work on the Nightlife chapter; Sandra Bernstein for hers on the Shopping chapter; the author's wife, Merle, for all her help and patience; and his children, Judah and Elisheva, for enjoying Toronto with him.

While every care has been taken to ensure the accuracy of the information on this guide, the passage of time will always bring change, and consequently, the publisher cannot accept responsibility for errors that may occur.

All prices and opening times quoted here are based on information supplied to us at press time. Hours and admission fees may change, however, and the prudent traveler will avoid inconvenience by calling ahead.

Fodor's wants to hear about your travel experiences, both pleasant and unpleasant. When a hotel or restaurant fails to live up to its billing, let us know and we will investigate the complaint and revise our entries where the facts warrant it.

Send your letter to the editors of Fodor's Travel Publications, 201 E. 50th Street, New York, NY 10022.

Highlights and Fodor's Choice

Highlights

As we progress slowly and unsurely into the last decade of this century—the recession of 1990–92 hit this city exceedingly hard—Toronto continues to be Canada's version of New York City: in wealth, poverty (and extremes of both), costly housing, horrendous traffic jams, sports, communications, industry, theater, and film.

The most exciting cultural news to hit Toronto in several years is the projected opening of two major new theaters in 1993.

The $45 million **North York Performing Arts Centre,** scheduled to open in the fall or summer of 1993, will be located in the suburban city of North York, just a 20-minute drive up Yonge Street from midtown Toronto. The complex will house a 1,850-seat theater, a 1,025-seat recital hall, a 250-seat studio, and a two-story, 5,000-square-foot art gallery. Garth Drabinsky, the arts entrepreneur—who created and later lost the Cineplex movie-house empire and who now runs the Pantages Theatre—will be in charge of the complex. There are plans to stage a Broadway-bound, Hal Prince-directed musical, *Show Boat,* at the center in November 1993, an extravaganza not to be missed.

Even more extraordinary, Ed and David Mirvish, the brilliant owners/operators of the Royal Alexandra Theatre, are building (from scratch) a 2,000-seat theater, right across the street from the Alex, their beautiful, antique, jewel box of a theater, and their many restaurants; they plan to open in May 1993 with *Miss Saigon,* the international monster hit created by the same French fellows who gave us *Les Miserables.* Top price for tickets will be $91, and the popular musical drama is expected to run to the end of this century. Plan ahead to buy tickets, of course; this is Big Culture, Big Business, and a Big Headache for anyone who has to drive along King Street, between University and Spadina avenues, for the next several decades.

The magnificently refurbished 1920ish **Pantages Theatre,** as well as the once-vaudevilled **Elgin** and **Winter Garden theatres** (the latter two stacked upon each other), all recently opened to rave reviews, if only for the buildings. The former is showing the worldwide-hit musical *Phantom of the Opera,* which should continue its run well into the mid-'90s. The other two theaters—no less beautiful to behold and to enjoy performances in—tend toward road shows of musicals, dramas, comedies, and concerts, with the Elgin Theatre showing Andrew Lloyd Weber's latest, *Aspects of Love.* Plan way ahead for tickets.

People who work in or who avail themselves of the services of **Pearson International Airport,** just northwest of downtown, have been breathing sighs of relief ever since the February 1991 opening of its third terminal, relieving Terminals 1 and 2 of their incredible volume. Its primary tenant, **Canadian Airlines International,** is one of Canada's two major carriers; Terminal 2, the home of Air Canada, the country's other primary flight operator, has concluded a two-year-long, $50 million-plus face-lift. It's still an unpleasant airport, and there have been a lot of complaints about such things as the high cost of cabs to the newest terminal, but at least the miserable overcrowding is a thing of the past.

There is more airline news, much of it known to North Americans already: Midway Airlines of Chicago is no longer with us, nor is Eastern. And Torontonians are still mourning the loss of City Express, their own little version of the late, lamented People's Express of the United States. Furthermore, throughout the past few years struggles have been going on between Canada and the United States over which country gets to fly where. In other words, will U.S. companies get the right to fly *between* Canadian cities? And vice versa? If the two countries work out their differences, there could be a lot more choices, and potentially lower prices, for Canadians, and possibly even Americans. Still, it's nice to see Alaska Airlines fly in and out of Toronto from Los Angeles and San Francisco.

The **Underground City** was completed in late 1990. Pedestrians can now walk in a continuous path from Union Station on Front Street (near the Lake Ontario waterfront) all the way north to Dundas and Yonge streets, enjoying more than 1,000 stores and services, without ever having to brave the sometimes-brutal elements. The seemingly endless underground mall is 11 kilometers (7 miles) long, making it the longest in North America.

In 1993 Torontonians are finally celebrating the two towers of **BCE Place**—BC refers to Bell Canada—one at Bay and Front streets, the other on Wellington Street. Canada's five largest banks and two biggest trust companies (Canada Trust and Royal Trust) will be doing business in these two major new additions to the skyline. The beautiful 1885 **Bank of Montreal,** standing majestically at the northwest corner of Front and Yonge streets, is being restored and will be incorporated into one of the new, modern towers, as the new home of the Hockey Hall of Fame. Be sure to go inside and enjoy its exquisite, huge main-floor Galleria.

Begun in late 1988 but not completed until 1992 is the $380 million Toronto headquarters for the **Canadian Broadcasting Corporation.** The $1 billion complex on a 9.3-acre gravel parking lot next door to Roy Thomson Hall—and just across from SkyDome—includes two office towers, a hotel, a retail plaza, and a condominium complex. This should destroy all driving within downtown Toronto, once and for all.

The entire year of 1992 has been a series of horror stories for the Canadian economy in general and the Toronto economy in particular. **Creed's,** this city's most glamorous, ritzy store, actually went belly-up in 1991, to the horror of its well-heeled patrons. **Simpson's,** a century-plus-old chain of department stores, has now been folded into (and under the name of) The Bay. And here's a *real* sign of the times: A massive, new, twin-towered building, the **Bay-Adelaide Centre,** which was to open by late 1992, was deliberately delayed for two full years, due to a decline in office demand.

A further attack on the country's economy has been the much-debated, much-hated new Goods and Services Tax (alias "the GST," or Grab and Soak Tax). Even though it has replaced quite a bit of other, previously hidden, federal taxes (e.g., Canadian car prices have actually dropped a bit), the impact on tourism to this country has been brutal. Furthermore, the GST not only applies to various services, such as that of barbers and lawyers, for the first time, but it also hits books, which has been devastating to the always-struggling publishing industry. Several firms have gone under in the last few months, with more teetering on the edge. Still, tourists need not be crushed by this new tax (or by the all-time-high 8% Ontario sales tax); just be sure to inquire about rebates on hotel bills and any major purchases. You could save quite a bit of money.

For more than a hundred years, Sunday has been an enforced day of rest for large Toronto stores, with exceptions made for movie houses (and these only since the '60s), and, more recently, "designated tourist areas" such as Harbourfront Centre, Mirvish Village, and Chinatown. Well, despite its vow to "Keep the Stores Closed on Sunday," and after wild fluctuations in opening policies in the early '90s, the socialist NDP (New Democratic Party) government in Ontario reluctantly gave in to pressure from tourist officials and store owners (who have been losing millions of dollars weekly from cross-border shoppers), and **agreed to allow all stores in Ontario to open on Sunday,** if the owners so wish. This means that Eaton Centre (the city's number one tourist attraction) will now be open seven days a week, along with large grocery stores, suburban malls, and pretty much everything else in Toronto. There are still plenty of hold-outs, but visitors to Toronto need no longer squish all their shopping into six days, or fear that, by arriving in the city on a Sunday, they are doomed to try out the Metro Toronto Zoo and Science Centre, but little else.

Welcome to the secular 20th century, Toronto!

By the way, a dubious honor: In mid-1991, it was announced for the second straight year that Toronto is the most expensive city in the Western Hemisphere, outstripping pricey locales like New York, Chicago, Los Angeles, and Lima, Peru. And its house prices remain dizzingly high, compared with those of nearly all U.S. cities, despite the fact that many prices have plummeted over the past couple of years, thanks to the Great Recession. But visitors will undoubtedly find many of Toronto's food and clothing costs quite reasonable.

Still, while Toronto is expensive for those who live here, it need not be oppressively so for visitors. One simple example: From late 1990 through the end of March 1991, American Express ran a Toronto Doubles Your Adventure program that gave 50% off double-occupancy rooms at nearly five dozen hotels. And there are countless other ways to save money while in this wonderful, clean, safe, exciting city. Indeed, a further survey, conducted by the Washington-based Population Crisis Committee, rated living standards in the world's largest cities and placed Toronto in the top 10. Most inhabitants would put it closer to number one.

Fodor's Choice

No two people will agree on what makes a perfect vacation, but it's fun and helpful to know what others think. We hope you'll have a chance to experience some of Fodor's Choices yourself while visiting Toronto. For detailed information about each entry, refer to the appropriate chapters within this guidebook.

Sights Worth at Least a Quick Look

Casa Loma
CN Tower
Metro Toronto Library
New City Hall
Roy Thomson Hall
Royal Bank Tower
SkyDome

Sights Worth Two Hours or More

Black Creek Pioneer Village
Eaton Centre
Harbourfront Centre
Metro Toronto Zoo
Ontario Place
Ontario Science Centre
Royal Ontario Museum

Sights Worth a Two-Hour Drive

African Lion Safari
Algonquin Park
Marineland and Niagara Falls

Parks

Bluffers Park and Cathedral Bluffs Park, Scarborough
High Park (including the zoo)
Leslie Street Spit
Riverdale Farm
Toronto Islands and Centreville

Shopping Areas

Eaton Centre
Hazelton Lanes and Yorkville
Kensington Market/Chinatown
Mirvish (or Markham) Village
Queen's Quay Terminal on Lake Ontario
Queen Street West

Theaters and Cultural Events

Canadian Opera Company at the O'Keefe
Concerts and symphonies at Roy Thomson Hall
National Ballet of Canada at the O'Keefe
Phantom of the Opera at the Pantages Theatre
Shaw Festival (Niagara-on-the-Lake)
Stratford Festival
Theater at the Royal Alexandra
Theater at the St. Lawrence Centre

Seasonal Events

Caravan (June)
Caribana (July)
Canadian National Exhibition (August/September)
Festival of Festivals (September)
Harbourfront Reading Series (late October–November)
Royal Agricultural Winter Fair (November)

Drives

Cabbagetown
Forest Hill
Rosedale
Toronto Islands (by bike; cars not allowed!)

Hotels

The Four Seasons Toronto *(Very Expensive)*
The Harbour Castle Westin *(Very Expensive)*
King Edward Hotel *(Very Expensive)*
Sutton Place Hotel *(Very Expensive)*
Royal York *(Expensive)*
Sheraton Centre *(Expensive)*
Novotel Toronto Centre *(Moderate)*
Journey's End Suites *(Inexpensive)*

Restaurants

Centro *(Expensive)*
La Fenice *(Expensive)*
Le Bistingo *(Expensive)*
North 44 *(Expensive)*
Splendido *(Very Expensive)*
Thai Magic *(Moderate–Expensive)*
Avocado Club *(Moderate)*
BamBoo *(Moderate)*
Kensington Kitchen *(Moderate)*
Southern Accent *(Moderate)*
Pearl Court *(Inexpensive)*
Santa Fe Bar & Grill *(Inexpensive)*
United Bakers *(Inexpensive)*

Lake Muskoka

169

62

41

O N T A R I O

Orilla

7

N

Hawartha Lakes

QEW

Lake
Simcoe

Barrie

400

Peterborough

Belleville

Newmarket

Lake
Scugog

28

Rice Lake

Trenton

9

11

QEW

2

Oshawa

Lake Ontario

TORONTO

Brampton

401

Mississauga

QEW

Burlington

Hamilton

St.
Catharines

Erie Canal

Rochester

QEW

90

490

Niagara Falls, N.Y.

Niagara
Falls, Ont.

190

90

3

Welland

Buffalo

Port
Claiborne

390

N E W   Y O R K

90

17

17

P E N N S Y L V A N I A

Bathurst St.

Yonge St.

Finch East Park

Don Mills Rd.

Don Valley Pkwy.

Pharmacy Ave.

Finch Ave W.

Finch Ave. E.

Finch Ave. E.

Metro Toronto Zoo →

(11)

Bayview Ave.

Sheppard Ave. E.

(404)

SCARBOROUGH

Earl Bales Park

(401)

York Mills Rd.

Ellesmere Ave.

Avenue Rd.

Leslie St.

Lawrence Ave. E.

Don Mills Rd.

Pkwy.

Wigmore Park

Victoria Park Ave.

Warden Ave.

Birchmount Rd.

Kennedy Rd.

Eglinton Ave. E.

Laird Dr.

Sunnybrook Park

Don Valley

Mount Pleasant Rd.

EAST YORK

Pharmacy Ave.

St. Clair Ave. E

Danforth Rd.

Bayview Ext.

O'Connor Dr.

Greenwood Ave.

Coxwell Ave.

Taylor Creek Park

Dawes Rd.

(404)

Broadview Ave.

Pape Ave.

TORONTO

Bloor St. E.

Woodbine Ave.

Gerrard St. E.

Parliament St.

Gerrard St. E.

(2)

Dundas St. E.

Leslie St. E.

Queen St. E.

Eastern Ave.

Lake Shore Blvd. E.

Ashbridges Bay Park

Harbourfront Park

Inner Harbour

N

Toronto Islands

Aquatic Park

Subway Lines

•••••••• Bloor Danforth Line
━━━━ Yonge-University Line
═══ Scarborough Rapid Transit
Ⓜ Subway stop
── Railroad lines

World Time Zones

MONDAY
SUNDAY

International Date Line

+12   +13   -9

-10

-11   -10

+11

+12

1

3

7

4

14 15
13
5   8   9
6   10   17 16
11
12   18

19   22

-5   -4

-5

-4   -3

20

23

21   24

-3

| +11 | +12 | -11 | -10 | -9 | -8 | -7 | -6 | -5 | -4 | -3 | -2 |

Numbers below vertical bands relate each zone to Greenwich Mean Time (0 hrs.).
Local times frequently differ from these general indications,
as indicated by light-face numbers on map.

Algiers, **29**	Berlin, **34**	Delhi, **48**	Istanbul, **40**
Anchorage, **3**	Bogotá, **19**	Denver, **8**	Jerusalem, **42**
Athens, **41**	Budapest, **37**	Djakarta, **53**	Johannesburg, **44**
Auckland, **1**	Buenos Aires, **24**	Dublin, **26**	Lima, **20**
Baghdad, **46**	Caracas, **22**	Edmonton, **7**	Lisbon, **28**
Bangkok, **50**	Chicago, **9**	Hong Kong, **56**	London (Greenwich), **27**
Beijing, **54**	Copenhagen, **33**	Honolulu, **2**	Los Angeles, **6**
	Dallas, **10**		Madrid, **38**
			Manila, **57**

Introduction

A joke popular in the neighboring province of Quebec between the wars went "First prize, one week in Toronto. Second prize, two weeks in Toronto. Third prize, three weeks in Toronto." And who could blame them for laughing? Toronto was a deadly city right into the 1950s, at which time its half-million citizens used to rush off to Detroit (a four-hour drive to the southwest) and Buffalo (90 minutes to the south, around Lake Ontario) for a good time. Today, of course, the rush is in the opposite direction, for hundreds of reasons that are sprinkled through this volume.

Yet, is not Toronto the city that American novelist John Dos Passos called "a beastly place" in his letter to a friend in 1907? And the city that the great British poet Rupert Brooke, during a visit in 1913, gave halfhearted, one-handed applause to, by writing that "the only depressing thing is that it will always be what it is, only larger"? The city that Ernest Hemingway, while honing his writing craft at *The Toronto Star* in the 1920s, could not wait to escape from, for fear of going mad with boredom?

Even as late as 1960, the witty Irish dramatist Brendan Behan was letting the city have it: "Toronto will be a fine town when it is finished." And in the words of Leopold Infeld, the Polish-born mathematical physicist who worked with Einstein: "It must be good to die in Toronto. The transition between life and death would be continuous, painless and scarcely noticeable in this silent town. I dreaded the Sundays and prayed to God that if he chose for me to die in Toronto he would let it be on a Saturday afternoon to save me from one more Toronto Sunday."

What on earth could have happened in so short a period? And why was no one surprised (in Toronto, at least) when various participants at the 1982 International Conference on Urban Design, in Toronto, ran around spouting such superlatives as "This is the most livable city in North America" and "It is an example of how a city could grow"?

Much of Toronto's excitement is explained by its ethnic diversity. Nearly two-thirds of the 3.2 million people who now live in the metropolitan Toronto area were born and raised somewhere else. And that somewhere else was often very far away.

Nearly 500,000 Italians make metropolitan Toronto one of the largest Italian communities outside of Italy. It is also the home of the largest Chinese community in Canada and the largest Portuguese community in North America. More than 120,000 Jews. Nearly as many Muslims. Tens of thousands of Germans. Greeks. Hungarians. East Indians.

West Indians. Vietnamese. Maltese. South Americans. Ukrainians. More than 70 ethnic groups in all, speaking over 100 different languages. Certainly, a city worthy of inviting the United Nations to consider moving here from Manhattan.

What this has meant to Toronto is the rather rapid creation of a vibrant mix of cultures that has echoes of turn-of-the-century New York City—but without the slums, crowding, disease, and tensions. Toronto undoubtedly would have had this, too, had Canada been decent and wise enough to open its gates wide back then, as the Yanks had. (This fact the city continues to bemoan and tried to atone for by accepting more "boat people" in the 1970s than any other country in the world. Yet, there are still tensions over large immigration to this very day.)

Still, to give to its burgeoning ethnic population all, or even most, of the credit for Toronto's becoming a cosmopolitan, world-class city in just a few decades would be a kind of reverse racism, and not totally correct, either. Much of the thanks must be given to the so-called dour Scots who set up the banks, built the churches, and created the kind of solid base for commerce, culture, and community that would come to such a healthy fruition in the three decades following World War II. Now a minority in the city they helped make, the much-maligned white Anglo-Saxon Protestants had their noses tweaked mercilessly in an issue of *Toronto*, the free monthly magazine that comes with the *Globe and Mail*. In the March 1988 edition, a writer noted that the city was about to hold its first St. Patrick's Day parade ever: "But Toronto—Toronto was for generations known as the Belfast of the North, a city so firmly in the grip of Protestants, Loyalists, and Royalists that a Roman Catholic celebration would have been unthinkable. Well, it's not anymore." In a subsequent issue (*see* Chapter 2, Portrait of Toronto) historian William Kilbourn added, "Once, Toronto the Good was embodied by the masters of the Orange Order: defenders of abstinence, Protestantism, and the British race." His closing words are striking: "My own childhood was pure British colonial . . . But I know I couldn't stand living in that kind of Toronto now. Instead, I think of my two Italian grandsons and my Chilean granddaughter, and of this city as a welcoming and exciting place for them, and I celebrate my non-WASP home."

The letters to the editor in the next issue of the magazine were scathing, with many of the WASPs who had built the city screaming (perhaps justifiably), "Racist!" And one might fairly ask, would Toronto be the decent place it is today had it not been for those harshly criticized white Protestants? Who opened the gates to foreigners, if not those same, now-outnumbered, supposedly boring sons and daughters of what was once the British Empire?

The city that once united Canadians from the Atlantic to the Pacific in a shared hatred of Toronto's sanctimoniousness and industriousness now tends to draw their collective envy at how well the place works. Other critics insist that Toronto remains too smug (well, yes); too regulated (would they prefer chaos?); too provincial (actually, it's municipal; Ontario is provincial); too prim and proper (would they rather be mugged?); too young (as a major city, perhaps, but it was hardly born yesterday).

We have to laugh with the Montrealers—a wildly different culture of primarily French-speaking Catholics—who joke that "Toronto is a city where people go around saying 'Thank God it's Monday.'" To this day, indeed, Torontonians seem to actually enjoy working, and they appear to lack the ability to enjoy themselves doing anything else. But with the prices of houses, who can afford not to work? And as for "having a good time," there have never been more fine restaurants, theaters, movie houses, concerts, and bars to enjoy oneself in—even on Sunday!

The city officially became Toronto on March 6, 1834, more than 150 years ago, but its roots go back to 1615. A Frenchman named Etienne Brûlé was sent into the not-yet-Canadian wilderness in 1610 by explorer Samuel de Champlain to see what he could discover. And he discovered plenty: the river and portage routes from the St. Lawrence to Lake Huron, possibly Lakes Superior and Michigan, and, eventually, Lake Ontario.

His discoveries surprised the local Indians, who had known about all these places for centuries and had long since named the area between the Humber and Don rivers Toronto, which is believed to mean "a place of meetings." (How prescient!) It was later a busy Indian village named Teiaiagon, a French trading post, a British town named York (if the British hadn't won the Seven Years' War in the late 1700s, you would be reading this in translation from the French), and finally the city we know today, once again bearing the original Indian name of Toronto.

The city had the usual history of colonial towns of the last century: It was invaded by the Americans in 1812; there were many Great Fires; there was a rebellion in 1837; and there was a slow but steady growth of (you guessed it) white Anglo-Saxon Protestants, from about 9,000 in the 1830s to nearly 500,000 before World War II, at which time they outnumbered the non-WASPs by five to two.

And now, as we've noted, it has somehow metamorphosed into a great world city. There are countless reasons why this has happened, and we have touched on but a few. Toronto is clearly this country's center of culture, commerce, and communications—"New York run by the Swiss," according to Peter Ustinov's marvelously witty description of the place—and this is partly by chance. For example, Mikhail Baryshnikov chose to defect from the Bolshoi in Toronto in 1974 and has returned frequently to work with its ballet corps.

But far more of Toronto's success can be credited to thoughtful and sensitive government actions, such as the limits that the city council set in the 1970s on the number and size of new buildings, and the decision by the Ontario government to put a stop to a major (Spadina) expressway, which would have slashed like a knife through many precious, long-standing neighborhoods. Toronto is a collection of little neighborhoods united by an enlightened metropolitan form of city government.

With occasional lapses, metropolitan Toronto has encouraged urban renewal, and many of the city's building projects have mixed low-rent housing with luxury condos, restaurants, offices, and businesses. Somehow, Toronto has managed to avoid the situation in many North American cities, where the middle class has fled to the suburbs, taking their taxes and children with them. On the contrary, one can see tens of thousands of young couples eagerly moving back to the same areas in the heart of the city where they grew up, and where they know that they will have fine schools for their kids and a healthy community to live in.

There are a growing number of problems, to be sure. In late 1988, there were 303 vacant apartments available to rent in Toronto, out of a total of 234,568—in other words, a vacancy rate of .1%. And in a single month in late 1988, the average house price shot up $30,000, making the average resale cost of a home in the metropolitan Toronto area a towering $250,000 and more. In other words, one has to be upper class anywhere else to live even lower middle class in Toronto. As of late 1992 the apartment market had eased up a bit and house prices had drifted down, but there's still no question that the city remains a very expensive place to live.

Toronto has gained the nickname "Hollywood North" because literally dozens of major films have been made in this city, especially over the past decade, from *The Black Stallion* to *Three Men and a Baby* and from David Cronenberg's *Dead Ringers* and *Naked Lunch* to such TV series as *Degrassi High, Night Heat,* and many more. Indeed, it is hard to walk about the city nowadays without tripping over a movie crew and a number of famous people. A story is still told about one particular film made in the downtown area in 1987. Since it was a crime movie set in New York City, street signs had to be put up and several tons of garbage trucked in and spread around the city street. After filming all morning, the cast took a lunch break. When they returned barely an hour later, all the garbage had been cleaned up!

That's Toronto, in a nutshell: Clean. Safe. Orderly. Yet somehow dynamic and exciting. Groucho Marx sang an old vaudeville tune back in 1967 that went "It's better to run to Toronta/Than to stay in a place you don't wanta." And he was right. But more than a quarter-century later, we can honestly change the words to "It's best that you run to Toronta/There's no better place that you'd wanta."

1 Essential Information

Before You Go

Government Tourist Offices

The best source of specific information on travel to Toronto is the **Metropolitan Toronto Convention and Visitors Association** (Queen's Quay Terminal, 207 Queen's Quay W, Suite 509, Box 126, Toronto, Ont. M5J 1A7, tel. 416/368–9821).

American and Canadian visitors can also contact the **Ministry of Ontario Tourism/Ontario Travel** (Queen's Park, Toronto, Ont. M7A 2E5, tel. 800/668–2746).

British travelers can visit or write to the **Ontario Ministry of Tourism and Recreation** (21 Knightsbridge, London SW1X 7LY, England, no phone).

Another excellent source of free information on Toronto and all aspects of travel to Canada is the **Canadian Consulate General** offices (ask for the tourism department):

United States 1 CNN Center, Suite 400, South Tower, Atlanta, GA 30303, tel. 404/577–6815; 3 Copley Pl., Suite 400, Boston, MA 02116, tel. 617/536–1730; 310 S. Michigan Ave., 12th floor, Chicago, IL 60604, tel. 312/427–1666; St. Paul Tower, 17th floor, 750 N. St. Paul St., Dallas, TX 75201, tel. 214/922–9815; 300 S. Grand Ave., Suite 1000, Los Angeles, CA 90071, tel. 213/687–7432; 701 Fourth Ave. S, Minneapolis, MN 55415, tel. 612/333–4641; Exxon Bldg., 16th floor, 1251 Avenue of the Americas, New York, NY 10020, tel. 212/586–2400; 1 Maritime Plaza, Suite 1160, Alcoa Bldg., San Francisco, CA 94111, tel. 415/981–8515; 1211 Connecticut Ave., Suite 300, Washington, DC 20036, tel. 202/223–9710.

United Kingdom **Canada House,** Trafalgar Sq., London SW1Y 5BJ, England, tel. 01/629–9492.

Tour Groups

When considering an escorted tour, be sure to find out (1) exactly what expenses are included (particularly tips, taxes, side trips, additional meals, and entertainment); (2) ratings of all hotels on the itinerary and the facilities they offer; (3) cancellation policies both for you and for the tour operator; and (4) what the single supplement is, should you be traveling alone. Most tour operators request that bookings be made through a travel agent—there is no additional charge for this.

General-Interest **Talmage Tours** (1223 Walnut St., Philadelphia, PA 19107, tel.
Tours 215/923–7100) has a five-day Niagara Falls–Toronto package. **Maupintour** (Box 807, Lawrence, KS 66044, tel. 913/843–1211 or 800/255–4266) offers a week-long Toronto–Montreal tour. **Globus-Gateway/Cosmos** (95–25 Queens Blvd., Rego Park, NY 11374, tel. 718/268–7000 or 800/221–0090) offers a two-week tour of Niagara Falls, Toronto, Ottowa, Montreal, Quebec City, Bar Harbour, Boston, and Newport. **Domenico Tours** (751 Broadway, Bayonne, NJ 07002, tel. 201/823–8687 or 800/554–TOUR) has a four-day tour of Toronto and Niagara Falls, as well as longer trips that take in more Canadian sights and cities. **Bixler Tours** (Box 37, Hiram, OH 44234, tel. 216/569–3222 or 800/325–5087) gives you eight days of touring in Toronto, Montreal, Ottawa, and Quebec City. **Tauck Tours** (11 Wilton

Rd., Westport, CT 06881, tel. 203/226–6911 or 800/468–2825)
travels from Montreal to Niagara Falls, stopping in Toronto
along the way. **Gadabout Tours** (700 E. Tahquitz Way, Palm
Springs, CA 92262, tel. 619/325–5556 or 800/952–5068) puts together an 18-day fall-foliage tour that begins with two nights in
Toronto and includes stops in Montreal and Quebec City. **Bren-
nan Tours** (1402 3rd Ave., Suite 717, Seattle, WA 98101–2118,
tel. 206/622–9155 or 800/237–7249) takes in the sights of Ontario and Quebec on a nine-day deluxe tour.

Package Deals for Independent Travelers

Air Canada (tel. 800/776–3000) has two-night packages with a
choice of hotels. The cost depends on the hotel rating.
SuperCities (7855 Haskell Ave., 3rd floor, Van Nuys, CA 91406,
tel. 818/988–7844 or 800/333–1234) offers two-, three-, and
four-night packages. **GoGo Tours** (69 Spring St., Ramsey, NJ
07446, tel. 201/934–3500) has three-night city packages, which
include a "Taste of Toronto Dine-A-Round" sightseeing tour
and rental car. Also check with **American Fly AAway Vacations**
(tel. 800/321–2121) and **United Airlines** (tel. 800/328–6877) for
packages.

When to Go

The weather can often fall below freezing from late November
into March and can be brutal in January and February (although the snowfalls are almost never heavy). That simple fact
alone could repel some visitors while attracting ski and skating
enthusiasts. Some of the best theater, ballet, opera, and concerts take place between September and May; both the Stratford and Shaw festivals, in venues each about a 90-minute drive
from Toronto, are in full swing from May to October.

There is no single time when the city is unbearably crowded, or
disappointingly empty, in the way that Paris, say, can be. But
it cannot be denied that Toronto is most pleasant to walk
around, and simply enjoy, from late spring through early fall,
when there are outdoor concerts and open-air dining—and the
entire city seems to come to life. On the other hand, many hotels drop their prices up to 50% in the off-season, particularly
in December and January.

Climate   Jokes about Canadian polar bears and igloos notwithstanding,
Toronto's climate is really not that harsh, except in December,
January, and February. Okay, and March as well. (And sometimes in late November.) Indeed, a look at a map of North
America will prove that the city is farther south than about a
dozen states and that Toronto is not in the so-called Snow Belt,
in which heavy and often savage storms paralyze cities such as
Detroit, Buffalo, Syracuse, and Rochester. Surprising as it
may seem—and as heartbreaking as it is to our ski-lift operators—prolonged snowfalls rarely come to the northern shores
of Lake Ontario, and many a December and January snowfall
soon melts away.

Furthermore, should you arrive during those often-bleak winter months, you will be pleased to discover that the city does
not come to a frozen halt with the first sign of a snowflake—or
even a snowstorm. Underground shopping concourses allow

one to walk through much of the downtown area and avoid the cold.

Spring can be brief, and a (hot) summer can last through much of June, July, and August, even September. And then come the gorgeous autumn colors—seen best just north of the city and throughout our myriad parks—along with more moderate and pleasant fall temperatures, before the much-cursed winter months come blasting and howling in again.

Lake Ontario often cools the city air in the summer and warms it in the winter. The airport, therefore, being some distance from the lake, will be warmer in the summer than downtown, and colder in the winter.

The following are average daily maximum and minimum temperatures for Toronto.

Jan.	30F	−1C	May	63F	17C	Sept.	69F	21C
	16	−9		44	7		51	11
Feb.	30F	−1C	June	73F	23C	Oct.	56F	13C
	15	−9		54	12		40	4
Mar.	37F	3C	July	79F	26C	Nov.	43F	6C
	23	−5		59	15		31	−1
Apr.	50F	10C	Aug.	77F	25C	Dec.	33F	1C
	34	1		58	14		21	−6

Current weather information for foreign and domestic cities may be obtained by calling The Weather Channel Connection at 900/WEATHER from a touch-tone phone. In addition to offering the weather report, The Weather Channel Connection gives local time, travel tips, and hurricane, foliage, and ski reports. The call costs 95¢ per minute.

National Holidays

Though banks, schools, and government offices close for national holidays, many stores remain open. As in the United States, the move has been to observe certain holidays on the Monday nearest to the actual date, making for a long weekend.

New Year's Day (January 1); Good Friday (April 9); Easter Monday (April 12); Victoria Day (May 24); Canada Day (July 1); Labor Day (September 6); Thanksgiving (October 11); Remembrance Day (November 11); Christmas (December 25); and Boxing Day (December 26).

Festivals and Seasonal Events

Top seasonal events in Toronto include the International Boat Show in January, the Toronto Sportsman's Show in March, Caravan celebrations in June, Caribana in July, the Festival of Festivals in September, and the city's New Year's Eve Party. For further details, contact the Metropolitan Toronto Convention and Visitors Association (*see* Government Tourist Offices, *above*).

Mid-Jan.: Toronto International Boat Show is held annually at Exhibition Place.
Late Jan.: Molson Export Ice Canoe Race and Barrel Jumping Contests take place at Harbourfront.

Late Feb.: C.D.F.A. Championship Dog Shows are at Exhibition Place.
Mid-Mar.: Toronto Sportsmen's Show is set up at Exhibition Place.
Late Mar.: Annual Springtime Craft Show and Sale is held at Exhibition Place.
Apr.–Oct.: African Lion Safari is open.
Mid-May: Stratford Festival Season opens in Stratford.
Apr.–Oct.: Toronto Blue Jays season at the SkyDome.
Mid-June: Metro Toronto International Caravan takes place throughout Toronto. This is a unique celebration of the city's ethnic communities.
Late-June: du Maurier Jazz Festival is in its eighth year. Previous years have attracted such jazz greats as Sarah Vaughan, Miles Davis, Dizzy Gillespie, and Branford Marsalis.
Early July: The **Mariposa Festival** takes place in Molson Park, about an hour drive north of Toronto. Bob Dylan and Gordon Lightfoot have appeared in past years.
Mid-July: Toronto Outdoor Art Exhibition is held in Nathan Phillips Square by the New City Hall.
July: Caribana is a Mardi Gras–like festival held by the West Indian communities, with over 500,000 visitors and a striking parade of some 5,000 brightly dressed revelers.
Aug. 18–Sept. 6: Canadian National Exhibition is held at the Canadian National Exhibition Grounds by Lake Ontario and Ontario Place.
Early–mid-Sept.: Festival of Festivals is a film event that attracts cinematographers and stars from many countries.
Late October: The **International Festival of Authors** at Harbourfront brings in major writers from around the world, on the level of Saul Bellow, Jay McInerney, Jan Morris, and, yes, Salman Rushdie (in 1988). This is truly one of Toronto's major cultural experiences and should not be missed.
Mid-Nov.: Santa Claus Parade travels downtown Toronto.
Dec. 31: City of Toronto's New Year's Eve Party is thrown in Nathan Phillips Square. And, as of the last day of 1991, special No-Booze celebrations (fit for the entire family and very low-priced) take place in many theaters and other locations across downtown.

What to Pack

Pack light because porters and baggage trolleys are scarce and luggage restrictions are tight. Although restrictions may vary from one airline to another, passengers are usually allowed two pieces of check-in luggage and one carry-on piece. On Canadian planes, no piece of check-in luggage can weigh more than 70 pounds. The first piece cannot exceed 62″ (length + width + height), the second piece, 55″ (length + width + height). The carry-on luggage cannot exceed 45″ (length + width + height) and must fit under the seat or in the overhead luggage compartment. These are the requirements of Air Canada for travel between the United States and Canada; other airlines may have slightly different requirements.

What you pack depends more on the time of year than on any specific dress code. Toronto has extremely cold winters; hot, steamy summers; and lots of rain in between. Winter can extend from November through April. For winter, you'll need your warmest clothes, in many layers, and waterproof boots.

Salt will destroy leather shoes and boots; winter visitors will be wise to bring a cheap pair. In the summer, loose-fitting, casual clothing will see you through both day and evening events. Women should pack a sweater or shawl for summer evenings, which can get cool, and for restaurants that run their air conditioners full blast. Men will need a jacket and tie for the better restaurants and many of the night spots. Jeans are as popular in Toronto as they are elsewhere and are perfectly acceptable for sightseeing and informal dining. Toronto has an extremely low crime rate and is a wonderful place for wandering on foot, so bring comfortable walking shoes. Consider packing a bathing suit for your hotel pool.

The electrical current is the same as in the United States: 110 volts, 60 cycles.

Taking Money Abroad

Traveler's checks and major U.S. credit cards are accepted in Toronto. You'll need cash for some of the small restaurants and shops. Many establishments accept U.S. dollars. Although you pay more for Canadian dollars in the United States, it's wise to buy some before you leave home to avoid long lines at airport currency-exchange booths. If your local bank can't exchange your money into Canadian dollars, Thomas Cook Currency Services will. Its office at 630 Fifth Ave., New York, NY 10111 (tel. 212/757–6915) will inform you of the location of its branches.

The most recognized traveler's checks are American Express, Barclay's, Thomas Cook, and those issued through major commercial banks such as Citibank and Bank of America. Some banks will issue the checks free to established customers, but most charge a 1% commission fee. Buy part of the traveler's checks in small denominations to cash toward the end of your trip. This will save you from having to cash a large check and ending up with more foreign money than you need. (Hold on to your receipts after exchanging your traveler's checks; it's easier to convert foreign currency back into dollars if you have the receipts.) You can also buy traveler's checks in Canadian dollars, a good idea if the U.S. dollar is falling and you want to lock in the current rate. Remember to take the addresses of offices where you can get refunds for lost or stolen traveler's checks. American Express now issues **Traveler's cheques for Two**—a system that allows two people to sign and use the same checks. "The American Express Traveler's Companion," a directory of offices to contact worldwide in case of loss or theft of American Express traveler's checks, is available at most travel service locations.

Banks and bank-operated currency-exchange kiosks in airports, railway stations, and bus terminals are the best places to change money. Hotels and privately run exchange firms will give you a significantly lower rate of exchange.

Like the American dollar, the Canadian one floats (and often sinks) on the world's money markets, but it will probably remain in the United States 80¢–85¢ range over the next few years. Since 1987, the $1 bill has slowly been phased out in Canada and replaced with a funny-looking coin that has been nicknamed "the Loonie," after the illustration of a Canadian loon on one side. But these bills (as well as the far more useful $5, $10, and $20 bills—and, yes, the always welcome $2 Canadian denomination) should remain in circulation into the 1990s.

U.S. currency is eagerly accepted at most good-size stores and restaurants, and with good reason: owners are always happy to give far less exchange than the daily rate. So it is financially wise for all visitors to go to a Canadian bank or exchange firm within a few hours of arrival. The sooner you exchange your money for the worth-less (if not yet worthless) Canadian dollar, the more money you'll save. When you use your credit cards, you can be assured that your expenditures will automatically go through as Canadian funds, and you will get the proper exchange rate.

There are more bank branches in this country than there are pubs, which tells you something, does it not? But the banks have rather abbreviated hours—usually Monday to Thursday from 10 to 3, and Fridays 10 to 6. **Thomas Cook Currency Services** has longer hours. There are branches at 10 King St. E, near Yonge St., tel. 416/863–1611; in the Manulife Centre, 55 Bloor St. W at Bay St., tel. 416/961–9822; 60 Bloor St. W, tel. 416/923–6549; the Sheraton Centre hotel lobby, 123 Queen St. W, across from the New City Hall, tel. 416/363–4867; Yorkdale Pl., tel. 416/789–1827; and the Skyline Hotel lobby, 655 Dixon Rd., near the airport, tel. 416/247–4600.

Getting Money from Home

Cash Machines
Withdrawals
It's easy to use automated-teller machines (ATMs) to withdraw money from your checking account with a bank card. Just get the names of affiliated cash-machine networks before your departure. (For locations for two of the larger networks, Cirrus and Plus, call 800/4–CIRRUS or 800/THE–PLUS.) Note that you may be charged a fee for withdrawals away from your home turf. Of course, you need to get a personal identification number (PIN) if you don't have one already.

Cash Advances
You can also use ATMs to get cash advances on your credit card, providing you have a PIN number for your card. As with cash advances from tellers, you pay interest from the day of posting, and some banks tack on an additional service charge.

For both withdrawals and cash advances, there are usually limits on the amount you can access within given time periods. Know before you go.

Bank Transfers
Just have your bank send money to another bank in Toronto. It's easiest to transfer money between like branches; otherwise, the process takes a couple days longer and costs more.

American Express Cardholder Services
The company's **Express Cash** system links your U.S. checking account to your Amex card. Abroad you can withdraw up to $1,000 in a 21-day period (more if your card is Gold or Platinum). For each transaction there's a 2% fee (minimum $2, maximum $6). Call 800/227–4669 for information.

Cardholders can also cash personal or counter checks at any American Express office for up to $1,000, of which $500 may be claimed in cash and the balance in traveler's checks carrying a 1% commission.

Wiring Money
To send or receive up to $10,000, you can use an American Express MoneyGram, and you don't have to have an American Express card. The sender goes to an American Express

MoneyGram agent, specifies an amount, pays up to $1,000 with a credit card (anything over that in cash), and telephones the receiver with the reference number he or she is given. The receiver goes to the nearest MoneyGram agent, presents identification and the reference number, and picks up cash. Fees are 5% to 10%, depending on the amount and method of payment (AE, D, MC, V are accepted). For agent locations, call 800/543–4080.

If there are no American Express offices nearby, you can use **Western Union** (tel. 800/325–6000). A friend at home can bring cash or a check to the nearest Western Union office or pay over the phone with a credit card. Delivery usually takes two business days, and fees are roughly 5% to 10%.

Canadian Currency

The units of currency in Canada are the Canadian dollar (C$) and the cent, in the same denominations as U.S. currency. There are also a $2 bill and a $1 coin, nicknamed "the Loonie." At press time, the exchange rate was fluctuating at around C$1.15 to U.S. $1 and C$2.20 to £1.

What It Will Cost

Note: Throughout this guide, unless otherwise stated, prices are quoted in Canadian dollars.

It's true that the U.S. dollar is worth some 15%–20% more than the Canadian dollar, but this translates into upwards of a 15% savings only when goods in both countries are sold at the same price. The fact is that goods and services are priced slightly higher in Canada than in the United States, so the actual savings is closer to 10%. In Toronto, a can of Coke costs about 75¢; a taxi, as soon as the meter is turned on, $2.20; a movie, $8; and a glass of beer in a bar, more than $3.

The airport departure tax is 7% of the fare, plus $10, to a maximum of $40. In other words, if you are flying to Toronto and back from Los Angeles, and the flight costs an even U.S. $400, you will end up paying U.S. $438. You will rarely be made aware of this obnoxious little tax; it will be written into the total ticket cost at the time of purchase. But don't forget the new $5 (U.S.K.) immigration tax to be paid as you leave Canada.

Passports and Visas

Because there is so much border traffic between Canada and the United States (for example, many people live in Windsor [Ontario] and work in Detroit), entry requirements are fairly simple. Citizens and legal residents of the United States do not require a passport or a visa to enter Canada, but proof of citizenship (a birth certificate, valid passport, voter registration card, draft card, selective service card, or naturalization certificate) may be requested. If you return to the United States by air, possession of a passport can save a long wait on line. Resident aliens should be in possession of their U.S. Alien Registration or "green" card. U.S. citizens interested in visiting Canada for more than 90 days may apply for a visa that allows them to stay for six months. For more information, contact the Canadian Embassy, 501 Pennsylvania Ave., NW, Washington, DC 20001, tel. 202/682–1740.

British citizens should consult Tips for British Travelers, below.

Customs and Duties

On Arrival Clothing and personal items may be brought in without charge or restriction. American and British visitors may bring in the following items duty-free: 200 cigarettes, 50 cigars, and two pounds of tobacco; personal cars (for less than six months); boats or canoes; rifles and shotguns (but no handguns or automatic weapons); 200 rounds of ammunition; cameras, radios, sports equipment, and typewriters. A deposit is sometimes required for trailers and household equipment (refunded upon return). If you are driving a rented car, be sure to keep the contract with you. Cats may enter freely, but dogs must have proof of a veterinary inspection to ensure that they are free of communicable diseases. Plant material must be declared and inspected.

On Departure Passengers flying from Toronto to the United States will have to go through U.S. Customs in Toronto, so allow extra time before your flight. If you have brought any foreign-made equipment from home, such as cameras, it's wise to carry the original receipt with you or to register it with U.S. Customs before you leave home (Form 4457). Otherwise, you may end up having to pay duty on your return. U.S. residents visiting Canada for at least 48 hours may bring home up to $400 in foreign goods duty-free for each 30-day period. Each member of the family is entitled to the same exemption, regardless of age, and exemptions may be pooled. For the next $1,000 worth of goods, a flat 10% rate is assessed; above $1,400, duties vary with the merchandise. Travelers 21 or older may bring home one liter of alcohol, 100 cigars (non-Cuban), and 200 cigarettes. Only one bottle of perfume trademarked in the United States may be imported. There is no duty on antiques or art over 100 years old. Anything exceeding these limits will be taxed at the port of entry, and may be taxed additionally in the traveler's home state. Gifts valued at under $50 may be mailed to friends or relatives at home duty-free, but not more than one package per day to any one addressee, and not including perfumes costing more than $5, tobacco, or liquor.

Since the passage of the so-called Free Trade Agreement between the United States and Canada in late 1988, many people have come to think that all duties were being dropped overnight. *Au contraire, mon frère:* On the vast majority of goods, these duties are being eliminated gradually, many not before January 1, 1998. It is recommended that you pick up the brochure, "Free Trade and the Traveller," published by the government, outlining how the FTA will affect goods brought into Canada from the United States. It's available at Customs offices, airport departure lounges, and border crossing points.

Tips for British Travelers

Passports and Visas You will need a valid 10-year passport (cost: £15). Visas and vaccinations are not required.

Customs Upon returning to Britain you may bring home: (1) 200 cigarettes or 100 cigarillos or 50 cigars or 250 grams of tobacco; (2) two liters of table wine and, in addition, (a) one liter of alcohol over 22% by volume (most spirits) or (b) two liters of alcohol under 22% by volume (fortified or sparkling wine) or (c) two more liters of table wine; (3) 60 milliliters and 250 milliliters of toilet water; and (4) other goods up to a value of £32, but not more than 50 liters of beer or 25 lighters.

Insurance To cover health and motoring mishaps, insure yourself through **Europ Assistance** (252 High St., Croydon, Surrey CR0 1NF, tel. 081/680–1234).

It is also wise to take out insurance to cover lost luggage (though make sure this isn't already covered in your existing homeowner's policy). Trip-cancellation insurance is another wise buy. The **Association of British Insurers** (51 Gresham St., London EC2V 7HQ, tel. 071/600–3333) will give comprehensive advice on all aspects of vacation insurance.

Tour Operators **Kuoni Travel** (Kuoni House, Dorking, Surrey RH5 4AZ, tel. 0306/742222) offers holiday packages in Toronto hotels and features the city in several multicenter escorted tours. It also can arrange self-drive itineraries and motor-home holidays.

Premier Holidays (Premier Travel Center, Westbrook, Milton Rd., Cambridge CB4 1YQ, tel. 0223/355977) offers city stays in Toronto, plus self-drive and escorted tours.

National Holidays Ltd. (Clarendon House, Clarendon Rd., Eccles M30 9AA, tel. 061/707–4404) will put together a complete package to Canada, including airfare or a week's car rental. Similar plans are offered by **North American Vacations** (Acorn House, 172/174 Albert Rd., Jarrow, Tyne & Wear NE32 5JA, tel. 091/483–6226) and **Albany Travel** (Royal London House, 196 Deansgate, Manchester M3 3NF, tel. 061/833–0202).

Airfares Major airlines serving Toronto are **Air Canada** (tel. 081/759–2636), **British Airways** (tel. 081/897–4000), and **Northwest Airlines** (tel. 0345/747800). If you can afford to be flexible about when you travel, look for last-minute flight bargains, which are advertised in the Sunday newspapers.

Traveling with Film

If your camera is new, shoot and develop a few rolls of film before leaving home. Pack some lens tissue and an extra battery for your built-in light meter. Invest about $10 in a skylight filter and screw it onto the front of your lens. It will protect the lens and also reduce haze.

Film doesn't like hot weather. If you're driving in summer, don't store film in the glove compartment or on the shelf under the rear window. Put it behind the front seat on the floor, on the side opposite the exhaust pipe.

On a plane trip, never pack unprocessed film in check-in luggage; if your bags get X-rayed, you may ruin your pictures. Always carry undeveloped film with you through security and ask to have it inspected by hand. (It helps to isolate your film in a plastic bag, ready for quick inspection.) Inspectors at American airports are required by law to honor requests for hand inspection; abroad, you'll have to depend on the kindness of strangers.

The newer airport scanning machines used in all U.S. and Canadian airports are safe for anything from five to 500 scans, depending on the speed of your film.

Language

It amuses Canadians to see how many visitors assume (in fear) that "everyone will speak French to me." Canada is, indeed, a bilingual country, in that it has two official languages, French and English. And visitors are charmed, even fascinated, to see the cereal boxes and road signs in both languages. But Toronto is the Anglophone center of Canada, which means that 99% of the people living here will speak to you in English.

Staying Healthy

Shots and Medications There are no health risks associated with travel to Canada. No inoculations are needed. If you have a health problem that might require purchasing prescription drugs while in Canada, have your doctor write a prescription using the drug's generic name. Brand names vary widely from country to country.

In Washington, the Department of State **Citizens Emergency Center** (tel. 202/647–5225) provides information about health conditions in other nations; what U.S. citizens can do in the event of an emergency abroad; whether any notices, cautions, or warnings exist in the area to which you're traveling; and how to obtain passports and visas.

Doctors The **International Association for Medical Assistance to Travelers** (IAMAT) is a worldwide association offering a list of approved doctors whose training meets British and American standards. For a list of Canadian physicians and clinics that are part of this network, contact IAMAT, 417 Center St., Lewiston, NY 14092, tel. 716/754–4883. In Canada: 40 Regal Rd., Guelph, Ont. N1K 1B5. In Europe: 57 Voirets, 1212 Grand-Lancy, Geneva, Switzerland. Membership is free.

Insurance

Travelers may seek insurance coverage in four areas: health and accident, loss of luggage, flight, and trip cancellation. Your first step is to review your existing health and homeowner policies; some health-insurance plans cover health expenses incurred while traveling, some major medical plans cover emergency transportation, and some homeowner policies cover the theft of luggage.

Health and Accident Several companies offer coverage designed to supplement existing health insurance for travelers:

Carefree Travel Insurance (Box 310, 120 Mineola Blvd., Mineola, NY 11501, tel. 516/294–0220 or 800/323–3149) provides coverage for emergency medical evacuation and accidental death and dismemberment. It also offers 24-hour medical phone advice.

International SOS Assistance (Box 11568, Philadelphia, PA 19116, tel. 215/244–1500 or 800/523–8930), a medical assistance company, provides emergency evacuation services, worldwide medical referrals, and optional medical insurance.

Travel Guard International (1145 Clark St., Stevens Point, WI 54481, tel. 715/345–0505 or 800/782–5151), underwritten by Transamerica Occidental Life Companies, offers reimbursement for medical expenses with no deductibles or daily limits, and emergency evacuation services.

Wallach and Company, Inc. (Box 480, Middleburg, VA 22117–0480, tel. 703/687–3166 or 800/237–6615) offers comprehensive medical coverage, including emergency evacuation services worldwide.

Loss of Luggage Luggage loss is usually covered as part of a comprehensive travel-insurance package that includes personal-accident, trip-cancellation, and sometimes default and bankruptcy insurance. Several companies offer comprehensive policies:

Access America Inc. (Box 11188, Richmond, VA 23230, tel. 800/334–7525 or 800/284–8300), a subsidiary of Blue Cross/Blue Shield.

Near Services (450 Prairie Ave., Suite 101, Calumet City, IL 60409, tel. 708/868–6700 or 800/654–6700).

Travel Guard International (*see above*).

Trip-Cancellation and Flight Insurance Consider purchasing trip-cancellation insurance if you are traveling on a promotional or discounted ticket that does not allow changes or cancellations. You are then covered if an emergency causes you to cancel or postpone your trip. Trip-cancellation insurance is usually included in combination travel-insurance packages available from most tour operators, travel agents, and insurance agents. Flight insurance, which covers passengers in case of death or dismemberment, is often included in the price of a ticket when paid for with American Express, MasterCard, or other major credit cards.

Renting Cars

If you're flying into Toronto and planning to spend some time there before exploring the rest of Ontario, save money by arranging to pick up your car in the city and then head off into the province. You'll have to weigh the added expense of renting a car from a major company with an airport office against the savings on a car from a budget company with offices in town.

You could waste precious hours trying to locate the budget company in return for only a small financial savings. If you're arriving and departing from different airports, look for a one-way car rental with no return fees. Rental rates vary widely, depending on size and model, number of days you use the car, insurance coverage, and whether drop-off fees are imposed. In most cases, rates quoted include unlimited free mileage and standard liability protection. Not included are the Collision Damage Waiver (CDW), which eliminates your deductible payment should you have an accident; personal-accident insurance; gasoline; and an 8% sales tax.

Driver's licenses issued in the United States are valid in Canada. Although you can legally drive a car at age 16 in Toronto, you must be at least 21 to rent a car.

It's best to arrange a car rental before you leave home. You won't save money by waiting until you arrive in Toronto, and you may find that the type of car you want is not available at the last minute. Rental companies usually charge according to the exchange rate of the U.S. dollar at the time the car is returned or when the credit-card payment is processed. Rental companies that serve Toronto include **Avis** (tel. 416/964-2051 or 800/331–1212), **Budget Rent-a-Car** (tel. 416/673–3322 or 800/527–0700), **Hertz** (tel. 416/961–3320, 800/654–3001, or 800/263–0600), and **National Interrent** (tel. 416/922–2000 or 800/CAR-RENT).

Student and Youth Travel

Discount Cards   The **International Student Identity Card** (ISIC) entitles students to youth rail passes, special fares on local transportation, and discounts at museums, theaters, sports events, and many other attractions. If the card is purchased in the United States, the $14 cost also includes $3,000 in emergency medical insurance plus hospital coverage of $100 a day for up to 60 days, as well as a collect phone number to call in case of emergency. Apply to the **Council on International Educational Exchange** (CIEE) (205 E. 42d St., New York, NY 10017, tel. 212/661–1414). In Canada, the ISIC is available for C$13 from **Travel Cuts** (187 College St., Toronto, Ont. M5T 1P7, tel. 416/979–2406).

The **Youth International Educational Exchange Card** (YIEE) provides similar services to nonstudents under the age of 26. In the United States, the card is available from CIEE (address above) or from ISE (Europa House, 802 W. Oregon St., Urbana, IL 61801, tel. 217/344–5863). In Canada, the YIEE is available from the **Canadian Hostelling Association** (CHA) (1600 James Naismith Dr., Suite 608, Gloucester, Ont. K1B 5N4, tel. 613/748–5638).

Accommodations   An **International Youth Hostel Federation** (IYHF) membership card is the key to inexpensive dormitory-style accommodations at thousands of youth hostels around the world. Hostels provide separate sleeping quarters for men and women, at rates ranging from $7 to $20 a night per person, in a variety of facilities, including converted farmhouses, villas, and restored castles, as well as specially constructed modern buildings. There are more than 5,000 hostel locations in 70 countries around the world. IYHF memberships, which are valid for 12 months from the time of purchase, are available in the United States through **American Youth Hostels** (AYH, Box 37613, Washington, DC 20013, tel. 202/783–6161). The cost for a first-year membership is $25 for adults 18 to 54. Renewal thereafter is $20. For youths (under 18) and senior citizens (55 and older) the rate is $15. Family membership is available for two adults traveling with up to two children for $35. Every national hostel association arranges special reductions for members visiting its country, such as discounted rail fares or free bus travel, so be sure to ask for an international concessions list when you buy your membership.

Tours   Economical **bicycle tours** for small groups of adventurous, energetic students are another popular AYH student travel service. For information, contact the address above.

Council Travel, a CIEE subsidiary, is the foremost U.S. student travel agency, specializing in low-cost charters and serving as the exclusive U.S. agent for many student airfare bargains and student tours. CIEE's 72-page *Student Travel*

Catalog and "Council Charter" brochure are available free from any Council Travel office in the United States (enclose $1 postage if ordering by mail). There are Council Travel offices in the following cities: Tempe, AZ; Berkeley, La Jolla, Long Beach, Los Angeles, San Diego, San Francisco, and Sherman Oaks, CA; Boulder, CO; New Haven, CT; Washington, DC; Atlanta, GA; Chicago and Evanston, IL; New Orleans, LA; Amherst, Boston, and Cambridge, MA; Ann Arbor, MI; Minneapolis, MN; Durham, NC; Columbus, OH; Portland, OR; Providence, RI; Austin and Dallas, TX; Seattle, WA; and Milwaukee, WI.

Further Information CIEE publishes many books of interest to the student traveler, including *Work, Study, Travel Abroad: The Whole World Handbook* ($12.95 plus $1.50 book-rate postage or $3 first-class postage); and *Volunteer! The Comprehensive Guide to Voluntary Service in the U.S. and Abroad* ($8.95 plus $1.50 book-rate postage or $3 first-class postage).

The Information Center at the **Institute of International Education** (809 U.N. Plaza, New York, NY 10017, tel. 212/883–8200) has reference books, foreign university catalogues, study-abroad brochures, and other materials, which may be consulted by students and nonstudents alike, free of charge. It is open weekdays 10–4.

Traveling with Children

Publications *Family Travel Times* is an 8- to 12-page newsletter published 10 times a year by TWYCH (Travel with Your Children, 45 W. 18th St., 7th floor Tower, New York, NY 10011, tel. 212/206–0688). A subscription costs $35 and includes access to back issues and twice-weekly opportunities to call in for specific advice. *Toronto Loves Kids*, by M. Weisman (The Can-Do Publishing Co., Inc., Toronto; $6.95), is filled with activities, sights, resources. Another resource is *Kid-Bits: Dini Petty's Guide to Toronto for Children*, by Merike Weiler and Dini Petty (Methuen; $9.95). *Kids Toronto* (Kids Canada Publishing, 540 Mt. Pleasant Rd., Suite 202, Toronto, Ont. M4S 2M6, tel. 416/481–5696) is a newspaper for parents, with complete listings of activities, resources, etc. It's free at libraries, bookstores, supermarkets, and nursery schools. It also publishes *Kids Toronto Directory*, which is available at Toronto bookstores.

Hotels **The Delta Chelsea Inn** (33 Gerrard St., Toronto, Ont. M5G 1Z4, tel. 800/268–1133) maintains a supervised Children's Creative Center and allows children under 18 to stay free with their parents. **The Inn on the Park,** a Four Seasons hotel (1100 Eglinton Ave. E, North York, Ont. M3C 1H8, tel. 416/444–2561), has a supervised children's program. The friendly **Town Inn Hotel** (620 Church St., Toronto, Ont. M4Y 262, tel. 416/964–3311) offers reliable baby-sitting services.

Home Exchange Exchanging homes is a surprisingly low-cost way to enjoy a vacation abroad, especially a long one. The largest home-exchange service, **Intervac U.S./International Home Exchange Service** (Box 590504, San Francisco, CA 94159, tel. 415/435–3497 or 800/756–4663) publishes three directories a year. Membership costs $45 and entitles you to one listing and all three directories. **Loan-a-Home** (2 Park La., 6E, Mount Vernon, NY 10552, tel. 914/664–7640) is popular with the academic community on sabbatical and businesspeople on temporary assignment. There's no annual membership fee or charge for listing your home; however, one directory and a supplement costs $35.

Getting There On international flights, children under 2 not occupying a seat pay 10% of adult fare. Various discounts apply to children 2 to 12 years of age. Regulations about infant travel on airplanes are in the process of changing. Until they do, however, if you want to be sure your infant is secure and traveling in his or her own safety seat, you must buy baby a separate ticket and bring your own infant car seat. (Check with the airline in advance; certain seats aren't allowed.) Some airlines allow babies to travel in their own car seats at no charge if there's a spare seat available; otherwise, safety seats will be stored and the child will have to be held by a parent. (For the booklet *Child/Infant Safety Seats Acceptable for Use in Aircraft*, write to the Federal Aviation Administration, APA-200, 800 Independence Ave., SW, Washington, DC 20591, tel. 202/267–3479.) If you opt to hold baby on your lap, do so with the infant outside the seat belt so he or she won't be crushed in case of a sudden stop.

Also inquire about children's special meals and snacks. The February 1990 and 1992 issues of *Family Travel Times* include "TWYCH's Airline Guide," which contains a rundown of the children's services offered by 46 airlines.

Baby-Sitting **Active Home Services** (110 St. Clair Ave. W, tel. 416/962–0296)
Services has been around for two decades, providing sitters as far west as Jane Street, a few miles east of the airport. There's a five-hour minimum by day and a four-hour minimum at night.

Christopher Robin Services (5 Whitecap Blvd., Scarborough, tel. 416/265–2212) covers all of Metro Toronto. Service is also based on a five-hour daily and a four-hour nightly minimum.

Kingsway Household Services (tel. 416/233–9983) has been offering trustworthy sitters for more than three decades. There's a four-hour minimum plus a transportation charge.

Also check *Kids Toronto* (*see* Publications, *above*) for local agencies, or make child-care arrangements through your hotel concierge (*see* Hotels, *above*).

Hints for Disabled Travelers

Guide to Ontario Government Programs & Services for Disabled Persons is a superb new—and free—72-page booklet available from the Office for Disabled Persons, 3rd floor, 700 Bay St., Toronto, Ont. M5G 1Z6, tel. 416/965–3165 (voice/TDD for the hearing-impaired) or 800/387–4456 (voice/TDD). To obtain the booklet in French, call 800/387–4456 (*voix*/ATS).

Toronto with Ease is a free booklet available from the Metropolitan Toronto Convention and Visitors Association (*see* Government Tourist Offices, *above*). Or call 416/485–4308. To have it mailed before you go to Canada, send $3.75 to Ontario March of Dimes, Information Services, 60 Overlea Blvd., Toronto, Ont. M4H 1B6.

The **Toronto Transit Commission** (TTC) offers a bus service, called Wheel-Trans, for disabled people (and friends) who are unable to use regular public vehicles. For advance reservations, phone 416/393–4222; for same-day requests, 416/393–4333; TTD number 416/393–4555.

Transportation to and from Pearson International Airport is available for the handicapped through Wheel-Trans (tel. 416/393–4111). Three limousine companies—**Aaroport, MacIntosh** (tel. 416/741–5466 for both) and **Airline Limousine** (tel. 416/676–3210)—operate wheelchair-accessible vans. By prearrangement, a disabled person can be picked up or dropped off at points in all three of the airport's terminals.

For information on governmental services for the hearing impaired, the TTY-TDD numbers are 416/392–8069 and 416/392–7354. For general information about handicapped-accessible transportation and buildings, call the accessibility planner, weekdays 8–5, tel. 416/392–7339.

Freedom in Traveling (tel. 416/234–8511) is a liaison between the disabled and the travel industry, providing accessibility information. Many travel agents across North America are affiliated with it.

The **Community Information Centre** (tel. 416/392–0505) provides information on various facilities, as well as social and health services for the disabled.

The **Advocacy Resource Centre for the Handicapped** (tel. 416/482–8255 or TTY number 416/482–1254) is a responsible and responsive legal center that defends the rights of the mentally and physically disabled.

The Information Center for Individuals with Disabilities (Fort Point Pl., 1st floor, 27–43 Wormwood St., Boston, MA 02110, tel. 617/727–5540) offers useful problem-solving assistance, including lists of travel agents that specialize in tours for the disabled. The center is open 10–4.

Moss Rehabilitation Hospital Travel Information Service (1200 W. Tabor Rd., Philadelphia, PA 19141–3099, tel. 215/456–9603) provides information on tourist sights, transportation, and accommodations in destinations around the world for a small fee.

Mobility International USA (Box 3551, Eugene, OR 97403, tel. 503/343–1284) is an internationally affiliated organization with 500 members. For a $20 annual fee, it coordinates exchange programs for disabled people around the world and offers information on accommodations and organized study programs.

The Society for the Advancement of Travel for the Handicapped (347 5th Ave., Suite 610, New York, NY 10016, tel. 212/447–7288, fax 212/725–8253) offers access information. Annual membership costs $45, or $25 for senior travelers and students. Send a stamped, self-addressed envelope.

The Itinerary (Box 2012, Bayonne, NJ 07002, tel. 201/858–3400) is a bimonthly travel magazine for the disabled.

Greyhound/Trailways (tel. 800/752–4841) will carry a disabled person and companion for the price of a single fare. **Amtrak** (tel. 800/USA–RAIL) requests 24-hour notice to provide Redcap service and special seats. Disabled passengers are entitled to a 15% discount on the lowest available coach fare.

Hints for Older Travelers

The American Association of Retired Persons (AARP, 601 E St., NW, Washington, DC 20049, tel. 202/434–2277) has two programs for independent travelers: (1) the Purchase Privilege Program, which offers discounts on hotels, airfare, car rentals, and sightseeing; and (2) the AARP Motoring Plan, provided by Amoco, which offers emergency aid and trip routing information for an annual fee of $39.95 per couple. The AARP also arranges group tours through **AARP Travel Experience from American Express** (400 Pinnacle Way, Suite 450, Norcross, GA 30071, tel. 800/927–0111). AARP members must be 50 or older. Annual dues are $8 per person or per couple.

When using an AARP or other identification card, ask for a reduced hotel rate at the time you make your reservation, not when you check out. At participating restaurants, show your card to the maître d' before you're seated, since discounts may be limited to certain set menus, days, or hours. When renting a car, be sure to ask about special promotional rates, which may offer greater savings than the available discount.

Travel Industry and Disabled Exchange (TIDE, 5435 Donna Ave., Tarzana, CA 91356, tel. 818/368–5648) is an industry-based organization with a $15-per-person annual membership fee. Members receive a quarterly newsletter and information on travel agencies and tours.

National Council of Senior Citizens (1331 F St., NW, Washington, DC 20004, tel. 202/347–8800) is a nonprofit advocacy group with some 5,000 local clubs across the country. Annual membership is $12 per person or per couple. Members receive a monthly newspaper with travel information and an ID card for reduced-rate hotels and car rentals.

Mature Outlook (6001 N. Clark St., Chicago, IL 60660, tel. 800/336–6330), a subsidiary of Sears, Roebuck & Co., is a travel club for people over 50, with hotel and motel discounts and a bimonthly newsletter. Annual membership is $9.95 per couple. Instant membership is available at participating Holiday Inns.

Golden Age Passport is a free lifetime pass to all parks, monuments, and recreation areas run by the U.S. government. People 62 and over should pick them up in person at any national park that charges admission. A driver's license or other proof of age is required.

Further Reading

Don't miss Michael Ondaatje's award-winning *In the Skin of a Lion*, about Toronto in the 1940s and 1950s. The best literary and geographic history of the area is *Toronto Remembered* by William Kilbourn. *Toronto Observed*, by William Dendy and William Kilbourn, is an award-winning book on Toronto's 100 most interesting buildings. Eric Arthur's *No Mean City* is a penetrating look at the city's 19th-century architecture.

Robertson Davies wrote a series of novels about the supernatural, set in Toronto. One is *Fifth Business*.

Margaret Millar's *Wall of Eyes* and Hugh Garner's *Death in Don Mills* are mystery/thrillers set in the area.

Austin Clarke's *Nine Men Who Laughed* and *The Storm of Fortune* are novels about immigrants from the West Indies to Toronto. Mordecai Richler's *The Inconquerable Atuk* is about the life of an Inuit (Eskimo) in Toronto; the picture it paints of the city is rather dated.

The best encapsulation of today's Toronto, albeit fictional, is Margaret Atwood's *Cat's Eye*. It is highly entertaining, as well written as her other fine books—including the dystopian *Handmaid's Tale*, and *Life Before Man*—and punctures all the city's pretensions and foibles with a devastatingly satiric vision. Harry J. Pollack's *Gabriel: A Novel* is an autobiographical novel about a Toronto man involved in the literary life. Other suggested titles include *Hunger Trace* by Adrienne Clarkson, and *A Casual Affair: A Modern Fairytale* by Sylvia Fraser.

Arriving and Departing

From the United States by Plane

The Airlines There are three types of flights to Toronto: nonstop—no changes, no stops; direct—no changes but one or more stops; and connecting—two or more planes, two or more stops.

Toronto is served by **Alaska Airlines** (tel. 800/426–0333), **American** (tel. 800/433–7300), **Delta** (tel. 800/843–9378), **Northwest** (tel. 800/225–2525), **United** (tel. 800/241–6522), **US Air** (tel. 800/428–4322), **Air Canada** (tel. 800/422–6232), and **Canadian Airlines International** (tel. 800/387–2737).

Discount Flights The major airlines offer a range of tickets that can increase the price of any given seat by more than 300%, depending on the day of purchase. As a rule, the further in advance you buy the ticket, the less expensive it is and the greater the penalty (up to 100%) for canceling. Check with airlines for details.

It's important to distinguish between companies that sell seats on charter flights and companies that sell one of a block of tickets on scheduled airlines. Charter flights are the least expensive and the least reliable—with chronically late departures and not infrequent cancellations. They also tend to depart less frequently (usually once a week) than regularly scheduled flights. A wise alternative to a charter is a ticket on a scheduled flight purchased from a wholesaler or ticket broker. It's an unbeatable deal: a scheduled flight at up to 50% off the APEX fare. Tickets can usually be purchased up to three days before departure (but in high season expect to wait in line an hour or so).

The following brokers specialize in discount sales; all charge an annual fee of about $20–$50: **Discount Travel International** (114 Forrest Ave., Narberth, PA 19072, tel. 215/668–7184 or 800/334–9294), **Moment's Notice** (425 Madison Ave., New York, NY 10017, tel. 212/486–0500), **Travelers Advantage** (CUC Travel Service, 49 Music Sq. W, Nashville, TN 37203, tel. 800/548–1116), and **Worldwide Discount Travel Club** (1674 Meridian Ave., Miami Beach, FL 33139, tel. 305/534–2082).

Flying Time Flying time from New York is about 1 hour; from Chicago, about 1½ hours; from Miami, 3 hours; from Los Angeles or San Francisco, 5 hours. One should know that Toronto's Pearson airport, in deference to the tens of thousands of nearby residents who must suffer the regular roar of jets, has an evening curfew, and one cannot expect to land there much after 11 PM or before 8 AM. Travelers who are arriving from the West Coast will therefore not be able to get flights after 2 or 3 PM. A handful of airlines offer the infamous "red-eye" service, which leaves west-

ern cities after midnight, local time, and arrives in Toronto about
8 or 9 AM, sometimes via Chicago.

Luggage
Regulations
Checked Luggage

U.S. airlines generally allow passengers to check in two suit-
cases. The total dimensions (length + width + height) of each
bag should not exceed 62″, and the weight per bag should not be
more than 70 pounds.

Rules governing foreign carriers vary from airline to airline, so
check with your travel agent or the airline itself before you go.
All the airlines allow passengers to check in two bags. In general, expect the weight restriction on the two bags to be not more
than 70 pounds each, and the size restriction per bag to be not
more than 62″ in total dimensions.

Carry-on Luggage

Passengers aboard major U.S. carriers are usually limited to
two carry-on bags. For a bag you wish to store under the seat,
the maximum dimensions are 9″ × 14″ × 22″, a total of 45″. For
bags that can be hung in a closet or on a luggage rack, the maximum dimensions are 4″ × 23″ × 45″, a total of 72″. For bags you
wish to store in an overhead bin, the maximum dimensions are
10″ × 14″ × 36″, a total of 60″. Each carryon must fit one of
these sets of dimensions, and any item that exceeds them may
be rejected as a carryon and handled as checked baggage. Keep
in mind that an airline may adapt these rules to circumstances,
so on an especially crowded flight don't be surprised if you are
allowed only one carry-on bag.

In addition to the two carryons, passengers may also bring
aboard: a handbag (pocketbook or purse); an overcoat or wrap;
an umbrella; a camera; a reasonable amount of reading material; an infant bag; and crutches, a cane, braces, or other pros-
thetic device upon which the passenger is dependent. Infant/
child safety seats can be brought aboard if parents have purchased a ticket for the child or if there is space in the cabin.

These regulations are for U.S. airlines only; foreign airlines
generally allow one piece of carry-on luggage in tourist class,
plus bags filled with duty-free goods. Passengers in first and
business class may also bring aboard a garment bag. It is best
to check with your airline ahead of time to find out what its exact rules are regarding carry-on luggage.

Luggage Insurance

Airlines are responsible for lost or damaged property only up
to $1,250 per passenger on domestic flights, $9.07 per pound for
checked baggage on international flights, and $400 per passen-
ger for unchecked baggage on international flights. If you're
carrying valuables, either take them with you on the airplane
or purchase additional insurance for lost luggage. Some airlines will issue additional luggage insurance when you check in,
but many do not. One that does is American Airlines. Rates are
generally $2 for every $100 valuation, with a maximum of
$5,000 valuation per passenger. Hand luggage is not included.

Insurance for lost, damaged, or stolen luggage is available
through travel agents or directly through various insurance
companies. Two that issue luggage insurance are **Tele-Trip**
(Box 31685, 3201 Farnam St., Omaha, NE 68131–0618, tel. 800/
228–9792), a subsidiary of Mutual of Omaha, and **The Traveler**
(Ticket and Travel Dept., 1 Tower Sq., Hartford, CT 06183–
5040). Tele-Trip operates sales booths at airports and also issues insurance through travel agents. It will insure checked
luggage for up to 180 days; rates vary according to the length of

the trip. The Travelers Insurance Corporation will insure checked or hand luggage for $500 to $2,000 valuation per person, also for a maximum of 180 days. The rate for 1–5 days for $500 valuation is $10; for 180 days, $85. Both companies offer the same rates on domestic and international flights. Check the travel pages of your Sunday newspaper for the names of other companies that insure luggage. Before you go, itemize the contents of each bag in case you need to file an insurance claim. Be certain to put your home address on each piece of luggage, including carry-on bags. If your luggage is stolen and later recovered, the airline will deliver the luggage to your home free of charge.

Toronto's airport, unlike many in the States, does not have a person checking each passenger's luggage against his tag as he leaves the baggage-claim area. So someone *could* walk off with your luggage. (Of course, it would probably not be a Canadian!) So go directly from the plane to the baggage-claim area, and catch your luggage as it sails around the room on the conveyor belt.

Enjoying the Flight Drinking lots of nonalcoholic liquids can help one survive the usually dry air on planes; booze usually adds to jet lag, as does eating heavy meals in flight. Since feet swell at high altitudes, it can be more comfortable to remove your shoes (but be prepared to struggle to get them back on). If you are the wandering type, be sure to ask for an aisle seat; if you like to sleep— and not be disturbed by those crazy wanderers—then book a window seat.

Bulkhead seats—those in the front row of each cabin—have more legroom, but they also have no place in front to store bags or briefcases, and trays do not fold down from the seats in front. Furthermore, in some planes the last row in the first-class section is for smokers, and the residue of their pleasure tends to drift straight back to those nonsmokers who sit in the seats behind them.

Dietary Needs Most airlines offer a wide variety of food services. Vegetarians, lacto-vegetarians, diabetics, and Jews and Muslims with special dietary needs all should remember to ask for their own particular foods at the time they book their flights. Be sure to call again two or three days before the flight, to make sure this request was properly entered in the master computer.

Smoking It is best to request a no-smoking seat at the time you book your ticket. If a U.S. airline representative tells you there are no seats available in the no-smoking section, insist on one: Department of Transportation regulations require U.S. flag carriers to find seats for all nonsmokers on the day of the flight, provided they meet check-in time restrictions. On foreign carriers, ask for a seat far from the smoking section.

The Airports With a handful of exceptions—such as planes from Montreal, Ottawa, and London, Ontario, that land at Toronto's tiny **Island Airport**—flights into Toronto land at the **Lester B. Pearson International Airport,** so named in 1984 to honor Canada's Nobel Peace Prize–winning prime minister of a quarter-century ago. It's commonly called "the Toronto airport" or "Malton" (after the once-small town where it was built, just northwest of the city), but it's just as often called "impossible," since its terminals are inadequate for the number of travelers who use it. Waits for bags are often lengthy—although the free carts are a human touch—and Pearson can be dreadfully overcrowded, both coming and going. Terminal 1, which opened in 1964 to handle 3 million passengers, handled over *10 million* in 1990. The sorely needed Terminal 3 opened in early 1991 after many delays, and it is the only airline terminal in the world to ban smoking (with a few exceptions, such as in pubs). And, thank heavens, the ugly and uncomfortable Terminal 2 has undergone a $52 million renovation, which included replacing the endless walks with moving sidewalks and adding skylights and atria.

From the Airport to Center City Although Pearson is not far from the downtown area (about 32 km, or 18 mi), the drive can take well over an hour during Toronto's weekday rush hours (7–9 AM and 3:30–6:30 PM). Taxis and limos to a hotel or attraction near the lake can cost $30 or more. You may negotiate a fare, but the meter *must* be used, and the passenger pays whichever amount is less. Many airport and downtown hotels offer free buses to their locations from each of Toronto's three terminals. Travelers on a budget should consider the express coaches offered by **Grey Coach** (tel. 416/393–7911), which link the airport to three subway stops in the southwest and north-central areas of the city. Buses depart several times each hour, from approximately 6 AM to 11:30 PM. Fares average $6–$7. Even better is the service to and from several downtown hotels, which operates every 30 minutes from 6 AM to midnight daily and costs approximately $11.

Should you rent a car at the airport, be sure to ask for a street map of the city. Highway 427 runs south, some 3.6 miles to the lakeshore. Here you pick up the Queen Elizabeth Way (QEW) east to the Gardiner Expressway, which runs east into the heart of downtown. If you take the QEW *west*, you'll find yourself swinging around Lake Ontario, toward Hamilton, Niagara-on-the-Lake, and Niagara Falls.

From the United States by Train and Bus

Amtrak (tel. 800/872–7245) runs a daily train to Toronto from Chicago (a 10-hour trip), and another from New York City (11 hours). From Union Station you can walk underground to many hotels—a real boon in inclement weather.

Greyhound (check your local telephone directory) and **Grey Coach** (tel. 416/393–7911) both have regular bus service into Toronto from all over the United States. From Detroit, the trip takes five hours; from Buffalo, two to three hours; from Chicago and New York City, 11 hours. Buses arrive at 610 Bay Street, just above Dundas Street.

From the United States by Car

Drivers should have proper owner registration and proof of insurance coverage. There is no need for an international driver's license; any valid one will do.

Drivers may be asked several questions at the border crossing, none of them terribly personal or offensive: your place of birth; your citizenship; your expected length of stay. Border guards will rarely go beyond that. Expect a slight wait at major border crossings. Every fourth or fifth car may be searched, and this can increase the wait at peak visiting times to 30 minutes. However, a recent explosion of cross-border shopping has seen thousands of Canadians shooting across the border every month to take advantage of cheaper gas, food, and appliances, so expect the Detroit/Windsor and Buffalo/Fort Erie crossings to take even longer, especially on weekends and holidays.

The wonderfully wide Highway 401—it reaches up to 16 lanes as it slashes across Metro Toronto from the airport on the west almost as far as the zoo on the east—is the major link between Windsor, Ontario (and Detroit), and Montreal, Quebec. It's also known as the Macdonald–Cartier Freeway but is really never called anything other than "401." There are no tolls anywhere along it, but you should be warned: Between 6:30 and 9:30 each weekday morning and from 3:30 to 6:30 each afternoon, the 401 can become dreadfully crowded, even stop-and-go. Plan your trips to avoid these rush hours.

Those who are driving from Buffalo, New York, or Niagara Falls should take the Queen Elizabeth Way (fondly called the QEW or Queen E), which curves up along the western shore of Lake Ontario and eventually turns into the Gardiner Expressway, which flows right into the downtown core.

Yonge Street, which divides the west side of Toronto from the east (much like Manhattan's Fifth Avenue and Detroit's Woodward), begins at the Lakefront. Yonge Street is called Highway 11 once you get north of Toronto, and continues all the way to the Ontario–Minnesota border, at Rainy River. At 1,896.2 km (1,178.3 mi), it is the longest street in the world (as noted in the *Guinness Book of World Records*).

The distances are, from New York City, 851 km (532 mi); from Washington, DC, 899 km (562 mi); from Miami, 2,741 km (1,713 mi); from Montreal, 558 km (349 mi); from Detroit, 378 km (236 mi); from Chicago, 854 km (534 mi); from St. Louis, 1,310 km (1,023 mi); from Denver, 2,485 km (1,553 mi); from Los Angeles, 4,384 km (2,740 mi).

From the United Kingdom by Plane

Toronto is served by several airlines that fly daily from London's Heathrow and Gatwick airports. **British Airways** and **Air Canada** have regularly scheduled flights out of Heathrow. Air Canada has the most flights daily—three—two of them direct, and a third that stops at Montreal's Mirabel airport. **KLM** and **Air France** also fly between London and Toronto, the former stopping in Amsterdam on the way, the latter in Paris. Gatwick is the home of many charters, often at heavily discounted prices.

The flying time from London to Toronto is approximately seven hours and 45 minutes, to which one must add (or subtract) the five-hour time difference between the Mother Country and Her Former Colony.

Staying in Toronto

Important Addresses and Numbers

Tourist Offices The **Metropolitan Toronto Convention and Visitors Association** has its office at Queen's Quay Terminal (207 Queen's Quay W, Suite 509, M5J LA7, tel. 416/368–9821). Booths providing brochures and pamphlets about the city and its attractions, as well as accommodations, are set up in the summer outside the Eaton Centre, on Yonge Street just below Dundas Street, and outside the Royal Ontario Museum.

The **Traveller's Aid Society** is not just for the down-and-out. This is a nonprofit group whose 130 volunteers can recommend restaurants and hotels, and distribute subway maps, tourist publications, and Ontario sales tax rebate forms. *In Union Station, the society is located in Room B23, on the basement level (there is also a booth on the Arrivals level); tel. 416/366–7788. Open daily 9 AM–9 PM. In Terminal 1 at Toronto's Pearson International Airport, the society has its booth on the Arrivals level, directly across from the exit, just past Customs, near Area B; tel. 416/676–2869. Open daily 9 AM–10 PM. In Terminal 2, the booth is located between International and Domestic Arrivals, on the Arrivals level; tel. 416/676–2860. Open daily 9 AM–10 PM. In Terminal 3, the booth is located on the Arrivals level, close to the International side; tel. 416/612–5890. Open daily 9 AM–10 PM.*

Embassies   The **Consulate General of the United States** (360 University Ave., just north of Queen St., M56 1S4, tel. 416/595–1700).

The **Consulate General of Britain** (777 Bay St., at the corner of College St., M56 2G2, tel. 416/593–1267).

For all other consulates—there are dozens of countries represented in Toronto—look up "Consulate Generals" in the white pages of the phone book.

Emergencies   Dial 911 for **police** and **ambulance.**

Physicians and Dentists. Check the Yellow Pages or ask at your hotel desk. Also, call *Dial-a-Doctor* (tel. 416/492–4713), or the *Dental Emergency Service* (tel. 416/924–8041).

24-Hour Pharmacies. *Pharma Plus Drugmart* (Church St. and Wellesley Ave., about a mile from New City Hall, tel. 416/924–7760). *Lucliff Place,* 700 Bay and Gerrard Sts. (tel. 416/979–2424). *Shoppers Drug Mart* (2500 Hurontario St., Mississauga, near the airport, tel. 416/277–3665).

24-Hour Pet Emergency Service. *Veterinary Emergency Clinic,* 201 Sheppard Ave. E, about a half-mile east of Yonge St., and a few blocks north of Highway 401, tel. 416/226–3663.

Road Emergencies. The *CAA* (the Canadian version of AAA) has 24-hour road service (tel. 416/966–3000).

24-Hour Gas Stations and Auto Repairs. *Texaco Stations,* at 153 Dundas St. W, behind New City Hall, near Bay St.; 333 Davenport, just south of Casa Loma; and 601 Eglington Ave. E, west of the Ontario Science Center. *Cross Town Service Center,* 1467 Bathurst St., at the corner of St. Clair Ave. W, is well-known and respected for both gas and repairs. *Jim McCormack Esso,* 2901 Sheppard Ave. E, in the Scarborough area, heading toward the Metro Zoo. *Guido's Esso,* 1104 Albion Rd., not far from the airport.

Poison Information Center. *The Hospital for Sick Children* (tel. 416/598–5900) or for the hearing-impaired (tel. 416/597–0215).

Other Numbers   **Black Traveler's Information Hotline.** In early 1988, a Torontonian set up a hotline for black visitors, with the aim of helping them get to know Toronto (tel. 416/255–2072).

Concert Line. For a list of upcoming musical events, primarily rock and pop, tel. 416/870–1045.

Road Report. Call the CAA, tel. 416/966–3000.

Ski Information and Weather. Tel. 416/362–4151.

Weather Information. For a taped three-day forecast, phone 416/676–3066, 24 hours a day. If you want to hear a human voice, try 416/676–4567.

Camera Repairs. Queen Street Camera Exchange (tel. 416/862–0300).

24-Hour Restaurants. Golden Griddle (Jarvis and Front Sts.), Fran's Restaurant (20 College St., just a few steps west of Yonge St.).

Staying in Touch

Telephones Phones work as they do in the United States. Drop 25¢ in the slot (the machine eagerly accepts American change, unlike U.S. phones, which spit out Canadian money), and dial the number. There are no problems dialing direct to the United States; U.S. telephone credit cards are accepted. For directory assistance, dial 411.

Mail The Canadian mail service leaves a great deal to be desired. Indeed, many in Canada like to say that "Postal Service" is an oxymoron—a contradiction in terms. Within Canada, postcards and letters up to 30 grams cost 42¢, though this will undoubtedly rise a few cents at the start of 1993. From 30 to 50 grams, the cost is 65¢. Letters and postcards to the United States cost 48¢ for up to 30 grams, 70¢ for 30–50 grams. International mail and postcards run 84¢ for up to 20 grams, $1.26 for 20–50 grams. These prices, too, should increase a few pennies at the start of 1993.

Mail may be sent to you care of General Delivery, Toronto Adelaide Post Office, 36 Adelaide St. E, Toronto, Ont. M5C 1J0. American Express clients—cardholders and those who purchase traveler's checks or travel services—may pick up mail (with proper I.D.) without charge at American Express, 12 Richmond St. E, Toronto, Ont. M5C 1M5.

Getting around Toronto

Most of Toronto is laid out on a grid pattern. The key street to remember is Yonge Street (pronounced "young"), which is the main north–south artery. Most major cross streets are numbered east and west of Yonge Street. In other words, if you are looking for 180 St. Clair Avenue West, you want a building a few blocks *west* of Yonge Street; 75 Queen Street East is a block or so *east* of Yonge Street.

At press time, the fare for buses, streetcars, and trolleys was $2 *in exact change*. However, one can purchase 10 adult tickets/tokens for $11, which lowers the price per journey a bit. All fares will undoubtedly rise at least a nickel during the first week of 1993, if not before. Two-fare tickets are available for $3 for adults. Visitors who plan to stay in Toronto for more than a month should consider the **Metropass**, a photo-identity card that costs $56.50 for adults, plus $2.50 extra for the photo. (And, yes, probably a few bucks more than that as of January

1993). Children (2–13) pay only 50¢, though, and may purchase eight tickets for only $2.50.

Families should take advantage of the savings of the so-called **Day Pass.** It costs $5 and is good for unlimited travel for one person, Monday–Friday after 9:30 AM, and all day Saturday. On Sunday and holidays, it's good for up to six persons (maximum two adults), for unlimited travel. These fares could go up slightly in late 1992 or early 1993. For information on how to take public transit to any street or attraction in the city call 416/393–INFO from 7 AM to 11:30 PM.

A very useful **Ride Guide** is published by the Toronto Transit Commission each year. It shows nearly every major place of interest in the city and how to reach it by public transit. These guides are available in most subways and many other places around the city.

The subway trains stop running at 2 AM, but the Toronto Transit Commission runs bus service from 1 to 5:30 AM on most major streets, including King, Queen, College, Bloor, Yonge, and as far north as Sheppard, Finch, and Steeles.

By Subway There is little argument that the Toronto Transit Commission runs one of the safest, cleanest, most trustworthy systems of its kind anywhere. (It keeps winning international awards, which must mean something.) There are two major subway lines, with 60 stations along the way: the **Bloor/Danforth Line,** which crosses Toronto about 3 miles north of the Lakefront, from east to west, and the **Yonge/University/Spadina Line,** which loops north and south, like a giant "U," with the bottom of the "U" at Union Station. Tokens and tickets are sold in each subway station and at hundreds of convenience stores along the many routes of the TTC. Get your transfers just after you pay your fare and enter the subway; you'll find them in machines on your way down to the trains.

By Bus All buses and streetcars accept exact change, tickets, or tokens. Paper transfers are free; pick one up at the time that you pay your fare.

By Taxi The meter begins at $2.20, and includes the first .2 kilometer. Each additional .2 kilometer is 20¢—as is the fare for each additional passenger in excess of four. The waiting time "while under engagement" is 20¢ for every 33 seconds—and in one of Toronto's horrible traffic jams, this could add up. Still, it's possible to take a cab across downtown Toronto for little more than $5. The largest companies are **Beck** (tel. 416/467–0067), **Co-op** (tel. 416/364–8161), **Diamond** (tel. 416/366–6868), and **Metro** (tel. 416/363–5611).

By Car Seat-belt use is mandatory in the province of Ontario; although there was a negative response in the United States, where this is often seen as an infringement on one's right to die, the vast majority of Canadians welcomed this governmental move some years ago. The law applies to everyone in the car, and hefty fines have been known to be given. And that means infants as well; holding one upon the lap is as illegal as it is risky. Canada went metric some years ago, so gas is sold by the liter, and signs are in kilometers. The "100 km" signs on various highways are not an invitation to accelerate but, rather, a warning not to go more than 60 miles per hour.

Pedestrian crosswalks are sprinkled throughout the city; they are marked clearly by overhead signs and very large painted Xs. All a pedestrian has to do is stick out a hand, and cars screech to a halt in both directions. And they must do it, too. Naturally, if you happen to be the pedestrian, don't be foolish; wait until the traffic acknowledges you, and begins to stop, before venturing into the crosswalk. You'll be amazed at your power.

Right turns on red lights are nearly always permitted, except where otherwise posted. You must come to a complete stop before making the turn.

Opening and Closing Times

Most retail stores are open Monday–Saturday 10–6, and they now have the right to open on Sundays as well (*see* Highlights, *above*). Downtown stores are usually open until 9 PM. Some shops are open Friday evenings, too. Shopping malls tend to be open 9:30 AM to 9 or 9:30 PM.

Banks are open Monday to Thursday 10–3 and Friday 10–6. Some banks and trust companies open as early as 8:30 AM and on Saturdays as well, and some remain open as late as 8 PM.

The main civic and national holidays observed in Toronto are: New Year's Day; Good Friday, Easter Sunday, and Easter Monday; Victoria Day—the fourth Monday in May; the country's birthday—Canada Day, or Dominion Day—on July 1; Simcoe Day—the first Monday in August; Labor Day—the first Monday in September; Thanksgiving—the second Monday in October (note that this is more than five weeks earlier than the U.S. Thanksgiving; the harvest and the frost arrive much earlier in Canada); Remembrance Day on November 11; Christmas Day; and since the old Blue Laws prevent shopping until *the day after* Boxing Day, this means that December 27 is the big sale day.

Guided Tours

Orientation Tours **Toronto Harbour and Islands Boat Tours** are provided by **Gray Line** (tel. 416/364–2412) on attractive, sleek, Amsterdam-style touring boats, with competent tour guides. The hourly tour visits the Toronto Islands, with lovely views of the Toronto cityscape. Boats leave from the Queen's Quay Terminal daily from early May through mid-October, noon–5; tours leave as late as 7 during the summer months. Other boats depart from the Harbour Castle Westin. Fares are $9.95 adults, $7.95 students and senior citizens, $5.95 children 4–14.

Toronto Tours (tel. 416/869–3109) also provides one-hour boat tours of the Toronto harborfront for similar prices from mid-May through October. It also runs an informative 90-minute tour aboard a restored 1920s trolley car; the tour goes by both city halls, and through the financial district and the historic St. Lawrence area (*see* Tour Operators, *above*).

Insight Planners (tel. 416/868–6565) has been providing creative and reliable tours, particularly to art galleries, since 1974.

Reception Ontario (tel. 416/636–0082) provides complete tour-planning services, including sightseeing tours, entertainment packages, hotel accommodations, and even guides in various languages.

Happy Day Tours (tel. 416/593–6220) runs half-day tours of Toronto for about $30 per person, which include admission to Black Creek Pioneer Village and visits to the mansions of Forest Hills, Casa Loma, Chinatown, Queen's Park, Yorkville, and Harbourfront. Book ahead.

Gray Line Sightseeing Bus Tours (tel. 416/393–7911) leave from the Bus Terminal (Bay and Dundas Sts.) and spend 2½ hours visiting such places as Eaton Centre, both city halls, Queen's Park, the University of Toronto, Yorkville, Ontario Place, and Casa Loma—the latter, for a full hour. Costs run about $17 for adults, $11 for children under 12.

Special-Interest Tours **Antours** (tel. 416/481–2862) provides several tours of Niagara-on-the-Lake, which include lunch and tickets to major performances at the Shaw Festival.

Art Tours of Toronto (tel. 416/845–4044) offers a series of fall and spring gallery and walking tours. Most tours include lunch, and range from $40 to $50 per person.

The **Toronto Stock Exchange** (tel. 416/947–4676) has tours of its exciting new facilities weekdays at 2 PM.

The **Bruce Trail Association** (tel. 416/690–4453) arranges day and overnight hikes around Toronto and environs.

June–September, **Toronto Architecture Tour** offers a "Downtown Toronto Walking Tour," a two-hour tour of the area's architectural gems, including works by I. M. Pei and Ludwig Mies van der Rohe.

Tipping

Restaurants. Fifteen percent of the total bill is what most waiters and waitresses expect.

Taxis. We have always found the taxi and airport limousine drivers in Toronto to be a decent, polite lot, so a tip of 10% to 15% is usually in order.

Porters and doormen. Around 50¢ a bag; $1 or more in luxury hotels.

Room service. In moderate hotels, $1 per day; in luxury hotels, $2.

American money is always welcome (a U.S. $1 tip is worth about C$1.15–C$1.20), so don't worry if you run out of Canadian money.

Smoking

Nonsmokers may be pleased to learn that Toronto's stringent "no smoking" regulations apply to all public areas, sections of most restaurants, and even in all taxis.

Credit Cards

The following credit-card abbreviations are used: AE, American Express; D, Discover; DC, Diners Club; MC, MasterCard; V, Visa.

2 Exploring Toronto

Well, now you're in Toronto, and probably in the downtown area. It's rather confusing, isn't it? We're not talking about Avenue A, B, and C here, or 33rd, 34th, and 35th streets, either, so to begin with we're on somewhat shaky ground.

But once you establish that Lake Ontario runs along the south of the city, and that the fabulous Harbourfront Centre complex is there, as well as the ferry to the lovely Toronto Islands, you are well on your way to orienting yourself.

It's a shame to turn your back on our now-blossoming waterfront, but when you do, you meet the striking, often magnificent high-rise buildings that give Toronto so much of its skyline. Banks, banks, and banks: Yes, the church may have stood the highest and proudest in most western towns since medieval times, but today it is the god Mammon who towers over what was once called (both mockingly and with reverence) Toronto the Good. (May we remind you that there were no movies shown on Sundays until the late 1950s and no Sunday newspapers until the late 1970s.)

Every one of the major banks of Canada, which are far wealthier and more powerful than most of their U.S. counterparts, has its headquarters in downtown Toronto, between University Avenue and Yonge Street.

This preoccupation with massive buildings first expressed itself in the black 54-story tower of the **Toronto-Dominion Bank** (T-D Centre), designed by the justly admired German-American architect Mies van der Rohe. There are four towers there now, eclipsed by I. M. Pei's silver and mirrorlike **Bank of Commerce** building, right across the street.

Only a few years later—and only a few feet away—came the **Bank of Montreal**'s tower, covered with handsome marble and now holder of the title "Tallest Building in the Whole British Commonwealth." In the end, Toronto's most stunning bank building would be not the tallest but the most extraordinary: the **Royal Bank Building,** designed by the very gifted Torontonian Boris Zerafa. Born in Cairo to parents of Italian and English descent—which is late 20th-century Toronto in a nutshell—Zerafa is also the designer of Toronto's Richmond–Adelaide Centre and the **Bank of Nova Scotia,** which opened in 1989.

The new **Scotiabank Tower** looks like another winner, but it would be hard to beat the Royal Bank for sheer beauty. Its golden exterior, coated with fully 2,500 ounces of real gold (purchased when it was only $100 an ounce) in order to keep the heat in and the cold out (or vice versa, depending on the season), truly defines the skyline of Toronto. It's "a palette of color and texture as well as mass," in Zerafa's own words; "It has a cathedral feeling, due to natural light." It is certainly worth a visit.

After seeing all the bank buildings, the next best place to get a sense of orientation would be, without doubt, the **CN Tower.** One local wag suggested that the 180-story, 130,000-ton structure was built to teach Canadian men humility. Perhaps. But for all its basic ugliness, the CN Tower is the ideal place to get a sense of the layout of Toronto. The food here is terrible, but those of you who enjoy an overpriced drink now and then should

Toronto Exploring *(Boxes Refer to Detail Maps)*

YORK

Lawrence Ave. W.

Dufferin St.

Allen Expwy.

Avenue Rd.

Mount Pleasant Rd.

Eglinton Ave. W.

Eglinton Ave. E.

Laird Dr.

Oakwood Ave.

Rogers Rd.

St. Clair Ave. W.

EAST YORK

Landsowne Ave.

Dufferin St.

O'Connor

Davenport Rd.

Dupont St. St.

404

Bayview Ext.

Broadview Ave.

Pape Ave.

Tours 2 and 3

Bloor St. W.

Danforth Ave.

College St.

Dundas St. W.

Bathurst

Parliament St.

Gerrard St. E.

Queen St. W.

Dundas St. E.

King St. W.

Eastern Ave.

Lake Shore Blvd. E.

2

2

Canadian National Exhibition

Harbourfront Park

✈ **Toronto Island Airport**

Inner Harbour

Toronto Islands

Aquatic Park

Tour 1

N

Lake Ontario

0   2 miles

0   3 km

make a reservation and head up the tower any clear day between noon and 5.

Back on terra firma, imagine the downtown area of Toronto as a large rectangle. The southern part is, as you already know, Lake Ontario. The western part, shooting north to Bloor Street and beyond, is Spadina Road, near the foot of which stand the CN Tower, Harbourfront, and the spectacular new SkyDome Stadium. On the east, running from the lakefront north for hundreds of miles (believe it or not), is Yonge Street, which divides the city in half. University Avenue, a major road that parallels Yonge Street, for some reason changes its name to Avenue Road at the corner of Bloor Street, next to the Royal Ontario Museum. A further note: College Street, legitimately named since many of the University of Toronto's buildings run along it, becomes Carlton Street where it intersects Yonge Street, then heads east.

Tour 1: The Waterfront, St. Lawrence, the Financial District, and the Underground City

Numbers in the margin correspond with points of interest on the Tour 1 map.

Since, as we noted, Toronto has a waterfront as its southernmost border, it seems logical that we begin there. And it shouldn't be too hard to get there, since it's just south of Union Station. Unfortunately, only a handful of the city's major north–south streets—Bay, Jarvis, and York streets—go right to Lake Ontario from the city center. A new streetcar line between Union Station and the lakefront came into operation in the summer of 1990. It stops at Harbourfront, and continues on westward to Spadina Avenue, before looping back to Union Station—which is the beautiful terminus of both the University and Yonge north/south subway lines, and where trains leave for Stratford, Niagara-on-the-Lake, and Niagara Falls. The very fact that this new streetcar line was built at all underlines civic awareness of the growing importance of the central waterfront, both residentially and recreationally.

It was not always thus. Indeed, until quite recently, Toronto was notoriously negligent about its waterfront. The Gardiner Expressway, Lakeshore Boulevard, and a network of rusty rail yards stood as hideous barriers to the natural beauty of Lake Ontario. The city wished it could drop the expressway underground, but an estimated cost of several billion dollars put a rapid halt to that discussion.

Just over a decade ago, thank heaven, the various levels of government—city, Metro, provincial (Ontario) and federal (Ottawa)—began a struggle to change this unfortunate situation. By that time, most of the area just south of the Gardiner Expressway and Lakeshore Boulevard was overflowing with grain silos, various warehouses, and most unattractive (and unsweet-smelling) towers of malt, used by local breweries.

Part of the answer was the building of a handsome hotel, the Harbour Castle Westin (which, until the fall of 1987, was a Hilton hotel), and an attractive tower of condominiums. The hotel has an exterior, glassed-in elevator that offers guests a view of the waterfront and the Toronto Islands.

Toronto Islands   Just behind the giant Harbour Castle Westin is the embarka-
❶   tion point for ferries to the **Toronto Islands,** surely one of the
highlights of any trip to the city—especially from May to October. It takes only eight minutes for the quaint little ferries to
chug across the tiny bay. The islands make up one of the world's
great parks.

The four thin, curved, tree-lined islands—Centre, Ward's, Algonquin, and Hanlan's Point—have been attracting visitors
since 1833, four years before Victoria became queen and just a
year before the town of York changed its name to Toronto. And
the more than 550 acres of parkland are irresistible, especially
during the hot summer months, when downtown Toronto
seems to be melting as rapidly as the ice cream cones sold
everywhere on the islands.

Be warned: The crowds always head to Centre Island, since
that's where most of the amusements are located. It gets so
crowded, in fact, that no bicycles are allowed on the ferry to
that island during summer weekends. Take one of the equally
frequent ferries to Ward's or Hanlan's, both of which are quiet,
delightful places to picnic, sunbathe, read under a tree, or simply escape the city. You'll enjoy spectacular views of Toronto's
majestic skyline, especially as the setting sun turns the Royal
Bank Tower and other downtown skyscrapers to gold, silver,
and bronze.

The beaches on Ward's tend to be the least crowded. They're
also the cleanest, although there have been problems with the
cleanliness of Lake Ontario's water over the past decade. Except for the hottest days in August, the Great Lake tends to be
uncomfortably chilly, so bring appropriate clothing. You'll be
wise to rent a bike for an hour or more and work your way
across the interconnected islands. (Students of the petty politics of the petit bourgeois might enjoy hearing about the endless controversy over the hundred or so homes on Ward's and
neighboring Algonquin Island that many city politicians have
been fighting to tear down for years. Some argue that having
people living in a much-used park makes it safer to visit; others
insist that the "squatters" are using up precious parkland.
Whoever is "right," it appears that the homes on the islands are
safe for the next decade, at least.)

If you are traveling with children, Centre Island is the one to
check out first. Signs everywhere read "Please Walk on the
Grass," which should charm visitors to pieces, even before they
begin to explore. A few hundred yards from the ferry docks lies
Centreville, an amusement park that's supposed to be a turn-of-
the-century children's village. The concept works wondrously
well: True, the pizza, fries, and hot dogs are barely edible—
pack a lunch!—but on the little Main Street there are charming
shops, a town hall, a little railroad station, and more than a doz-
en rides, including a restored 1890s merry-go-round with over
four dozen hand-carved animals. And there's no entrance fee to
the modest, 14-acre amusement park, although you'll have to
pay a nominal charge for each ride or buy an all-day pass. Perhaps most enjoyable for children is the free **Far Enough Farm,**
which is near enough to walk to. It has all kinds of animals to
pet and feed, ranging from piglets to geese, cows to birds. *Tel.
416/363–1112. Centreville: open weekends Apr. 30–May 15 and
Sept. 10–25; daily Victoria Day (mid-May)–Labor Day.*

All transportation on these islands comes to you compliments of your feet: No cars are allowed anywhere. Your nostrils will wonder at the lack of exhaust fumes, while your feet will wonder why you walked all the way along the boardwalk from Centre to Ward's Island (1.5 mi).

There you'll find **Gibraltar Lighthouse,** built back in 1808, making it the oldest monument in the city that is still standing on its original site. Right next to it is a pond stocked with rainbow trout, and a concession for buying bait and renting rods.

Sandy beaches circle the islands, the best ones being those on the southeast tip of Ward's, the southernmost edge of Centre, and the west side of Hanlan's. There are free changing rooms near each of these areas, but no facilities for checking your clothes. Swimming in the various lagoons and channels is prohibited. The winter can be bitter cold on the island, but snowshoeing and cross-country skiing with downtown Toronto over your shoulder will be irresistible to many. In the summer, there are rowboat and canoe rentals, tennis courts, gardens, playgrounds, and a wildlife sanctuary.

The ferries run irregularly during the winter: every hour or so until 10 or 11 AM, and then every few hours thereafter. In the summer, the ferries leave three times an hour at the foot of Bay Street. The cost is $2.50 adults, $1.25 senior citizens, 75¢ children under 15. For a recording giving the schedule and prices, call 416/392–8193; for other information, call 416/392–8186.

Harbourfront Centre ❷ Back at the ferry docks on the mainland, your next move should be to **Harbourfront Centre.** This is a trip that is well worth planning ahead—check *Now, eye,* and *Toronto Life* magazines, as well as daily newspaper listings, to see what concerts, dances, art shows, festivals, etc., are taking place there, and build your visit around them.

For many years, as we said, Toronto had good reason to be ashamed of its God-given, man-taken-away waterfront. Today Harbourfront Centre has become a 100-acre culture-and-recreation center, drawing over 3 million visitors each year. Stretching from just west of the Harbour Castle Westin for nearly a mile to Bathurst Street, the complex has become the scene of fabulous entertainment, exquisite buildings, glorious attractions—a true match for San Francisco's Pier 39 and Baltimore's Inner Harbor. Sadly, there have been numerous problems with funding this wonderful concept: All three levels of government—federal, provincial, and local—are fighting over who should pay and what may have to be closed. Still, even if some of the attractions are lost in the bureaucracy, this is still one of the highlights of Toronto.

Highlights are many. The **Queen's Quay** (pronounced "key") **Terminal** is a must: The 57-year-old food warehouse was transformed in 1983, at a cost of over $60 million, into a magnificent eight-story structure with delightful specialty shops, eateries, and the handsome 450-seat Premiere Dance Theatre.

Contemporary art exhibits of painting and sculpture, architecture and video, photography and design, now take place at the **Power Plant,** just west of Queen's Quay. (The building started in 1927 as a power station for an ice-making plant; you can spot it by the tall red smokestack.)

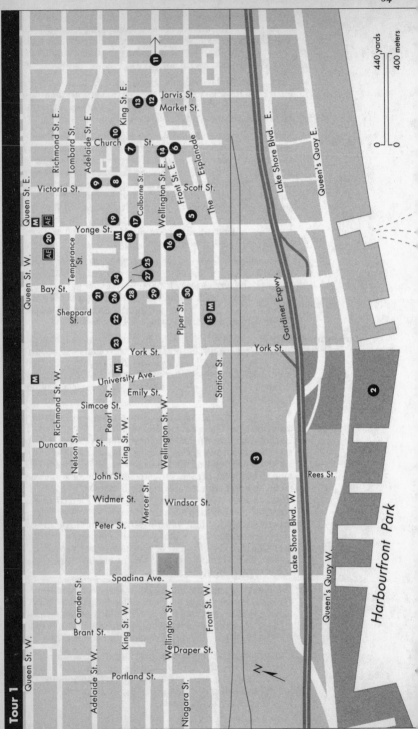

Tour 1

Harbourfront Park

Queen St. W.
Queen St. E.
Richmond St. E.
Lombard St.
Adelaide St. E.
King St. E.
Jarvis St.
Market St.
Church St.
Victoria St.
Colborne St.
Wellington St. E.
Front St. E.
Scott St.
The Esplanade
Yonge St.
Temperance St.
Bay St.
Sheppard St.
York St.
University Ave.
Emily St.
Simcoe St.
Pearl St.
Duncan St.
Nelson St.
John St.
Widmer St.
Mercer St.
Windsor St.
Peter St.
Spadina Ave.
Camden St.
Brant St.
Adelaide St. W.
King St. W.
Wellington St. W.
Portland St.
Niagara St.
Draper St.
Front St. W.
Queen's Quay W.
Lake Shore Blvd. W.
Lake Shore Blvd. E.
Queen's Quay E.
Gardiner Expwy.
York St.
Station St.
Piper St.
Richmond St. W.
Rees St.

N

440 yards
400 meters

1 Toronto Islands

Argus Corp., **8**
Bank of Commerce, **26**
Bank of Montreal/
BCE Place, **4**
Bank of Nova
Scotia, **24**

Canada Permanent
Trust Building, **21**
CN Tower, **3**
Commerce Court, **27**
Dominion Bank, **18**
15 Wellington
St. West, **16**

First Canadian
Place, **22**
Flatiron Bldg., **14**
Former Stock
Exchange, **29**

Gooderham and
Worts, **11**
Harbourfront
Centre, **2**
King Edward Hotel, **7**
O'Keefe Centre, **5**

"Old" Bank of
Commerce Tower, **25**
Royal Bank, **19**
Royal Bank Plaza, **30**
St. James
Cathedral, **10**

St. Lawrence
Centre, **6**
St. Lawrence Hall, **13**
St. Lawrence Mkt., **12**
Simpsons, **20**
Toronto-Dominion
Centre, **28**

Toronto Islands, **1**
Toronto Stock
Exchange, **23**
Traders Bank, **17**
Union Station, **15**
York County
Magistrate's
Courthouse, **9**

KEY

AE American Express Office

York Quay Centre has concerts, live theater, readings, even skilled artisans at work in open craft studios. A shallow pond at the south end is used for canoe lessons in warmer months, and as the largest artificial ice-skating rink in North America in more wintry times. The Nautical Centre nearby has many private firms offering lessons in sailing and canoeing, and vessels for rent.

On **Maple Leaf Quay,** the very popular **Antique Market** takes place every day but Monday. The 70 dealers triple in number each Sunday.

Here are some of the seasonal highlights: *Late January:* an Ice Canoe Race. *February:* two weekends of Winterfest. *April:* an Easter program. *May:* the Milk International Children's Festival and the Canoe Festival. *June:* a Jazz Festival. *July:* Canada Day celebrations and a Parade of Lights. *August:* the Zingy Dingy Boat Race and Teddy Bears Fair. *September:* a youth-oriented Labor Day weekend. *October:* the world-acclaimed Authors' Festival, a Harvest Festival, and Francophone Week. *November:* the Swedish Christmas Fair. *December:* Festive Trees, the Cavalcade of Lights, and a New Year's Eve Party.

Harbourfront Centre is within walking distance of Union Station. Drivers should head for the foot of Bay Street or Spadina Avenue and park in one of the many lots. For information, call 416/364–5665. The "Traffic Hotline" will give you current information on "the fastest and easiest route to Queen's Quay," 24 hours a day, seven days a week, tel. 416/363–4411. There's now a streetcar that swings around from Union Station to Harbourfront Centre, and on to Spadina Avenue.

❸ From Harbourfront Centre, it's a short walk to the **CN Tower,** an attraction second only to Eaton Centre.

The CN Tower, the tallest free-standing structure in the world, is tall with a cause: So many high buildings had been built over the past few decades that lower radio and TV transmission towers were having trouble broadcasting over them.

And so the tower stands, rather arrogantly, on Front Street near Spadina Avenue, not far from the waterfront. It's fully 1,815 feet, 5 inches high and it really is worth a visit, *if the weather is clear.* And it's in the *Guinness Book of World Records.*

Four elevators zoom up the outside of the $57 million tower, which weighs 130,000 tons and contains enough concrete to build a curb along Highway 401 from Toronto to Kingston, some 163 miles to the west. The ride takes but a minute, going at 20 feet a second, a rate of ascent similar to that of a jet-plane takeoff. But each elevator has only one floor-to-ceiling glass wall, preventing vertigo.

The **Skypod,** about two-thirds up the tower, is seven stories high, and it has two observation decks, a nightclub, and a revolving restaurant. It also has oodles of microwave equipment that is not open to the public but is its true *raison d'être.*

Level 2 is the **outdoor observation deck,** with an enclosed promenade, and an outdoor balcony for looking straight down at the ground. Level 3 of the Skypod, the **indoor observation deck,** has not only conventional telescopes, but high-powered peritelescopes that almost simulate flight. Also here is a unique Tour

Wand System, which provides an audio tour of the City of Toronto. A minitheater shows a presentation on the CN Tower.

The **Space Deck,** which is 33 stories higher, costs $2.35 extra; at an elevation of 1,465 feet, it is the world's highest public observation gallery. But even from the Skypod below, you can often see Lake Simcoe to the north, and the mist rising from Niagara Falls to the south. All the decks provide spectacular panoramic views of Toronto, Lake Ontario, and the Toronto Islands.

CN Tower, 301 Front St. W, tel. 416/360–8500. Observation deck $10.95 adults, $5.35 senior citizens and children 13–16, $4.25 children under 13. Audio Tour Wand included in price. Peak visiting hours: between 11 AM and 4 PM, especially on weekends. Open summers, 10 AM–midnight; the rest of the year, weekdays 10–10, weekends 9:30 AM–11 PM.

A charming one-hour experience is **Tour of the Universe,** located at the base of the CN Tower. It's a simulated space-shuttle journey to Jupiter in the year 2019, with everything from a 64-screen Multivision Wall that briefs you on your upcoming flight, to a laser "inoculation," to an InterPlanetary Passport souvenir, and a too-brief ride in a flight simulator that provides physical motion to match the spectacular special-effects film. It's very well done and a pleasant break before or after the CN Tower visit. *Admission: $7 adults, $6.50 senior citizens and children 13–16, $5.35 children under 13. Call 416/360–8500 for more information.*

St. Lawrence From Harbourfront Centre and the CN Tower, you may wish to experience the area of **St. Lawrence,** where the 19th century meets the 21st, before you head back into the 20th century of the financial district. Back when the city fathers divided up the city, in 1834, they gave each district a saint's name. They christened the area that lay farthest to the south, extending from the lake up to King Street and from Yonge Street east to Parliament, St. Lawrence.

Much like the waterfront before Harbourfront Centre, it was for years a depressing, tacky section of old, dirty buildings, factories, and railway tracks. But like so many parts of this city, it has been born again, as any area with a saint's name should be capable of doing.

During any walk through the St. Lawrence area, you will jog between the centuries: from strikingly beautiful, centuries-old buildings to the new St. Lawrence project, just south of the Esplanade, designed to house close to 10,000 people. It's part of Toronto's genius, this peaceful coexistence of classy condominiums and low-cost (alias subsidized) housing. No, downtowns do not necessarily have to be dead, dirty, and dangerous.

This area is where Toronto began, as the village of York, back in 1793. Start at the northwest corner of Yonge and Front streets ④ at the **Bank of Montreal building,** an early example of ostentatious bank architecture. Built in the mid-1880s by the architects Darling & Curry, it is a significant city landmark. Note the richly carved Ohio stone, and don't miss the Hermes figure supporting the chimney near the back of the building. It's a beauty. Be sure to walk through the Galleria of **BCE Place,** a modern complex built around this magnificent heritage building. The new complex stretches from Front Street up to Wellington Street and from Yonge Street over to Bay Street.

On the southeast corner of Yonge and Front streets is one of the major showcases for live theater, opera, and ballet in the city: the gigantic **O'Keefe Centre.** Another block east, at the corner of Church Street, is the two-theater complex of the **St. Lawrence Centre,** which has a number of repertory companies and many concerts year-round (*see* Concert Halls and Theaters in Chapter 7).

Walk up to King Street and admire the attractive (and ritzy) **King Edward Hotel,** built in 1903 and recently refurbished in grand fashion. Note the details both inside and out; the architect was none other than E. J. Lennox, who also designed Old City Hall, Massey Hall, and Casa Loma.

Looking north from King Street, on the west side of Toronto Street, is the very understated head office of **Argus Corporation,** one of Canada's major conglomerates. It was originally built in 1853 as a post office. Still farther to the north is the **York County Magistrate's Courthouse,** built in 1852 and restored in 1982.

At the corner of Church and King streets stands **St. James Cathedral** (Anglican), with its noble, gothic spires. The steeple is the tallest in Canada—even if the bank towers dwarf it now—and its illuminated spire clock once guided ships into the harbor (which was once far closer; everything south of Front Street is landfill). This is the fourth St. James Cathedral on this site; the third one burned down in the Great Fire of 1849.

Continue east to Trinity Street and walk south. The first distillery in Canada—**Gooderham and Worts**—celebrated its 185th birthday in 1987. The massive limestone building is still used today to make rum spirits from molasses. The brothers-in-law started their company as a flour mill but soon began making alcohol out of the surplus grain.

Return along Front Street to the corner of Jarvis Street. There it is—the **St. Lawrence Market.** Built in 1844 as Toronto's first city hall (what other city has four extant?), it now has an exhibition hall upstairs where the original council chambers stood. It continues to serve the citizens of the city, although in a more delicious fashion—as a food market. It grew up around the city hall at the turn of the century. (Who says governments never produce anything?)

Renovated in 1978, the market is renowned for its wide range of foods—from kiwi fruit to Ontario cheddar, from homemade bread to conch meat. Its four dozen stalls are open each Tuesday through Saturday, and are an ideal place to create lunches for the Metro Zoo, Canada's Wonderland, or the nearby Toronto Islands—three places where the excellence of the attractions in no way guarantees excellence in cuisine.

The plain brick building just across Front Street, on the north side, is another superb farmer's market, but it is open only on Saturdays. As early as 4 AM, the finest produce from farms just north of Toronto pours into this cornucopia.

Walk just behind the market, one block north, and you'll find, on the south side of King Street, another treasure: the second city hall of Toronto, today called **St. Lawrence Hall.** This is Victorian architecture at its finest (built in 1850). Erected originally for musical performances and balls, this is where Jenny Lind sang and where P. T. Barnum first presented the midget Tom

Thumb. For the last several years, it has been the home of the National Ballet of Canada. Take time to admire its interior and its exterior; it is an architectural gem.

Back on Front Street, heading west toward Yonge Street and the heart of downtown, you'll encounter a building that has relatives in pie-shaped lots all over North America—the **Flatiron Building.** There it stands, on the little triangle of Wellington, Church, and Front streets. It was erected in 1892 as the head office of the Gooderham and Worts distilling company, and it is now a prestigious office building. You may wish to take a ride in its original elevator.

One more treat before we head into Toronto's financial district: As you walk west along the sweet little park that sits behind the Flatiron Building, look back at the witty mural by Derek Besant (on the west side of the Flatiron Building). It's a giant painting of a painting of windows, drawn around the real windows of the structure; it looks as though it's been tacked up on the wall and is peeling off. It plays tricks with your eyes, makes children and adults giggle, and is a pleasant way to end your walk through St. Lawrence.

Financial District   One doesn't always recommend visits to a train station, but **Union Station** is special. On the south side of Front Street, between Bay and York streets (and across from the handsome Royal York Hotel), Union Station is a most historic building, though it is of this century. It was designed back in 1907, when trains were still as exciting as space shuttles are today, and it was opened in 1927 by the Prince of Wales. As the popular historian Pierre Berton has written, its planning recalls "the love lavished on medieval churches." Of course, the latter used to take centuries to build; this shrine to Our Lady of the Train was put up in less than two decades.

Put up? More like erected. Established. Created. Try to imagine the awe of the immigrants who poured into Toronto between the two world wars by the tens of thousands, staring up at the towering ceiling of Italian tile or leaning against one of the 22 pillars, each one 40 feet tall and weighing 75 tons. Walk along the lengthy concourse and study the mellow reflection in its walls. Get a sense of the beauty of the light flooding through the high, arched windows at each end of the mammoth hall.

When you look up, you almost expect to see a rose window; instead, you can read the names of the towns and cities of Canada that were served by the two railroads that used Union Station when it first opened. Many of those places are no longer served by trains, which take too long in a world that now seems to travel at the speed of light. That the remarkable structure still remains, its trains (and, more recently, hundreds of very modern subway cars) still chugging back and forth several levels below its glorious canopy, is no thanks to the many local politicians of the 1970s who wanted it torn down. But once again, Torontonians rallied, petitioned, and won the day.

As you come out of Union Station, walk back to Yonge Street and the beautiful **Bank of Montreal** building, at the northwest corner of Front Street. Just steps north of it is a shabby row of shops, which are among the oldest surviving commercial buildings in the city. Many of the original Georgian facades have been drastically altered, but the one- and two-story buildings give you a sense of the scale of buildings from the 1850s and are the last remnants of the early business community of the then brand-new city of Toronto. As of early 1993 the giant **BCE Place,** built around and above the bank, finally should be completed. By then, the Hockey Hall of Fame and Museum will have found its home in the old bank's rooms.

(16) Make a left turn at the first intersection, which is Wellington Street West. **Number 15** is the oldest building on this walk, an elegant stone bank designed in the Greek Revival style. It's one of the earliest (1845) projects of William Thomas, the talented architect who also designed the St. Lawrence Hall, which we recently visited.

Head back a few steps to Yonge Street and go north again, away from Front Street. On the northeast corner of Yonge and **(17)** Melinda streets, at 67 Yonge Street, is **Traders Bank,** the first "skyscraper" of the city when it went up in 1905–06, complete with an observation deck. It's fun to see what was considered the CN Tower of the turn of the century. The next building to the north (69 Yonge St.) was built in 1913, and it helped turn the intersection into a grouping of the tallest buildings in North America, outside of Manhattan. After more than 75 years, it is still owned by **Canadian Pacific,** the largest private employer in Canada (planes, trains, hotels, and more).

Just across the street, at the southwest corner of King and **(18)** Yonge streets, is the **Dominion Bank building** (1 King St. W), erected in 1913 by the same architects who designed the voluptuous Bank of Montreal building we saw at Yonge and Front streets. It's a classic Chicago-style skyscraper and is well worth a visit inside. Climb the marble-and-bronze stairway to the opulent banking hall on the second floor, and enjoy the marble floor, marble walls, and the ornate plaster ceiling, which features the coats of arms of the then nine Canadian provinces. (Newfoundland did not join the Confederation until 1949). No, they most certainly do not build places like this anymore.

On the northeast corner of Yonge and King streets (2 King St. **(19)** E) is the original **Royal Bank building,** also put up in 1913. Note the distinctive cornice, the overhanging roof, the decorative pattern of sculpted ox skulls above the ground-floor windows, and the classically detailed leaves at the top of the Corinthian columns. Greek culture lives!

Walking several blocks farther north along Yonge Street, you **(20)** reach the original **Simpsons department store,** on the northwest corner of Richmond Street West and Yonge Street (176 Yonge St.). Built in 1895, it was one of the city's first buildings with a steel-frame construction. There are attractive terra-cotta decorations in the section closest to Yonge Street, which went up in 1908; the part along Richmond Street, near Bay Street, added in 1928, is a fine example of the Art Deco style, popular between the two world wars. In the fall of 1991, Simpsons was bought by The Hudson Bay Company; it is now called The Bay.

Continue a few steps west to Bay Street, a name synonymous with finance and power in Canada, as Wall Street is in the United States. Head south (left), back toward the lakefront. Just south of Adelaide Street, on the west side of Bay Street, is **(21)** the **Canada Permanent Trust Building** (320 Bay St.). Built in the very year of the stock-market crash (and we don't mean the 1987 one), it's a skyscraper in the New York wedding-cake

style. Look up at the ornate stone carvings both on the lower
stories and on the top, where carved, stylized faces peer down
to the street below. Walk through the imposing vaulted entrance with its polished brass doors, and note that even the elevator doors in the foyer are embossed brass. The spacious
banking hall has a vaulted ceiling, marble walls and pillars, and
a marble floor with mosaic borders. Those were the days—or so
they thought.

Turn right (west) along King Street, and you arrive at the first
of the towering bank buildings that have defined Toronto's sky-
②② line over the past two decades. This is **First Canadian Place** (100
King St. W), built in the early 1970s by the firm of Bregman and
Hamann, architects, with consultation from Edward Durrell
Stone. Also called the Bank of Montreal tower, its 72 stories
were deliberately faced with white marble to contrast with the
black of the Toronto-Dominion Centre, to the south, and with
the silver of the Commerce Court Tower. The second phase of
②③ the project, opened in 1983, houses the ultramodern **Toronto
Stock Exchange (TSE)**.

The Exchange Tower (2 First Canadian Pl.) has a Visitors' Center that should be visited by anyone interested in the world of
high finance. Enter the Exchange Tower and proceed to the
TSE reception area on the ground floor. The nearby escalator
and circular staircase lead to the Visitors' Center and observation gallery.

This is the pulse of the Canadian economy, where papers fly,
traders scoot about, tickers tick away, phones ring off the
hooks, and fortunes are made or lost. Here, visitors can learn
about the securities industry through colorful displays, or even
join in daily presentations. The attractions are many: a 100-foot
public gallery, a 140-seat auditorium, recorded tours, a mini
slide show of the TSE 300 Composite Index (an echo of the Dow
Jones Average). *Tel. 416/947–4670. Admission free. Public
tour daily at 2 PM. Open weekdays 9:30–4.*

On the northeast corner of King and Bay streets (44 King St.
②④ W) is the **Bank of Nova Scotia.** Built between 1949 and 1951,
and partially replaced by the recently completed Scotia Tower
just to the east, it has sculptural panels inspired by Greek my-
thology above the large, exterior windows. In the lobby, there
are reliefs symbolizing four regions of Canada and a brightly
colored gilded plaster ceiling. The original stainless steel and
glass stairway with marine motifs is attractive, as are the marble counters and floors. The north wall relief depicts some of
the industries and enterprises financed by the bank.

②⑤ On the southeast corner of King and Bay streets is the **"Old"
Bank of Commerce Tower,** which for a third of a century was the
tallest building in the British Commonwealth. Its base has bas-
relief carvings, and marvelous animal and floral ornamentation
around the vaulted entrance. Because the top is set back, you
must look up to see the huge, carved human heads on all four
sides of the building. These are "the wise old men of commerce," who are supposed to be looking out over the city.

②⑥ The **Bank of Commerce building** (25 King St. W) was built in the
two years following the stock-market crash of 1929, but the
hard times didn't prevent the creation of a stunning interior of
marble floors, limestone walls, and bronze vestibule doors decorated with masks, owls, and animals. In the alcoves on either

side of the entrance are murals that trace the history of transportation. The bronze elevator doors are richly decorated, the vaulted banking hall is lit by period chandeliers, and each desk has its own lamp. What a difference from the often cold, brittle skyscrapers of today!

㉗ Just south of the "old tower," at 243 Bay Street, is **Commerce Court,** the bank's 57-story stainless-steel sister. And due west, just across Bay Street, also on the south side of King Street, **㉘** are the two black towers of the **Toronto-Dominion Centre,** the first International-style skyscrapers built in Toronto, thanks to the "less is more" man, Mies van der Rohe. The two towers went up in the mid-1960s, and they are starkly plain and stripped of ornament. The only decoration consists of geometric repetition and the only rich extravagance is the use of rich materials, such as marble counters and leather-covered furniture.

Immediately south of the T-D Centre towers, at 232 Bay **㉙** Street, is the **former Toronto Stock Exchange building,** which, for close to half a century, was the financial hub of Toronto. Built in 1937 of polished pink granite and smooth buff limestone, it's a delightful example of Art Deco design. The stainless steel doors are a wonder, as is the wise and witty stone frieze carved above them. Don't miss the hilarious social commentary up there—the banker with the top hat marching behind the laborer, his hand sneaking into the worker's pocket. Only in Canada, where socialism has always been a strong political force, would you find such an artistic statement on the side of a stock exchange.

Walk south another block, still heading toward Lake Ontario, to the northwest corner of Bay and Front streets: There, in all **㉚** its golden glory, is the **Royal Bank Plaza,** built only in 1976 but already a classic of its kind. Be sure to go into the 120-foot-high banking hall and admire the lovely hanging sculpture by Jesús Raphaél Soto.

And there you have our tour of the waterfront, St. Lawrence, and the financial district, which could take anywhere from several hours to one or two days, depending on whether or not you head off to the Toronto Islands, spend several hours shopping at Harbourfront Centre, or catch some theater and meals along the way. But in all three portions of this walk, you have encountered what makes Toronto so admirable: the coexistence of the city's oldest and newest buildings, often side by side. The fact that many of the older properties have been included on the city's Inventory of Buildings of Architectural and Historical Importance proves just how determined Toronto is not to destroy its history. Only two cheers, though. There was massive destruction of great 19th-century buildings throughout the first quarter of this century; many of their still-striking facades, porticoes, and columns can be seen on the grounds of the Guild Inn, in Scarborough, about a half-hour's drive to the northeast of downtown Toronto (*see* Off the Beaten Track in Chapter 6 for more information about that forlorn and often moving collection of architectural artifacts).

If you cross Front Street to its south side and return to Union Station, you can begin another rather fascinating walk—and a very welcome one, should the weather be windy, cold, snowy, slushy, or even too hot: Toronto's Underground City.

Underground City   The origins of Toronto's **Underground City**—purportedly the
largest pedestrian walkway in the world—go back over a gen-
eration, and it somehow all came about with very little assistance from the powers that be. As each major new building
went up, the respective developers kept agreeing to connect
their underground shopping areas, until it finally all came together. One can walk—and shop, eat, browse, etc.—without
ever seeing the light of day, from beneath Union Station to the
Royal York Hotel, the Toronto-Dominion Centre, First Canadian Place, the Sheraton Centre, The Bay, the Eaton Centre, and
the Atrium. Altogether, it extends through nearly 3 miles of
tunnels and seven subway stops. But these are not the depressing, even dangerous subway tunnels that one encounters in
Paris, London, and New York; they are sparklingly clean, and
the underground is wall-to-wall with more than 300 eateries,
shops, banks, even dental offices and theaters.

One can respond with civic pride ("The world's only weatherproof city!" "The ultimate in climate control!") or with cyni-
cism, echoing King Lear's lament over Cordelia: "Why should
cars and animals have fresh air while we are forced to live,
breathe, and shop underground?" But one is *not* forced, which
is part of the Underground City's charm. Shop along the main
streets of Toronto as you wish—but isn't it nice to know that
there's a subterranean complex, running for dozens of blocks,
just a few feet below you? And with Toronto's weather—so often inclement—it's kind of an insurance policy against sudden
or insistent storms, or merely the exhaust fumes of cars.

The Underground City has been called a must-see for visitors,
but that's debatable; Toronto overflows with attractions and
first-class shopping that it's hard to recommend that one rush
"downstairs." And, indeed, there are numerous other, but far
smaller, underground retail passageways: beneath Bloor
Street, running east of Yonge Street; and along College Street,
between Yonge and Bay streets. There are offshoots of the Underground City reaching all the way to the New City Hall and
beyond. Enter the subterranean community from anywhere
between Dundas Street on the north and Union Station on the
south, and you'll encounter everything from art exhibitions to
buskers (the city actually auditions young musicians and licenses the best to perform throughout its subway system and
elsewhere) to walkways, fountains, and trees growing as much
as two stories high. Because up to 50% of the complex lies underneath Toronto's multibillion-dollar financial district, you
will keep bumping into men and women in business suits,
browsing or on lunch breaks.

So don't see this so much as a walking tour but rather as a very
pleasant option to escape sun, rain, snow, or heat. It's just another example of Toronto's architectural ingenuity—making a
city that occasionally lacks a livable climate more livable.

Tour 2: From Eaton Centre to the City Halls and the Far and Middle East

*Numbers in the margin correspond with points of interest on
the Tours 2 and 3 map.*

From the corners of Yonge and Queen streets, one can begin a
tour that will include several of this city's most popular attractions, as well as some of its most interesting neighborhoods.

Alas, one of these, Eaton Centre, is closed on Sunday, as of this writing, while others thrive on what is still considered the Lord's Day in the province of Ontario. Still, the following walking/driving tour should make for a very pleasant day in the central and western portions of Toronto's downtown.

Eaton Centre and City Hall

❶

Eaton Centre, a 3-million-square-foot building that extends along the west side of Yonge Street all the way from Queen Street up to Dundas Street (with subway stops at each end), has quickly become the number-one tourist attraction of Toronto. Even people who rank shopping with the flu will still be charmed, even dazzled, for this is a beautiful environment indeed.

The handsome collection of over 300 stores and services, just a few blocks from Toronto's New City Hall, was quite controversial in the late 1970s, when some Torontonians attacked it as "a sterile and artificial environment." Yet others, like Jane Jacobs, author of *Death and Life of Great American Cities*, wrote that "people like the environment of the Galleria. Its popularity has lessons for Yonge Street."

And lessons for most cities of the world, as well. From its graceful glass roof, arching 127 feet above the lowest of the mall levels, to Michael Snow's exquisite flock of fiberglass Canada geese floating poetically in the open space of the Galleria, to the glass-enclosed elevators, porthole windows, and nearly two dozen long and graceful escalators, there are plenty of good reasons for visiting Eaton Centre.

Such a wide selection of shops and eateries can be confusing, however, so here's a simple rule: Galleria Level 1 contains two food courts; popularly priced fashions; photo, electronics and record stores; and much "convenience" merchandise. Level 2 is directed to the middle-income shopper, while Level 3, suitably, has the highest elevation, fashion, and prices. **Eaton's,** one of Canada's classic department-store chains, has a nine-floor branch here. At the southern end of Level 3 is a skywalk that connects the centre to the seven-floor **The Bay** (formerly Simpsons) department store, across Queen Street.

Dozens of restaurants, from snack to full-service, can be found here. A 17-theater cinema complex—the initial unit of the now worldwide Cineplex chain—is located at the Dundas Street entrance. (Tuesdays are half-price days for movie tickets, and it's a cheap 90-minute break from shopping.)

There are safe, well-lighted parking garages sprinkled around the centre, with spaces for some 1,800 cars. *Admission free. Open weekdays 10–9, Sat. 9:30–6.*

Exit the Eaton Centre at Queen Street and walk just one long block west to Toronto's city halls. Yes, the plural is correct.

❷ **Old City Hall** is the beautiful building at the northeast corner of Queen and Bay streets, sweetly coexisting with the futuristic **❸** **New City Hall,** just across the street, on the west side.

The creator of the old one, which opened in 1899, was none other than E. J. Lennox, who would later design Casa Loma. It was considered one of North America's most impressive municipal halls in its heyday, and since the opening of its younger sister, it has been the site of the provincial courts, county offices, and thousands of low-cost marriages. Do note the hideous gargoyles above the front steps, which were apparently the architect's witty way of mocking certain politicians of the time. The designer also carved his name under the eaves on all four faces of the building—a cry for recognition from nearly a century ago. The great stained-glass window as you enter is attractive, and the handsome old structure stands in delightful contrast to its daring and unique sibling.

The New City Hall—humorously described by many as "a urinal for the Jolly Green Giant"—was the result of a massive international competition in 1958, to which some 520 architects from 42 countries submitted designs. The winning presentation by Finnish architect Viljo Revell was controversial: two towers of differing height, and curved, yet! But there was and is a logic to it all: An aerial view of the New City Hall shows a circular council chamber sitting like an eye between the two tower "eyelids."

Within months of its opening in 1965, the New City Hall became a symbol of a thriving city, with a silhouette as recognizable as, say, the Eiffel Tower. How sad that architect Revell died before his masterwork was opened to the public.

The entire area is a living, breathing environment, with Nathan Phillips Square (named after the mayor who initiated the project) spreading across a 9-acre plaza in front of the building. It has become a true gathering place for the community, whether for royal visits, protest rallies, picnic lunches, or concerts. The reflecting pool is a delight in the summer, and even more so in the winter, when office workers come down and skate during lunch. There is a Peace Garden for quiet meditation, a striking bronze sculpture by famed British sculptor Henry Moore (*The Archer*), and a remarkable mural within the main entrance of the New City Hall, *Metropolis*, put together by sculptor David Partridge from 100,000 common nails.

Annual events at the New City Hall include the Spring Flower Show in late March; the Toronto Outdoor Art Exhibition early each July (the 32nd annual one will be held in the summer of 1993); and the Cavalcade of Lights from late November through Christmas each year, when over 100,000 sparkling lights are illuminated across both city halls.

Tel. 416/392–7341 for details; for information on facilities for the disabled, 416/392–7732. Underground garage for 2,400 cars. Open to public weekdays 8:30–4:30. Free 30-minute guided tours on weekdays. Cafeteria in basement of New City Hall open daily 7:30–4.

Chinatown and the Museums Just north of the New City Hall begins Toronto's main **Chinatown**, which is the largest in all of North America—and that includes San Francisco. There are more than 100,000 Chinese living in the city, which is quite impressive, considering that just over a century ago there was only one—Sam Ching, who ran a hand laundry on Adelaide Street.

Today Chinatown covers much of the area of Spadina Avenue from Queen Street to College Street, running along Dundas Street nearly as far east as Bay Street. The old Chinatown used to be stuck behind the Old City Hall, but it was uprooted by the building of the New City Hall, and began to spread to the west. This was helped by the huge influx of Chinese immigrants, which began some two decades ago and still continues. Most

Tours 2 and 3

KEY

AE American Express Office

0   440 yards

0   400 meters

come from Hong Kong, bringing money, skills, and intelligence to the already burgeoning community that had been here before.

One of the best times to explore Chinatown is on a Sunday, when, up and down Spadina Avenue and along Dundas Street, Chinese music blasts from storefronts, cash registers ring, abacuses clack, and bakeries, markets, herbalists, and restaurants do their best business of the week.

But whatever day you wander through Toronto's impressive Chinatown—we recommend that you start on Elizabeth Street, just north of the New City Hall, and walk north to Dundas Street, east toward Bay Street, and west to Spadina Avenue—you will be thrilled by the diversity, the excitement, the liveliness: the sheer foreignness of it all. (Remember the cliché: If the United States is a melting pot, Canada is a mosaic—with each piece maintaining its individuality and differences.)

❹ The **Shing Wah Daily News** on Hagerman Street, near Bay Street, due north of the New City Hall (tel. 416/977–3745), will show you some of the 10,000 Chinese characters being typeset and printed, plus samples of Blondie and Dagwood speaking
❺ Cantonese. **Mon Kuo Trading Co. Ltd.** (120 Elizabeth St., also just north of New City Hall) cultivates bean sprouts under a sprinkler system in the basement, on their one-week growth to maturity.

On Dundas Street, you'll pass shops selling reasonably priced silk blouses and antique porcelain; silk kimonos for less than half the price elsewhere; exquisite sake sets; and women's suits
❻ made from silk. Huge Chinese characters hang over the **52nd Division police station,** a large building on the west side of University Avenue, on the south side of Dundas Street. Many of the banks still have abacuses, to help those who prefer to use 4,000-year-old "hand-held calculators" over the modern ones.

❼ Just to the north, on St. Patrick Street, is the **Chinese Catholic**
❽ **Church.** Over on D'Arcy Street is the modern **Chinese home for the aged,** with charming crafts rooms, hydroponic gardens, and lots of goldfish, because an Eastern tradition has it that every time a goldfish dies, a human being is guaranteed long life.

❾ Just to the south of Dundas Street is the **Ontario College of Art** (100 McCaul St.), one of the major institutions specializing in animation, design, advertising art, tapestry, glassblowing, sculpture, and painting in Canada. Directly across the street is
❿ **Village by the Grange** (89 McCaul St.), an apartment-and-shopping complex that contains more than a hundred shops selling everything from ethnic fast food to serious art. It's a perfect example of what more cities need in their downtown areas: a wise, careful blending of the commercial and the residential.

⓫ Return to Dundas Street, and head west to the **Art Gallery of Ontario,** which has been slowly but steadily evolving into one of the better art museums in North America. From extremely modest beginnings in 1900, the AGO is now in the big leagues in terms of exhibits and support. Its membership of over 25,000 is one of the largest among the continent's museums, and recent international exhibits of King Tut, van Gogh, Turner, Judy Chicago, William Blake, and Picasso will give you an idea of the gallery's importance, image, and profile.

In 1988, the AGO began its $28 million "Stage 3 expansion," completed in 1991. This has increased its exhibition space by nearly 50% and now includes new galleries for contemporary art, Inuit art, and an indoor sculpture court. Even before its expansion, the AGO was noted for the excellence of its art treasures.

The **Henry Moore Sculpture Centre** on the second floor has the largest public collection of the sculptor's work in the world. (Do not miss Moore's large *Two Forms,* which stands outside the AGO, at the southwest corner of McCaul Street. Adults as well as children love to climb in and around it.)

Also on the second floor is the **Samuel and Ayala Zacks Wing,** with its fine collection of 20th-century sculpture. The **Canadian Wing** includes major works by such northern lights as Emily Carr, Cornelius Krieghoff, David Milne, and Homer Watson, plus a broad selection from the Group of Seven, which is no rock group—although they *did* paint rocks—rather a group of Ontarian painters famous for developing "Canadian Impressionism." On the lower level is a hands-on room where children are invited to paint, make slides, and otherwise creatively muck about (open Sundays, summers, and holidays).

The Art Gallery of Ontario also has a growing collection of Rembrandt, Hals, Van Dyck, Hogarth, Reynolds, Chardin, Renoir, de Kooning, Rothko, Oldenburg, Picasso, Rodin, Degas, Matisse, and many others. And it also has **The Grange,** a historic house located just behind the AGO, in a large park (*see* Historic Buildings and Sites in Sightseeing Checklists, *below*). In early 1989, the AGO unveiled a new, computerized reinstallation of paintings and sketches by Tom Thomson and the Group of Seven. Installed near some of the oil sketches, there are computers and telephones that give simple messages about the paintings and related topics as well as explanatory material.

The AGO, 317 Dundas St. W, 3 blocks west of St. Patrick station of University subway line; tel. 416/977–0414. Admission: $4.50 adults, $2.50 senior citizens and children 12–18, $9 families. Free Wed. after 5:30 PM; free Fri. for senior citizens. Open Tues.–Sun. 11–5:30, Wed. until 9; Mon. late May–Labor Day. Closed Christmas, Dec. 26, New Year's Day, Jan. 2.

Across from the AGO and The Grange is Village by the Grange, as noted above. It is a perfect place to browse, either before or after a visit to the art gallery.

Check out some of the commercial art galleries on the north side of Dundas Street, across from the AGO, many of which display classical and contemporary Chinese paintings. Then head west, back through Chinatown. **Champion House** (478 Dundas St. W, near Spadina) is a good bet for lunch.

Spadina and the Marketplaces Toronto's widest street, **Spadina Avenue,** has been pronounced "Spa-*dye*-nah" for a century and a half, and we are too polite to point out that it really should be called "Spa-*dee*-na." To explain why it's 48 meters (149 ft) wide, double the width of almost every other vintage street in town, we have to go back to 1802, when a 27-year-old Irish physician named William Warren Baldwin came to Muddy York. He soon married a rich young woman, built a pleasant home where Casa Loma now sits, and decided to cut a giant swath through the forest from Bloor Street down to Queen Street so they could look down—literally

and socially—on Lake Ontario. Alas, their view disappeared in
1874, when a thankless granddaughter sold the land at the
crescent just above College Street for the site of Knox College,
which moved to the University of Toronto campus several decades later. Now covered with vines, the Victorian college
building still sits in the crescent, a number of the chestnut trees
planted by Dr. Baldwin still standing on the west side of the
crescent. Little else remains of Dr. Baldwin's Spadina, except
for a handful of Victorian mansions.

Spadina, running from Queen Street north to College Street,
has never been fashionable, or even worth a visit by most tourists. Way back, it was just a collection of inexpensive stores,
factories that sold to you wholesale if you had connections, ethnic food and fruit stores, and eateries that gave you your 2¢
worth, usually plain.

And so it remains, with the exception of some often first-class,
if modest-looking, Chinese restaurants sprinkled throughout
the area. Each new wave of immigrants—Jewish, Chinese,
Portuguese, East and West Indian, South American—added
its own flavor to the mix, but Spadina-Kensington's basic bill of
faré is still "bargains galore." Here you'll find gourmet cheeses
at gourmet prices, fresh (no, not fresh-frozen) ocean fish, fine
European kitchenware at half the price of stores in the
Yorkville area, yards of fabric remnants piled high in bins, designer clothes minus the labels, and the occasional rock-and-
roll night spot and interesting greasy spoon.

For any visitor who plans to be in Toronto for over four or five
days, a few hours exploring the ins and outs of the garment district could bring great pleasure—and even greater bargains.
Park your car at the lot just west of Spadina Avenue on St. Andrew's Street (a long block north of Dundas St.), or take the
College or Queen streetcar to Spadina Avenue. Be warned:
This area can be extraordinarily crowded on weekends, when
smart suburbanites head here for top-quality luggage and
handbags at unbelievably low prices; wholesale dry-goods
stores overflowing with brand-name socks, underwear, and
towels; designer jeans and jackets; women's evening wear,
coats, sportswear, and dresses; new and used furs; and more.

We cannot resist mentioning a few of our favorites. **Fortune
Housewares** (388 Spadina Ave., tel. 416/593–6999) is possibly
the best kitchenware shop in Toronto. There's a good selection
of cookbooks, too, and the staff is both knowledgeable and helpful. Also recommended is the new **Dragon City Food Court** (tel.
416/977–2368), located on the southwest corner of Dundas and
Spadina, where 11 independent outlets offer a variety of exotic
Asian foods. It is open daily 10 AM–midnight.

⑫ And then there's **Kensington Market,** a delightful side tour off
Spadina Avenue. Here, the bargains are of the more edible
kind. All your senses will be titillated by this old, steamy,
smelly, raucous, colorful, European-style marketplace. Come
and explore, especially during warmer weather, when the
goods pour out into the narrow streets: Russian rye breads,
barrels of dill pickles, fresh fish on ice, mountains of cheese,
bushels of ripe fruit, and crates of chickens and rabbits that
will have your children both giggling and horrified.

Kensington Market sprang up just after the turn of the century, when Russian, Polish, and Jewish inhabitants set up stalls

in front of their houses. Since then, the market—named after the area's major street—has become a United Nations of stores. Unlike the UN, however, these people get along fabulously with one another. Jewish and Eastern European stores sit side by side with Portuguese, Caribbean, and East Indian stores—with Vietnamese, Japanese, and Chinese establishments sprinkled throughout. Most shops are open every day except Sunday, from as early as 6 AM.

⓭ Lovers of religious architecture may wish to visit the two hauntingly attractive old synagogues in the market area: **Anshei Minsk** (10 St. Andrew's St., just west of Spadina Ave.) and, just a few **⓮** short blocks away, the **Kiever Synagogue** (corner of Denison Sq. and Bellevue Ave.).

Afterward, you can rest in **Bellevue Square** (corner of Denison Sq. and Augusta Pl.), a lovely little park with shady trees, benches, and a wading pool and playground for kids.

⓯ **Mirvish** (or **Markham**) **Village** (*see* Shopping Districts in Chapter 3) is a small, delightful tourist area— but no tourist trap— one block west of Bathurst Street, running south from Bloor Street. It is open on Sundays.

The history is interesting: Ed Mirvish is an inspired capitalist who has run a big, ugly, barnlike bargain-basement store called **Honest Ed's** for the past four decades. The place is nothing special; Americans have its equivalent in every city (although his sheer vulgarity is disarming; the world's largest neon sign on his store screams out such sayings as "Honest Ed's no midwife . . . but the bargains he delivers are real babies"). As if to make up for the crudeness of his selling techniques (which include daily "door crashers," such as five pounds of white flour for 79¢), Mirvish saved the magnificent Royal Alexandra Theatre from destruction, and he even decided to purchase the venerable Old Vic, in London, England. When Mirvish tried to tear down all the houses on the block behind his store to build a parking lot, he was prevented by zoning bylaws. No problem: He thought up the brilliant alternative of Mirvish, or Markham, Village. By officially being declared a tourist attraction, the village could legally be open on Sundays; and so, though it is in the unfashionable Bloor/Bathurst area, it can be a lifesaver for weekend visitors with time to kill. Most stores are open daily 10–6.

Ed's Ice Cream Parlour (corner of Bloor and Markham Sts.) has cappuccino and, of course, the cold stuff. **The Children's Book Store** calls itself the largest children's bookstore in the world, and carries books from all over the world. Folksingers, artists, and writers often make personal appearances to sing, show off, or read from their works, usually on Sundays. This place is a beauty—the Louvre of kiddie lit. The irresistible **Memory Lane** sells vintage movie posters and old comic books and magazines. **David Mirvish Books on Art,** run by Ed's son, has many remaindered books at shockingly low prices, as well as a fine collection of new volumes.

Before you turn back to Bloor Street, note the wonderful house at the corner of Markham and Lennox streets: the hexagonal corner tower, the fine leaded-glass butterfly window to one side of its front door, and the stunning oval window on the other. This is old Toronto architecture at its most attractive.

Tour 3: Academia, Culture, Commercialism, Crassness

University Avenue, running from Front Street for about 3 miles north to Bloor Street, where it changes its name to Avenue Road and continues north, is one of Toronto's few mistakes. It's horribly boring, with hospital after office building after insurance company after office building. Yet it is still an interesting start for a healthy walk, because it does have lovely flowerbeds and fountains in a well-maintained strip along its middle. Still, you may wish to drive this part of the tour.

16 One highlight is **Campbell House** (northwest corner of Queen St. and University Ave.), the stately Georgian mansion of Sir William Campbell, the sixth chief justice of Upper Canada. Built in 1822 and tastefully restored with elegant 18th- and early 19th-century furniture, it is one of Toronto's most charming "living museums." Costumed hostesses will tell you about the social life of the upper class. Note the model of the town of York as it was in the 1820s, and the original, restored kitchen sans Cuisinart. *Tel. 416/597–0227. Admission: $2.50 adults, $1.25 students and senior citizens. Guided tours only. Open weekdays 9:30 AM–11:30 AM and 2:30 PM–4:30 PM; mid-May–mid-October, weekends noon–4:30 PM.*

17 College Street is the southern boundary of the **University of Toronto.** A city the size of Toronto is too large to be labeled a college town, but with a staff and student population of more than 50,000, and over 225 buildings on three campuses, the university is almost a city in itself.

It goes back to 1827, when King George IV signed a charter for a "King's College in the Town of York, Capital of Upper Canada." The Church of England had control then, but by 1850 the college was proclaimed nondenominational, renamed the University of Toronto, and put under the control of the province. And then, in a spirit of good Christian competition, the Anglicans started Trinity College, the Methodists began Victoria, and the Roman Catholics established St. Michael's; by the time the Presbyterians founded Knox College, the whole thing was almost out of hand.

But not really: The 17 schools and faculties are now united, and they welcome anyone who can pass the entrance exams and afford the tuition, which, thanks to generous government funding, is still only about $1,500 a year.

The architecture is interesting, if uneven—any place would be, too, if it had been built in bits and pieces over 150 years. We recommend a walking tour. Enter the campus just behind the Parliament buildings, where Wellesley Street ends. Go under the bridge, past the guardhouse (whose keeper will not let you pass if you are encased in an automobile), and turn right, around King's College Circle.

18 At the top of the circle is **Hart House,** a Gothic-style student center built during the teens of this century by the Masseys— the folks who brought us Massey-Ferguson farm equipment, Massey Hall, Vincent Massey (a governor-general of Canada), and Raymond Massey, the actor. It was once an all-male enclave; today anyone may visit the Great Hall and the library, both self-conscious imitations of Oxford and Cambridge. Check out the dining hall for its amazing stained-glass windows as well as its food, which is inexpensive and rather good.

As you continue around King's College Circle, you'll see on your right the Romanesque **University College,** built in 1859. **⑲ ⑳** Next is **Knox College,** whose Scottish origins are evident in the bagpipe music that escapes from the building at odd hours. It's been training ministers since 1844, although the building was put up only yesterday—1915.

㉑ You may well wish to tip your hat to the **Medical Sciences Building,** which is no beauty but is where, in 1921, Drs. Frederick Grant Banting, Charles H. Best, and others discovered the insulin that has saved the lives of tens of millions of diabetics around the world.

Just a few hundred yards west is St. George Street and the **㉒ ㉓** **Robarts Research Library,** and **Thomas Fisher Rare Books Library** (*see* Sightseeing Checklists, *below*).

There is lots more to see and do around the main campus of the **㉔** University of Toronto. Visit the **Public and Community Relations Office** (Room 133S, 27 King's College Circle, tel. 416/978–2021), across the field from Hart House, and pick up free maps of the school grounds. Guided one-hour walking tours are held on summer weekdays, setting out from the map room of Hart House at 10:30, 12:30, and 2:30 (tel. 416/978–5000).

Back at College Street and University Avenue, you can see the Victorian structure of the Parliament buildings to the north, with Queen's Park just north of them.

Queen's Park There are a number of meanings to **Queen's Park,** for the native **㉕** Torontonian as well as the visitor. The term can refer to a charming circular park just a few hundred yards southeast of the Royal Ontario Museum (on University Ave., just below Bloor St.). This is a grand place to rest your feet after a long day of shopping or visiting the Royal Ontario Museum. But **㉖** Queen's Park also refers to the **Ontario Legislative Building,** which is nothing less than what Albany is to New York State or Lansing is to Michigan: the home of the provincial parliament. The mammoth building was opened back in 1893 and is really quite extraordinary, with its rectangular towers, triangle roofs, and circular and oval glass. Like the New City Hall, it was the product of an international contest among architects; it was won by a young Briton who was residing in Buffalo, New York.

㉗ The **Parliament building** itself looks grotesque to some, with its pink exterior and heavy, almost Romanesque style. But a close look will show the beautifully complex detail carved in its stone, and on the inside there are huge, lovely halls that echo half a millennium of English architecture. (Its pinkness does not necessarily reflect the politics of the men and women who work within the building, by the way; that's simply the color of Ontario's sandstone.)

Do go inside; the long hallways are hung with hundreds of oils by Canadian artists, most of which capture scenes of the province's natural beauty. Should you choose to take one of the frequent (and free) tours, you will see the chamber where the 130 elected representatives from across Ontario, called MPPs (Members of Provincial Parliament), meet on a regular basis. There are two heritage rooms—one each for the parliamentary histories of Britain and Ontario—filled with old newspapers, periodicals, and pictures. And the lobby holds a fine collection of minerals and rocks of the province.

On the lawn in front of the Parliament buildings, facing College Street, are many statues, including one of Queen Victoria and one of Canada's first prime minister, Sir John A. Macdonald.

Tel. 416/965–4028. Guided tours mid-May–Labor Day, daily on the hour 9–4; frequent tours the rest of the year. On summer weekends, tours are every half hour 9–11:30 and 1:30–4. Queen's Park can be reached via University Ave. subway; get off at College St. and walk north 1 block. If you drive, there are parking lots in the area, and meters around Queen's Park Circle.

❷❽ Just to the northwest of Queen's Park is the world-class **Royal Ontario Museum.** Its supporters pointed out that "ROM wasn't built in a day" during a major fund-raising effort earlier this decade. How true. Although once labeled "Canada's single greatest cultural asset" by the Canada Council, the museum floundered throughout much of its existence, which began in 1912 (the same day the *Titanic* sank). It never stopped collecting—always with brilliance—reaching more than 6 million items altogether. But by the 1970s, the monstrous building had run out of room to display its glorious treasures; its roofs had started leaking; and it was deemed necessary to install a climate-control system.

What a difference just $80 million can make! Today, at last, the museum has the space it needs, and when expansion is completed sometime in the 1990s, the ROM will be the second largest museum in North America, after New York's Metropolitan Museum of Art.

What makes the ROM unique is the fact that its science, art, and archaeology exhibits are all under one roof. The **Dinosaur Collection** will stun children and adults alike. The **Evolution Gallery** has an ongoing audiovisual program on Darwin's theories of evolution. The **Roman Gallery** has the most extensive collection of Roman artifacts in Canada. The **Textile Collection** has been ranked fifth in the world in size and scope. The collection of **Chinese art and antiquities** is one of the finest this side of Beijing. And the **European Musical Instruments Gallery** has a revolutionary audio system and over 1,200 instruments dating back to the late 16th century.

The **Discovery Gallery** allows children (7 years and older) to handle objects from the ROM's collections and to study them, using microscopes, ultraviolet light, and magnifying glasses.

The new **Bat Cave,** opened in early 1988, contains 4,000 freeze-dried and artificial bats in a lifelike presentation. Piped-in narration directs visitors on a 15-minute walk through a dimly lit replica of an 8-foot-high limestone tunnel in Jamaica, filled with sounds of dripping water and bat squeaks. Yes, the dinosaurs and mummies have a new rival in popularity.

In early 1992 the ROM's brilliant **Ancient Egypt Gallery** reopened, joined by the brand-new **Nubia Gallery**—the only one in North America.

Containing fascinating exhibits that range from a massive Ming tomb to an Islamic home, from Egyptian mummies to a Buddhist temple, from a towering totem pole to suits of armor, the Royal Ontario Museum is simply fabulous. The **Mankind Discovering Gallery** tells about the museum itself and helps one choose what to see.

ROM, tel. 416/586–5549. Admission: $6 adults; $3.25 students, senior citizens, and children 5 and older; $13 maximum for a family of five. Free entry to senior citizens all day Tues. (including the Gardiner and Planetarium shows); free to the rest of the public Tues. after 4:30 PM. Open Tues. and Thurs. 10–8, Wed., Fri.–Sun. 10–6; closed Mon. Labor Day–mid-May; New Year's Day. Discovery Gallery open Sept.–June weekdays noon–4, weekends and holidays 1–5; July–Aug. weekdays 11–4. Call ahead for Discovery Gallery hours; school visits often necessitate changes in schedules. To get here, take University subway to Museum stop; parking is expensive.

㉙ The **George R. Gardiner Museum of Ceramic Art** has now merged with the ROM, meaning that it costs not a penny more to visit a magnificent $25 million collection of rare European ceramics. The collection features 17th-century English delftware and 18th-century yellow European porcelain. Most popular is the second-floor display of Italian commedia del l'arte figures, especially Harlequin. *Across the street from ROM, on east side of University Ave., just south of Bloor St. Same hours as ROM.*

㉚ Next door to the ROM, to its south, is the **McLaughlin Planetarium,** which attracts some 250,000 visitors a year. There are four new 45-minute star shows each year. Open since 1986 is the **Astrocentre,** which has hands-on exhibits, computer terminals designed for both adults and children, and an animated model of the star system. *Planetarium (tel. 416/586–5736) has the same hours as ROM, plus evening hours for star shows. Admission: $5.00 adults, $3.00 senior citizens, students, and children. Senior citizens free on Tues. Combined admission ticket available to ROM and planetarium, should you plan to visit both on same day. Tel. 416/586–5751 for taped description of current night sky.*

㉛ A five-minute walk due south of the planetarium will bring you to the **Sigmund Samuel Canadiana Collection,** which is also part of the ROM and may be seen at no extra charge. Here is where you can view early Canadian furnishings, glassware, silver, and six settings of furniture displayed in typical 18th- and 19th-century homes. *14 Queen's Park Crescent W, on northwest corner of University Ave. and College St. Open Tues.–Sat. 10–5, Sun. 1–5.*

㉜ After so much culture, you may wish to enjoy one of the most dynamic and expensive areas of Toronto—**Bloor and Yorkville.** A recent article in one of Toronto's newspapers began, "If Imelda Marcos came to Toronto, she would shop on Bloor St. W. This is the home of the $1,300 loafers, the $110,000 fur coat, the $350 belt, and the $14,000 travel trunk, a chic zone where style is everything and cost is no object."

Not every store on these half-dozen-plus blocks between University Avenue and Yonge Street—and the two blocks running north and parallel to them—is so costly, but when monthly rents go above $100 per square foot, one can't sell at discount rates, can one?

When Joseph Bloor made his brewery fortune and built his family home on this street over a century ago, how was he to know that his name would become synonymous with success and high fashion? Had he known, he would never have sold an inch of his property, that's for sure.

Some call it Toronto's Rodeo Drive; others call it Toronto's Fifth Avenue. (Smug Torontonians have been known to call Fifth Avenue New York's Bloor Street, but that may be pushing it.) One thing is certain: These blocks are packed with high-price stores specializing in designer clothes, furs, jewels, specialty shops, ritzy restaurants, and more.

33 **The Colonnade,** on the south side of Bloor Street, a few doors east of University Avenue, has recently undergone a $10 million face-lift. In addition to several levels of luxury residential apartments and private offices, it also has more than two floors of stores selling quality leather goods, perfumes, jewelry, and European apparel.

Along the south side of Bloor Street are such stores as **Zoe,** with haute couture designs; **Creed's,** for more than seven decades *the* place for quality furs, lingerie, shoes, etc., went bankrupt in 1990, to the shock and horror of its very wealthy patrons. Still, there is **The Bay** (at the northeast corner of Bloor and Yonge Sts.), a department store with elegant, high-fashion designer clothes for men and women; **Holt Renfrew,** possibly the most stunning store in Toronto, with marble, chrome, glass, and glittering fashions for both sexes; **Eddie Bauer,** selling sturdily made and cleverly designed clothing, equipment, and accessories for all sports; **William Ashley,** which has the finest quality china, crystal, and silver available in Canada, at competitive prices; **David's,** with the finest footwear at the highest prices; and **Bowring,** which has linens, cookware, woodenware, china, crystal, and interesting accessories. **110 Bloor Street West** (near the northeast corner of Avenue Rd. and Bloor St., almost across from The Colonnade) is a dazzling complex of condos, offices, and retail shops ranging from **Rodier Paris** to **Celine.**

A block north of Bloor and Yonge streets is the magnificent **34** **Metropolitan Toronto Library.** Arranged around a tall and wide interior atrium, the library gives a fabulous sense of open space. It was designed by one of Canada's most admired architects, Raymond Moriyama, who also created the Ontario Science Centre. Among the highlights is a fascinating fabric sculpture, *Lyra,* designed by artist Aiko Suzuki. Overhanging the pool and waterfall in the foyer, it was meant to create a transition from the bustle of Yonge Street to the quiet library. It took eight months to complete—the artist walking over 250 miles back and forth in her studio to create it. Glass-enclosed elevators glide swiftly and silently up and down one side of the atrium, allowing you to admire the beautiful banners that hang from the ceiling, announcing the collections on each floor.

Browsers will appreciate that fully one third of the more than 1.3 million books—spread across 28 miles of shelves—are open to the public. The many audio carrels have headphones, which you may use to listen to any one of over 10,000 albums.

The **Arthur Conan Doyle Room** will be of special interest to Baker Street regulars. It houses the finest public collection of Holmesiana anywhere, with records, films, photos, books, manuscripts, letters, and even cartoon books starring Sherlock Hemlock of "Sesame Street." *789 Yonge St., just steps north of Bloor St., tel. 416/393-7000. Open Mon.-Thurs. 9-9, Fri. 9-6, Sat. 9-5, Sun. (Oct.-Apr.) 1:30-5. To get an answer to any question, on any subject, tel. 416/393-7131.*

㉟ Back on the east side of Avenue Road, two blocks north of Bloor Street and two blocks west of the Metro Library, is a real don't-miss shopping area—**Hazelton Lanes** (416/968-8600). Offering everything from Swiss chocolates to Hermès silks and Giorgio Armani's latest fashions, this is a wonderful, magical paean to capitalism. And in 1989 it doubled, in size and glory, with the addition of some 80 new stores.

㊱ And then there is what is still called **Yorkville,** which runs along the street of the same name, between Avenue Road and Yonge Street, but also includes Cumberland, Bellair, Bay, Scollard, and Hazelton streets. This little gathering of low-rise buildings, mostly old Victorian town houses turned into marvelous storefronts, has gone through many changes over the years: from a conservative middle-class residential district, to the gathering place for Ontario's revolutionaries, drug pushers, hippies, runaway kids, and avant-garde artists, to what it is today—a chic, expensive shopping district. (A century ago, it was a real village, just north of Toronto, with its own town hall, planked sidewalks, and horse-drawn streetcars linking it to the city's downtown.)

All along these streets—especially Cumberland and Yorkville—you will find many of Toronto's finest commercial art galleries (*see* Sightseeing Checklists, *below*). Just to the south is the best shopping in the city (with the exception of Bloor St.).

For a sense of what all this costly beauty was like before haute couture moved in, walk along Scollard and Berryman streets, just north of Yorkville Street. The rows of Victorian houses will be a rest for your overworked eyes and pocketbooks. Should you want to experience the seedy side of this rather uptight town, simply head over to Yonge Street and walk slowly south from Bloor Street as far as you desire. It's called The Strip, although it really doesn't strip anymore; there was quite a movement to clean up the area back in the 1970s. (This is Toronto, Canada, not the average American city; when one cleans up in a place like this, one starts at a much cleaner level of dirtiness.)

Still, by the time you reach Dundas Street, some 2 miles to the south, you'll have passed the soft-core-porn bookstores, the movie houses, the pinball arcades, the harmonica-playing vagabonds, the street vendors peddling jewelry, the hustlers and whores, the endless rows of fast-food dives, the occasional future politician, and the ubiquitous patroling cops (who are, in Toronto, there when you need them, though you rarely do).

No, Times Square this isn't. Back in the early 1970s, The Strip did indeed radiate a sense of vulgarity, danger, and despair; today, it has more the air of a tacky carnival. Three million dollars was spent refurbishing streets adjoining Yonge Street, adding trees, benches, outdoor cafés, and Victorian-style lampposts to create a fresher look. And, in the great tradition of keeping the downtown of Toronto healthy, many thousands of people keep moving to within a few blocks of this major street, making it more and more a living community. The massage parlors have

long been closed and most heavy drug peddlers are gone.
Yonge Street today is a safe area packed with people—both
residents and visitors—enjoying the punk rockers, the far-out
clothing shops, and the raucous music blaring from many of the
storefronts. It's certainly Toronto's *liveliest* street, if also its
most vulgar and least "Toronto-like."

37 You really should not miss **College Park,** at the southwest corner of Yonge and College streets. This building, complete with
marble walls and brass railings, was a major Eaton's department store from 1930 to the late '70s, when the chain put most
of its marbles (and money) into the gigantic Eaton Centre, just
a few blocks to the south. But would Toronto *dare* to tear down
such an architectural wonder? Not on your life! They simply
redid it brilliantly, renamed it College Park, and filled it with
dozens of beautiful stores and eateries—one more example of
how cities can preserve their pasts while they march proudly
into the future.

Just before you reach the Eaton Centre, on the east side of
Yonge Street, are two major record stores—among the largest
38 on the North American continent—**Sam the Record Man** (347
39 Yonge St.) and **A & A Records and Tapes** (351 Yonge St.). Both
are open late every night but Sunday.

And that's the Yonge Street walk. Do you feel dirty all over?
Are you worried that we won't respect you anymore? Not at all.
If it will make you feel better, think historic: You have just
walked the street where Canada's first streetcar line was inau-
gurated in 1861; where the first section of road in British North
America was macadamized and tested in 1833; and where the
first subway line in all of Canada was built, in the early 1950s.

Feel better now?

Tour 4: Toronto's Finest Neighborhoods

*Numbers in the margin correspond with points of interest on
the Tour 4: The Neighborhoods map.*

The major reason for Toronto's success as a city is its inspired
preservation of handsome, clean, safe neighborhoods—often
just steps from the heart of its vibrant, booming downtown.
Many of these neighborhoods are practically little villages in
their own right (indeed, many of them began that way). But because they are sprinkled across the city, it is difficult to walk to
most of them, even if every single one is well worth walking
through.

What we've done is to gather together several of Toronto's most
interesting neighborhoods: (1) Rosedale, (2) Forest Hill, (3) the
Annex and Casa Loma, (4) the Beaches, (5) Cabbagetown, and
(6) others with a distinct ethnic flavor.

Rosedale Morley Callaghan, the Toronto author who used to box with Ernest Hemingway and quarrel with F. Scott Fitzgerald, called
the neighborhood "a fine and private place." Others have called
it Blueblood Alley or Millionaire Row. But whatever it is called,
most of it is exceptionally beautiful and, once again, just blocks
from the heart of downtown Toronto.

1 The place is **Rosedale,** the posh residential area of Toronto and
still the symbol of old money. For visitors, Rosedale is a lovely
place to walk, bike, or drive and admire the handsome, oversize

houses. The neighborhood is bounded by Yonge Street on the west, the Don Valley Parkway on the east, St. Clair Avenue to the north, and the Rosedale Ravine (just above Bloor St. E) to the south. It is as if Mother Nature herself planted ravines around the area to keep out the riffraff.

Some years ago, a child of the privileged wrote a pithy article entitled "Rosedale Ain't What It Used to Be," and, in fact, it ain't. Many of the old families have gone, and their mansions have been chopped up into expensive flats. Pseudo-Georgian town houses have sprouted up in side gardens, like so many weeds.

Speaking of gardens, that's where this original Suburb of the Rich and Famous got its name. Rosedale began as the country estate of Sheriff William Jarvis, one of the powers that were, back in the 1820s. He brought his wife, Mary, to settle on the 200-acre estate, and she named her home Rosedale because of the wild roses that bloomed in profusion. Most of the roses are gone now; so are the magnificent elms that once lined Elm Avenue—including the famous Rosedale Elm, planted by Mary Jarvis herself back in 1835. Dutch elm disease hit even the estates of the very rich during the last generation.

Yet, there is surely not another metropolis in North America that maintains such an upper-class neighborhood just steps from the city's heart—a jumble of Edwardian, Victorian, Georgian, and Tudor. And massive maple trees cast their heavenly shade upon it all.

The heart of Rosedale is just a few yards north of the Castle Frank subway station on the Bloor Line. Walk up Castle Frank to Hawthorne Gardens. On the northeast corner of the two streets stands the old Seagram (as in booze) mansion, which was converted into five condominiums back in the early 1980s. Two doors north, along Castle Frank, is the impressive home of the Thomson family, the people who brought us *The London Times*, the Hudson's Bay Company, and some three dozen papers across North America, including *The Globe and Mail*. From here, follow your inclination along Elm Avenue, Milkman's Road, Craigleigh Gardens, and South Drive.

Another way to get to Rosedale (other than inheriting several million dollars) is via Roxborough Street or Crescent Road, just eight blocks north of Bloor Street, going east from Yonge Street. It is easy to find, because there is a Rosedale subway stop on the Yonge Line. Just follow the streets down and around all the ravines. Some of our favorites—all blooming with gigantic mansions—are Beaumont Road, a cul-de-sac called Old George Place, and a little park called Craigleigh Gardens. Listen carefully and you may just hear the delicate clicking of teacups as they are set down on their Wedgwood saucers.

Forest Hill
2
The closest rival to Rosedale in prestige is an area about 2 miles to the north and west of Yonge and Bloor streets called **Forest Hill**. A sense of this community can be obtained by recalling a Great Controversy back in 1982: Would the former village of Forest Hill continue to have backyard garbage pickup, or would the villagers have to (gulp!) drag their rubbish out front like everyone else in Metro Toronto? The City Council finally voted to continue the special service, on the principle that "invisible

Tour 4: The Neighborhoods

The Annex, **3**
The Beaches, **5**
Cabbagetown, **6**
Casa Loma, **4**
East Indian
community, **11**
Forest Hill, **2**
German/Ukrainian
community, **8**
Greek community, **12**

Italian community, **9**
Polish community, **7**
Rosedale, **1**
West Indian
community, **10**

Yonge St.

Mount Pleasant Rd.

Bayview Ave.

Laird Dr.

Don Mills Rd.

Wigmore
Park

Victoria Park Ave.

Eglinton   Ave. E.

Sunnybrook
Park

Don Valley Pkwy.

AE

Moore Ave.

EAST YORK

Don R.

O'Connor Dr.

Taylor Creek
Park

Bayview Ext.

404

Broadview Ave.

Pape Ave.

Greenwood Ave.

Coxwell Ave.

Woodbine Ave.

Massey Cr.

Dawes Rd.

1

E

M   M   M   M **12** M   M   M   M   M   M   M

Bloor St. E.

Danforth Ave.

Gerrard St. E.

Parliament St.

6

Gerrard St. E.

11

2

Dundas St. E.

Leslie St.

Queen St. E.

AE

Eastern Ave.

5

Lake Shore Blvd. E.

Ashbridges
Bay Park

Lake Ontario

Harbour

KEY
AE American Express Office

garbage" was one of the unwritten terms of Forest Hill's amalgamation with Toronto, in 1968.

This golden square of about 940 acres is bounded by Bathurst Street on the west, Avenue Road on the east, Eglinton Avenue on the north, and St. Clair Avenue West on the south. Today Forest Hill is home to approximately 25,000 rather well-heeled people, although it numbered but some 2,100 souls in 1923 when it chose to become a village on its own. Its first reeve passed a bylaw requiring that a tree be planted in front of every house; you can see the shady results of his campaign today. At that time, there were no paved streets. Eglinton Avenue was a wagon trail, and Old Forest Hill Road was part of an old Indian path that meandered from the Humber River to Lake Ontario.

Forest Hill remained its own little village, with its own police and fire departments and school system, until it was incorporated into Toronto. Today, apart from the green street signs and the right to leave the garbage where it properly belongs, it is mainly a state of mind.

You don't need a car to see Forest Hill. Either bike or walk along some of the streets, and you are in for an enjoyable hour or two. It lacks the gorgeous ravines of Rosedale, but you'll see some of this city's grandest homes and gardens. A good place to start is **Forest Hill Road,** just west of Avenue Road and St. Clair Avenue (and only a few blocks northeast of **Casa Loma**). You are now entering the thick of Forest Hill, with its handsome English manors and splendid Georgian homes. Just up the street is **Upper Canada College,** one of the country's most prestigious private schools, which has educated the likes of humorist Stephen Leacock, author Robertson Davies, the Eatons, and numerous bankers, mayors, and prime ministers.

A few blocks west of Upper Canada College is **Bishop Strachan** (rhymes with "yawn") **School.** It is one of the select private girls' schools in the city, and it is much admired, much attended, and much paid for. It's fitting that BSS shares a Forest Hill address with UCC; they both conjure up other initials: M.B.A., MP, MPP, and, in general, VIP.

Admire the homes along Old Forest Hill Road, then head up and down the streets that run north–south: Dunvegan, Warren, and Russell Hill. South of St. Clair Avenue, Russell Hill Road becomes a showpiece of mansions that really should be seen.

The only stores are on Spadina Road (it's Spadina Ave. south of Bloor St.), a few blocks north of St. Clair Avenue. This shopping area, with its fine shops and a superb bakery, still retains the feeling of a small village, which seems proper for the very proper people of Forest Hill.

It's a special part of Toronto, Forest Hill, and like Rosedale, a rare North American example of peacefulness, all within a short distance of Bloor and Yonge streets. Come to think of it, a lot of Forest Hill's inhabitants *own* stores at Bloor and Yonge streets. That is why they can afford to live in Forest Hill.

The Annex and Casa Loma ❸ The origin of **the Annex's** name is hardly the stuff of romance. It was born in 1887, when the burgeoning town of Toronto annexed the area between Bathurst Street and Avenue Road— north from Bloor Street to the Canadian Pacific railway tracks, alias Dupont Street.

The Annex was still country then, so it soon became an enclave for the well-to-do. Timothy Eaton (of department-store fame) and the Gooderham family (of liquor fame) escaped the masses and built north of Bloor Street. Eaton built a handsome structure at 182 Lowther Avenue; the Gooderhams erected a lovely red castle at the corner of St. George Street and Bloor Street, now the home of the exclusive York Club.

As Queen Victoria gave way to King Edward, the old rich gave way to the new rich in the Annex, and the Eatons headed farther north. Ethnic groups came and went, until the arrival of the ultimate neighborhood wrecker—the developer. Now began a war between the 19th and the 20th centuries that continues today. Alas, much of St. George Street has been lost to high rises; and as you near the Spadina subway entrance along Lowther Avenue and Walmer Street, you'll see that many Edwardian mansions have given way to apartment buildings whose architecture will forever remain 1960-ish—and *very* ugly.

Still, the Annex, with its hundreds of attractive old homes, can be cited as a prime example of Toronto's success in preserving lovely, safe streets within blocks of the downtown area. Even today, many examples of late 19th-century architecture can be enjoyed on Admiral Road, Lowther Avenue, and Bloor Street, west of University Avenue. Round turrets, pyramid-shape roofs, and conical and even comical spires are among the pleasures shared by some 20,000 Torontonians who live here—professors, students, writers, lawyers, and all the others who rightly find the area a vibrant place to live.

While the Annex is not number one on any visitor's checklist, it is an important part of the city, and it is lovely to visit. At the western end of the Annex—at Bathurst and Bloor streets— you come to Mirvish (or Markham) Village, described in Tour 2. And at the northern tip is the ultimate version of Your Home as Your Castle: Casa Loma.

❹ Casa Loma (1 Austin Terr.; on Spadina Rd., just south of St. Clair Ave. W and the St. Clair Ave. subway stop) is truly a stunner: an honest-to-goodness 20th-century castle, with 98 rooms; two towers; secret panels; long, creepy passageways; and some of the best views of Toronto—all just a short distance from the heart of the city.

The medieval-style castle was built shortly before the Great War by Sir Henry Pellatt, a soldier and financier who spent over $3 million to construct his dream (that's 1913 dollars, remember), only to lose it to the taxman just over a decade later. Today it's owned by the city of Toronto and has been operated by the Kiwanis Club of West Toronto since 1937, with profits going to aid its various charities.

Adults and children will be intrigued by the giant pipe organ; the reproduction of Windsor Castle's Peacock Alley; the majestic, 60-foot-high ceiling of the Great Hall; and the mahogany and marble stable—reached by a long, underground passage— with porcelain troughs worthy of Kohler. And architecture lovers will be fascinated by the rooms from English, Spanish, Scottish, and Austrian castles, which Sir Henry picked up during trips across Europe. The architect E. J. Lennox, who also designed Toronto's Old City Hall and King Edward Hotel, has created a remarkable structure; in a world of Disneyland-type plastic models, Toronto's "house on the hill" is a real treat.

There are no more guided tours of Casa Loma—you now get automatic tape recordings. That's all for the best, as you can drift through at your own speed while the children rush off to the stables or towers. You'll walk a good mile by the time you're done, so wear sensible shoes. *Tel. 416/923–1171. Admission: $8 adults, $4.50 senior citizens and children 6–16, 5 and under free with adult. Open daily 10–4; closed Christmas Day and New Year's.*

The Beaches   One of the most charming of all the neighborhoods that make up what we call Metropolitan Toronto is to the east of downtown, reached by the Queen Street streetcar. Called both the Beach **⑤** and **The Beaches,** the area is bounded by Kingston Road to the north, the Greenwood Raceway to the west, Victoria Park Avenue to the east, and the lake to the south. But The Beaches is really an *attitude,* as much as it is a neighborhood. The chance to live in a small town outside Toronto, with easy access to the city via public transport and even easier access to Lake Ontario, has attracted tens of thousands of residents over the years.

A soldier from London, Joseph Williams, first settled the area back in 1853, having arrived in Toronto with the 2nd Battalion Rifle Brigade five years earlier. His 25-acre grant was named Kew Farms, after London's Kew Gardens, and it was there that he raised vegetables, selling them along with pies and pickles at the St. Lawrence Market on Saturday mornings. (That market is discussed in Tour 1.) When Williams chose to turn his property into a park in 1879, he called it **Kew Gardens.** It was soon flooded by hundreds of hot and sticky Torontonians attracted by the advertisements for "innocent amusements" and the prohibition of "spiritous liquors." Only Canadians would be drawn to such promised innocence!

The youngest son of the *paterfamilias,* suitably named Kew Williams, built a handsome house of stone with a circular staircase and a tower. It stands in Kew Gardens today, The Beaches' own modest version of Casa Loma, serving as home to the park's keeper.

The cottages that once stood on the lakeshore vanished with the waves in 1932, at which time Kew Gardens, Scarborough Beach Park, and Balmy Beach were incorporated into one large park. But on a leisurely walk along the charming streets that run north from the lake to Queen Street, you will still find— and be charmed by—hundreds of New England–style clapboard-and-shingle houses, often standing next door to formal stucco mansions in the Edwardian tradition.

Ride east to the end of the 501 Queen Street streetcar line, to what's called the Neville Park Loop. From here, stroll down to the lake, and walk west toward the city along the delightful, safe, and often crowded (in the summer) boardwalk. Remember, July and August are the only months when one does not risk frostbite when dipping a toe into Lake Ontario. But merely sunbathing can be magical beside The Beaches' boardwalk, which is graced by huge, shady trees. And if you get too warm, there is the free Olympic-size **Somerville Pool** at Woodbine Avenue.

A return walk back up to Queen Street, window shopping along the way, is well worth the time, before grabbing the 501 car westbound and back into the last decade of the 20th century.

Cabbagetown Anyone with less than a week to spend in Toronto may wish to put this way down on their list of must-dos, but anyone with the time and a healthy interest in what makes the city of Toronto so healthy (and interesting) really should take an hour or so to walk through **Cabbagetown**—a cozy neighborhood just east of the downtown area.

We're not talking about major historic landmarks here, but it has the charm of street after street of 19th-century houses, giant trees, and the loveliness of its natural boundaries—two fascinating cemeteries and the Don Valley, now slashed through by the parkway of the same name.

Cabbagetown was originally populated by poor Irish immigrants, who gave it its very prosaic name: They used to grow cabbages in their front yards. Today, that name is used with almost wistful irony; the "white painters" eventually descended on the area, brushes and hammers waving, turning houses that sold in the $25,000 range just two decades ago into ones that will fetch $250,000 and more. In other words, Cabbagetown is yet another good example—along with Yorkville (in the Bloor/Avenue/Yonge district) and the St. Lawrence area (near Front/Church/Jarvis)—of the insistent gentrification of Toronto's downtown.

And so, the area that the late Cabbagetown-born-and-bred writer Hugh Garner once described as "the world's largest Anglo-Saxon slum" has Cinderellaed into one of the most popular areas in the city. (Being within walking distance from the Eaton Centre, at least in good weather, hasn't hurt.)

The borders of Cabbagetown are not terribly well defined. They extend roughly from Parliament Street on the west (about a mile due east of Yonge St.) to Broadview Avenue on the east, and from Bloor Street (aka The Danforth) on the north to Queen Street East on the south.

Our tour will point out only the highlights, but we think that you might well find the entire neighborhood of interest, especially if you are fond of small-scale domestic Victorian architecture.

The "main street" of Cabbagetown is Parliament, so we'll begin there, at the southeast corner of Carlton Street (alias College St., but on the east side of the city). The street was so named because the first government buildings were built near its foot in the closing years of the 18th century.

Walk south from Carlton and Parliament streets, through the busiest part of the Parliament Street commercial area. Most of the buildings on the west side date from the 1890s, though the fronts of the stores are more recent.

Turn left on Spruce Street, which is the first block you come to. The little brick cottage at **number 35,** set far back from the street, was built in 1860–61 and was once the home of the dean of Trinity College Medical School. Note the fence, as well, which also dates from the last century.

From 1856 to 1914, the entire block to your south was the site of the Toronto General Hospital (which now stands, along with most of the city's other major and modern hospitals, along University Ave., south of College St.). The building at **41 Spruce Street** was built in 1871, served until 1903 as a medical school, and has now been recycled as part of a residential development. Its history is outlined on the Toronto Historical Board plaque on its front lawn.

Continuing east, to the corner of Spruce and Sumach streets, you'll see **Spruce Court** on the northwest corner. It's one of the earliest and most attractive of Toronto's low-income housing projects. Constructed for the Toronto Housing Company between 1913 and 1926, the individual units not only provided modern conveniences and street access but also opened to a grassy courtyard. Today, it's a residential cooperative, and the humanity of the city continues to flourish.

Around that corner to the right, at **289 Sumach Street,** is the building that once housed the Ontario Women's Medical College, built in 1889 and a forerunner of Women's College Hospital. (Yes, fellow feminists, Toronto was slow to educate female doctors.) The attractiveness of this brick-and-stone building demonstrates well the success with which Victorian architects and builders managed to integrate institutions into streetscapes that were basically residential.

Now, turn around and walk north on Sumach Street. After crossing Spruce Street, look to your right, on the attractive row of small houses at **119–133 Spruce Street.** Erected in 1887, this terrace of workers' cottages is typical of the form of residential architecture built (to every scale) in Toronto between 1875 and 1890. The style, Second Empire, is typified by the high mansard roof punctuated by dormers with marvelous details, such as carved wooden brackets and metal decorative devices.

Continue north on Sumach Street back to Carlton Street, where you'll see some of the area's largest homes. (Note the redbrick surface of the street to the east.) Among the most outstanding is **number 288,** a solid brick house with white stone trim in the Second Empire style built in 1882. The house next door, **number 286,** was built the following year; it has the familiar Toronto-style steep gable and bargeboard trim. Check out the wrought-iron cresting over the round bow window.

The handsome residence at **number 297** is unusual for the area and is more like the stately homes of the Annex area of Toronto. Its interior, fully restored and exquisitely furnished, has been in more magazine pictorials than Elizabeth Taylor. Its neighbor at **295 Carlton Street** is an earlier house of Victorian Gothic design. It was originally the home of an executive of Toronto's first telephone company—be aware that the wondrous machine was invented by Alexander Graham Bell in Brantford, Ontario, just over an hour west of Toronto—and it had one of the first telephones in the entire city. It didn't cost a quarter to make a call back then.

Continue west on Carlton Street to Metcalfe Street, which, thanks to all its trees, fences, and unbroken rows of terraces, is one of the most beautiful streets in Toronto. On the sidewalk, on the east side nearest Carlton Street, is a utility-hole cover from the Victorian era, bearing the date 1889.

Proceed north to look at **37 Metcalfe Street,** a house that is unique due to its various additions. The renovations over the years (1891 and 1912) have created an array of beaux-arts classical forms, superimposed on the side of a simple but picturesque Victorian home. It's a fine example of the architectural diversity of the entire area.

Look north again. At the northeast corner of Metcalfe and Winchester streets is the handsome Romanesque **St. Enoch's Presbyterian Church,** erected in 1891. Its scale and style blend nicely with that of the surrounding homes of the same period. Today, it is the home of the Toronto Dance Theatre.

Turn left now, and walk west along Winchester Street, back to Parliament Street. As you amble along, admire the repeated sunburst patterns of carved wood in many of the gables and the very large amount of stained glass, much of it original, some of it recently installed by lovers of Victoriana.

At the southeast corner is the most prominent building in the area, the venerable but (alas) decaying **Winchester Hotel.** The old wing on the Winchester bears the plaque "Winchester Hall" and was put up in 1881; the large corner part was built seven years later.

South of the hotel stands an imposing row of large Victorian houses, numbered **502–508 Parliament Street.** Erected in 1879, they are among the largest and most elaborately decorated Second Empire structures still standing in Toronto.

To the north, at the northwest corner of Parliament and Wellesley streets—you can't miss them, sadly—loom the overwhelming apartment towers of **St. James Town,** built in the 1960s and reviled ever since. They wiped out many streets that had been lined with houses like the ones we have been walking by. Yes, Toronto, too, has been occasionally victimized by progress.

On the east side of Parliament Street, just north of Wellesley Street, is **St. James Cemetery,** which is worth a visit. This beautiful final resting place was laid out in the 1840s, making it the eternal home of many of the most prominent early citizens of the then town of York and the site of some of the most interesting funereal statuary in Toronto. While you are there, observe the small yellow-brick Gothic **Chapel of St. James-the-Less,** built in 1858 and considered to be one of the most beautiful church buildings in the entire country.

Turn right and walk east along Wellesley Street. Be sure to take note of **number 314,** built in 1889–90, with its stonework around the windows and carved stone faces above the door and in the keystones.

Farther east, turn north up the lane marked **Wellesley Cottages.** This row of workers' houses was built in 1886–87 by a carpenter of the time. Much of Toronto's most inexpensive housing of the 19th century was built in this simplified Gothic style, faced with wood lath and stucco. They may look unchanged to you, but some have been extensively modernized.

Back on Wellesley Street, walk north up the lane just east of number 402 to see the **Owl House,** named after the figure on a small terra-cotta plaque under one of its windows. This interesting little house was built in 1893–94.

Wellesley Street comes to an end at **Wellesley Park,** which was, from 1848 to 1888, the site of the area's only major industry, the P. R. Lamb Glue and Blacking Factory, just the thing one wouldn't want next door. Today, it's a small, pleasant neighborhood park and playground, framed by parts of the Don Valley, the Necropolis Cemetery, and the row of houses to the south, for whose occupants the park is a large and lovely front lawn.

Proceed south through Wellesley Park, and turn right along Amelia Street to Sumach Street. Walk south, past Winchester Street, and make a left (east) into **Riverdale Park.** The large stone gateposts on your left were the entrance to the Riverdale Zoo, a public zoo operated by the city from 1894 to 1974, when they finally moved all the animals—and brought in several thousand more—to the magnificent Metro Toronto Zoo, in Scarborough. It will warm your heart to know that this area was laid out on landfill that was dumped by prisoners of the Don Jail, as part of their work program.

It's now **Riverdale Farm,** one of Toronto's most delightful—and free—attractions, and a very special treat for children. Here is where they can find Herbie and Hughie Clydesdale, Morley and Honey Pony, Jasmine, and Sonny and Cher Goat.

The old birdhouse on the grounds is the last remnant of the old zoo, but the most interesting structure is the original, 19th-century Pennsylvania German–style barn, built in 1858 and moved to the farm in 1975. Inside are various implements, such as a light sleigh from the turn of the century and an exact replica of a Conestoga wagon, the kind used by German-speaking immigrants to this country early in the last century.

Bring along bathing suits for the very young children: There's a wading pond in the lovely park adjacent to the farm.

The Riverdale Farm, 201 Winchester St., near Wellesley and Parliament Sts.; tel. 416/392-6794. Open daily 9–5.

The **Necropolis** ("city of the dead") **Cemetery** lies just to the north of Riverdale Farm. The nonsectarian burial ground is filled with many of Toronto's early pioneers. Among the most famous (and notorious): Toronto's first mayor, William Lyon Mackenzie, who led a revolt against the city in 1837; Samuel Lount and Peter Matthews, two of Mackenzie's followers, who were hanged for their part in that rebellion; and George Brown, founder of the *Globe* newspaper and one of the fathers of Canada's confederation.

The beautiful chapel, gate, and gatehouse of the cemetery, erected in 1872, constitute one of the most picturesque groupings of small Victorian buildings in all of Toronto. The Necropolis is also known for its great variety of trees, flowering shrubs, and rare and exotic plants.

Other Neighborhoods As we never get tired of pointing out, part of Toronto's magic, and surely one of its major reasons for its success as a "city that works," is its quite extraordinary collection of neighborhoods. Here are a few others worthy of mention.

❼ A Polish community. The beauty of High Park is described at length in Sightseeing Checklists, below; let us merely say that one of North America's loveliest parks is but 3 or 4 miles due west of Bloor and Yonge streets, along the Bloor subway line. But just east of the park is a long street running north–south:

Roncesvalles Avenue. This is the commercial heart and soul of Toronto's Polish community, filled with butcher shop after butcher shop, each selling homemade sausages just like grandmother should have made, if she had had the skill and time. (Consider buying a few to grill in High Park.)

On the west side of the park is Runnymede Road. Here, and along Bloor Street West, you move both west and east across Europe: Both **German** and **Ukrainian** shops come into view, selling fine food and clothing.

⑧

⑨ **An Italian community.** From the College and Bathurst streets area, west to Dufferin Street and beyond, and north all the way to the city limits of Steeles Avenue, is the ever-widening Italian neighborhood, its numbers making Toronto one of the largest Italian communities outside the mother country. The streets here are filled with the passion and excitement of that great, vibrant Mediterranean culture—especially **St. Clair Avenue,** from Bathurst Street west to Dufferin Street. Here are many fine Italian restaurants and stores, including several that sell excellent ices and ice creams.

⑩ **A West Indian community.** West Indians and their fascinating food shops can be found along Eglinton Avenue, just east of Dufferin Street, and down along Bloor Street West near Christie Street. They can also be found along Bathurst Street, north from Bloor Street. Their snack bars selling *roti*—spicy Jamaican meat patties—can be found most everywhere in Toronto nowadays.

⑪ **An East Indian community.** East Indians are also fairly widely dispersed, although there is one quite concentrated row of Indian shops and restaurants—and movie houses—along Gerrard Street East, near Greenwood Avenue, a few miles east of Yonge Street.

⑫ **A Greek community.** The Danforth. This is a strange name for a street, but it is stranger still in its crazy-quilt ethnicity: Once English-settled (although it was named after Asa Danforth, an American contractor who cut a road in the area back in 1799), it is now Italian, Greek, East Indian, Latin American, and, increasingly, Chinese. But it is still called "Greek town," with its late-night taverns, all-night fruit markets, and some of the best ethnic restaurants in Toronto.

There are now well over a quarter-million Greek Canadians; more than 150,000 of them live in Ontario, and more than half of those live in Metropolitan Toronto. They created such major Canadian enterprises as Devon Ice Cream and Diana Sweets restaurants, and they gave the world internationally acclaimed opera star Teresa Stratas. For more than a decade, in fact, Toronto provided a home and a professorship (at York University, in the northwest part of the city, near Finch and Keele Sts.) for exiled Andreas Papandreou, who was Greece's socialist prime minister during much of the 1980s.

In the summer of 1982, 50 street signs in the Little Athens area of the Danforth, between Logan and Woodycrest avenues, went bilingual (English and Greek). When you've had a little too much souvlaki and Greek wine, the signs can help you find your way home.

What to See and Do with Children

Free Attractions The **Hilton,** at University Avenue and Richmond Street, and the **Harbour Castle Westin,** at the foot of Bay Street, both have outdoor, glass-enclosed elevators, which provide hair-raising rides and spectacular views of the city.

The **ferry boat** to the **Toronto Islands** offers a stunning panorama of downtown Toronto. The islands themselves offer swimming and biking (bikes can be rented) in the summer, skiing in the winter, and the delightful **Far Enough Farm** in Centreville (*see* Tour 1, *above*).

The **Riverdale Farm** in Cabbagetown is a working farm with animals and a wading pond (*see* Tour 4, *above*).

High Park has a sweet little zoo, swimming, skating, picnicking, and more (*see* Sightseeing Checklists, *below*).

Skating, skiing and **tobogganing** are all available for free in most of the major Toronto parks and ravines. And, still thinking about winter, don't forget the beautiful skating rink in front of the New City Hall and the often-terrifying hills at Winston Churchill Park, High Park, Earl Bales Park, and Riverdale Park.

The **Children's Bookstore** in Mirvish Village can provide an hour or more of free fun for children. It's the largest store of its kind in the world, and it frequently holds weekend concerts and readings in the summer (*see* Tour 2, *above*).

The **David Dunlap Observatory** in Richmond Hill, just north of Metro Toronto, and the **McLaughlin Planetarium,** right next to the Royal Ontario Museum, both provide outer-space experiences for preteens and teens (*see* Sightseeing Checklists, *below*).

Harbourfront Centre nearly always has free events and activities, from painting and sculpting to concerts and plays. Just being on the waterfront can be a thrill for children. Feeding the seagulls popcorn or hunks of bread is endlessly interesting, especially when the gulls catch the food in midair dives (*see* Tour 1, *above*).

Boys and Girls House is a superior library for children. The former Spaced-Out Library on the second floor, now called the **Merril Collection,** will thrill all teenage fans of science fiction (*see* Sightseeing Checklists, *below*).

Modestly Priced **Apple, strawberry,** and **raspberry picking** are available within a
Attractions short drive of downtown Toronto. Our favorite place is **Al Ferri's** (15 minutes west of the airport, near the corner of Mississauga Rd. and Steeles Ave.; tel. 416/455–8202). Check out a wonderful cross-bred apple at Ferri's called the Macoun, the result of crossing a Red Delicious with a MacIntosh. Glorious! For a free list of places to pick fruits and vegetables in the vicinity of Toronto, call 416/965–7701.

The *Haida,* at Ontario Place, is a giant World War II destroyer that children love to explore (*see* Sightseeing Checklists, *below*).

The **Art Gallery of Ontario** has a hands-on room that is marvelously creative and entertaining. Right behind it is the fascinating, historic **Grange** house. In front of the gallery is a Henry Moore sculpture that children love to climb (*see* Tour 2, *above*).

The **Royal Ontario Museum,** with its fantastic dinosaurs, towering totem pole, and other child-oriented exhibits, is ideal for children from 3 to 18 (and their parents).

Casa Loma. *See* Tour 4, *above.*

The **Puppet Centre,** near Yonge Street and Highway 401, has more than 400 puppets from all over the world.

More Expensive Attractions   The **Ontario Science Centre** is a must for children, especially those 5 years and older (*see* Sightseeing Checklists, *below*).

The **CN Tower** and the **Tour of the Universe** in its basement are not cheap, but they're a real treat for everyone, especially children (*see* Tour 1, *above*).

Black Creek Pioneer Village is a great place for children (*see* Sightseeing Checklists, *below*).

In their respective seasons, there are numerous events that are great for children: most especially, the **Frostfest** and **Winterfest** (January); the **Fort York Festival** (May); **Caravan** and **International Festival** (June); **Caribana** and **International Picnic** (July); the **Canadian National Exhibition** (mid-August–Labor Day); the **Bindertwine Festival** (September); the **Royal Winter Fair** and **Santa Claus Parade** (November); and the **Festival of Lights** (December).

From early April through September each year, the **Toronto Blue Jays** continue their eternal/infernal climb toward the American League pennant. Throughout the season, children 14 and younger are offered various freebies, such as bats, baseball caps, and sports bags. For ticket information, phone 416/341–1111.

The **Toronto Maple Leafs,** the only leaves that fall from October through April, can provide the occasional hockey thrill at Maple Leaf Gardens (tel. 416/977–1641).

For theater and concerts, the **Young People's Theatre** (tel. 416/864–9732) often has excellent fare, and there are frequent performances for children at **Roy Thomson Hall** (tel. 416/593–4828) and the **Minkler Auditorium** (tel. 416/491–8877), which is up north, near Finch Street and the Don Valley Parkway.

Pricey But Worth It   Just north of the city is **Canada's Wonderland,** Toronto's frozen version of Disneyland. It's uninspired but can provide a decent day's entertainment. There are many rock concerts here at the Kingswood Music Theatre. In past years, Shoppers Drug Mart has offered reduced-rate tickets with purchases amounting to more than a few dollars (*see* Sightseeing Checklists, *below*).

African Lion Safari, about an hour's drive west of Toronto, can provide marvelous entertainment, especially if the giraffe puts its head through your car window. Half-price tickets are often available in shops around the city (*see* Sightseeing Checklists, *below*).

Marineland, in Niagara Falls, is top-quality entertainment put on by underwater zoo crew. It's a world-class park, with thrilling amusement rides, dolphin shows, and aquariums (*see* Chapter 8).

Canada's Wild Water Kingdom, not far from the airport, Black Creek Pioneer Village, and Canada's Wonderland, is a welcome recent addition to every child's dream of a water-sports center: high water slides, river rapids, giant outdoor hot tubs, a fantastic wave pool, and a delightful area for younger children to splash around in. *Finch Ave. W and Hwy. 427; tel. 416/794-0468. Admission: $16 adults, $13 senior citizens and children 4–9. Open daily mid-June–Labor Day, weekends late May–June 30 and Labor Day–Sept. 30, 10 AM–8 PM; closed rest of year.*

The Metro Toronto Zoo The Metro Toronto Zoo was built for animals, not people. The Rouge Valley, just east of Toronto, was an inspired choice of site when it was built in the 1960s, with its varied terrain, from river valley to dense forest, where mammals, birds, reptiles, and fish have been grouped according to where they live in the wild. In most of the sections, you'll find remarkable botanical exhibits in enclosed, climate-controlled pavilions. Don't miss the 3-ton banyan tree in the Indo-Malayan Pavilion; the fan-shaped traveler's palm from Madagascar in the African Pavilion; or the perfumed flowers of the jasmine vines in the Eurasian Pavilion. The "round the world tour" takes some three hours and is suitable for any kind of weather, because most of the time is spent inside pavilions. It's been estimated that it would take four full days to see everything in the Metro Zoo, so study the map you'll get at the zoo entrance, and decide in advance what you wish to see most.

For the younger children, there is the delightful Littlefootland, a special area that allows contact with tame animals, such as rabbits and sheep. In the winter, cross-country skiers follow groomed trails that skirt the animal exhibits. Lessons and rentals are available. There is an electrically powered train that moves silently among the animals without frightening them. It can accommodate wheelchairs (available free, inside the main gate); all pavilions have ramp access.

Meadowvale Rd., just north of Hwy. 401, in Scarborough, a 30-minute drive from downtown. Or take Bus 86A from Kennedy subway station; tel. 416/392–5900 for information. Admission: $9 adults, $6 senior citizens and children 12–17, $4 children 5–11. Free parking in winter. Parking Mar.–Oct. $4. Family rates available. Open daily except Christmas. Summer 9:30 AM–7 PM; winter 9:30 AM–4:30 PM.

Off the Beaten Track

Watching the Italian promenade. St. Clair Avenue West, running from Bathurst Street to Dufferin Street and beyond, remains the heart of this city's vibrant Italian community. On many evenings, especially Sundays, the street is filled with thousands of men and women promenading between *gelaterias*, eyeing each other, and generally enjoying their neighbors. You'll think you're in Rome.

Chinatown on a Sunday morning. Spadina Avenue, from College Street south to Queen Street, and Dundas Street, from Spadina all the way east to Bay Street, are bustling most of the time, but on Sunday mornings—all day, really—the activity is nonstop. A great time to browse, buy, and just plain enjoy.

Greektown on a Sunday. The Danforth (Bloor St. east of the Don Valley Parkway) has great Greek restaurants, gift shops, and hundreds of Greek Canadians promenading. Welcome to the Mediterranean!

There's no hotel more romantic than the **Guild Inn** (*see* Chapter 6), and no view of Toronto more wonderful than from **Centre Island at sunset.**

Sightseeing Checklists

Historic Buildings and Sites
There are many attractive, even fascinating historic buildings and sites around the city of Toronto, a few of them rather far from the core of the downtown area. The following is a checklist for those who wish to make sure they see the most interesting ones. A number of these have been described before, in our Exploring chapter.

Black Creek Pioneer Village. Less than a half hour's drive from downtown Toronto is a rural, mid-19th-century village that makes one feel as if he or she has gone through a time warp. Black Creek Pioneer Village is a collection of over two dozen period buildings that have been moved to their current site: a town hall, weaver's shop, printing shop, blacksmith's shop, and a school, complete with dunce cap. The mill dates from the 1840s and has a 4-ton wood waterwheel that still grinds up to a hundred barrels of flour a day.

Visitors watch men and women in period costumes go about the daily routine of mid-19th-century Ontario life—cutting tin, shearing sheep, tending gardens (weather permitting), fixing and even making horseshoes, baking bread, weaving, printing a newspaper, stringing apple slices, and dipping candles. Most pleasantly, these knowledgeable souls explain what they're doing and how they do it, and they answer all questions about pioneer farm life.

Free wagon rides, a decent restaurant, and many farm animals all contribute to a satisfying outing. And in the winter, there's also skating, tobogganing, and sleigh rides. *Located in northwest Metro Toronto at Jane St. and Steeles Ave. By car, take Hwy. 401, then Hwy. 400 north to Steeles E, and follow signs. By bus, take #35B from Jane St. subway station in Toronto's west end and/or #60B or #60D from Finch Ave. subway station. Tel. 416/661–6610 for recorded message; 416/736–1733 for more information. Admission: $7 adults, $4.50 senior citizens, $3 children 5–14. Generally open 10–5. Phone for seasonal events, reduced winter hours, and extended summer hours. Closed early Jan.–school break (usually mid-Mar.).*

Campbell House. *See* Tour 3, *above.*

Casa Loma. *See* Tour 4, *above.*

Colborne Lodge. Visit this grand 19th-century home in conjunction with a trip to High Park. An architect named John Howard built this Regency-style "cottage" on a park hill overlooking Lake Ontario more than 150 years ago. Visitors will see the original fireplace, bake oven, and kitchen, as well as many of Howard's own drawings and paintings. *Colborne Lodge Dr., at south end of High Park. By subway, take Bloor St. Line west to High Park station. Tel. 416/392–6916. Admission: $3.25 adults, $2.50 senior citizens and children 13–18, $2.25 children*

*13 and younger. Open Jan. 1–Mar. 31, weekends noon–5; Apr.
1–Dec. 31, weekdays 9:30–4, weekends and holidays noon–5.*

Enoch Turner Schoolhouse. This building, just a few blocks
east of Union Station in the St. Lawrence area, helps us remember that free public education began only in the mid-19th
century. Back in the 1840s, Toronto parents paid two-thirds of
teachers' salaries, and the government picked up the rest.
When the Ontario legislature passed an act in 1848 authorizing
cities to provide free schools (paid for by property taxes), the
Toronto City Council balked at the radical concept and closed
down every public school in town. A brewer named Enoch Turner was outraged by the reactionary policy of the city elders,
and he created Toronto's first free educational institution.
Three years later, the politicians relented and absorbed the
Enoch Turner Schoolhouse into the public school system of Toronto. And so, this small red-and-yellow brick building remains, looking frightfully like today's schoolrooms, except for
the ancient desks. *106 Trinity St., near corner of King St. E
and Parliament St., tel. 416/863–0010. Admission free. Open
weekdays 9:30–4:30.*

Fort York. This remarkable historical site is in downtown Toronto, not far from Harbourfront Centre and Ontario Place. It
could well be combined with visits to either of those sites.

In 1813, a fierce battle took place between the Yankees and the
Queen's Rangers regiment in what was then York (now, Toronto). **Fort York** was torched, but the Canadians rebuilt it just
three years later, and it still stands, near the foot of Bathurst
Street, in downtown Toronto. The eight buildings, with their
brick, stone, and log frames, give visitors a good sense of what
it was like to be a British soldier stuck out in the boondocks
nearly two centuries ago.

You'll see the blockhouses, where dozens of men froze to death
in their beds over the years, and the mess, where women still
bake bread in the giant stone fireplace. There's a model of the
famous battle from the War of 1812, and, year-round, men get
rigged up in the uniforms of the era, call themselves the Fort
York Guard, and perform 19th-century drills, complete with
artillery salutes. Children will enjoy climbing on the various
cannons, and tour guides are both knowledgeable and friendly.
*By car, take Lakeshore Blvd. W to Strachan Ave. (pronounced
"strawn") north, and head east on Fleet St. By subway, take
Bloor St. train west to Bathurst St., then the streetcar south to
Garrison Rd. exit. The Bathurst St. #511 streetcar also goes
here. Tel. 416/392–6907. Admission: $4.75 adults, $3 senior citizens and children 13–18, $2.75 children 6–12. Open Oct.
1–May 15, weekdays 9:30–4, weekends and holidays 10–5;
May 16–Sept. 30, daily 9:30–5. Closed Jan. 1, Good Friday,
and Dec. 25–26.*

Gibson House. It's the Little House in the Suburbs, convenient
for people driving anywhere near Highway 401 and Yonge
Street. The 10-room country house was built in 1851 by one of
the supporters of William Lyon Mackenzie's 1837 rebellion.
True, David Gibson's original home was burned to the ground
by anti-Mackenzie men while the surveyor was off in a decade-
long exile in the United States (during which time he assisted in
constructing the Erie Canal), but when he returned to Toronto,
he built this. As in Fort York and Black Creek, there are men

and women in 19th-century costumes who demonstrate the cooking and crafts of the pioneers. *5172 Yonge St., about 1 mi north of Sheppard Ave. and Hwy. 401, tel. 416/225–0146. Admission: $2.14 adults, $1.61 students and senior citizens, $1.07 children, $5.35 families; senior citizens free Wed. Open Tues.– Fri. 9:30 AM–5 PM, weekends noon–5; also open on holiday Mon.*

The Grange. This fine living museum is located just behind the Art Gallery of Ontario. In 1911, a prominent lady donated her historic house (1817) to what was then the Art Museum of Toronto. It's been restored as a "Gentleman's House" of the mid-1830s, and it should not be missed. The columned Georgian front and the delicately balanced wings that flow from the sides of its porch only hint at the joys of the interior: Carefully refurnished in English regency style, it is a virtual stage set for "Upstairs/Downstairs," complete with music room and a row of bells to call the servants from the basement kitchen. Costumed hostesses bake bread in the 19th-century brick ovens and give out slices, and children can dress up in aprons and bonnets. *317 Dundas St. W, just west of University Ave.; tel. 416/977–0414. Admission free with admission to Art Gallery ($4.50 adults, $2.50 students and senior citizens, $9 families). Open Tues.– Sun. noon–4.*

Mackenzie House. This is in a deceptively modest row of houses, just blocks from the Eaton Centre. Its owner, William Lyon Mackenzie, was born in Scotland at the end of the 1700s and immigrated to Canada in 1820. He began a newspaper that so enraged the powers that be (they were known as "the Family Compact"—a powerful, smug group of politicians, *not* an economy car) that they broke into his print shop and dumped all his type into Lake Ontario. Undismayed, Mackenzie was elected the first mayor of Toronto, even designing the coat of arms of the new city. When he wasn't reelected in 1836, he gathered about 700 supporters and marched down Yonge Street to try to overthrow the government. They were roundly defeated, and Willie had to escape to the United States with a price on his head. When the Canadian government finally granted him amnesty, a dozen years later, Mackenzie was promptly elected to the legislative assembly—suggesting a daring on the part of Torontonians that few would imagine today—and began to publish another newspaper. By this time, though, Mackenzie was so down on his luck and cash that some friends passed the hat and bought him and his family the house we suggest you visit. His grandson, William Lyon Mackenzie King, became the longest-lasting prime minister of Canada.

Mackenzie enjoyed the place for but a few sickly and depressing years: He died here in 1861. Today it has been lovingly restored as a National Historic Site and is operated as a museum and library. There are dozens of 19th-century furnishings and treasures, even the wild man's printing press. *82 Bond St., two blocks east of Yonge St. and a few steps south of Dundas St., tel. 416/392–6915. Admission: $2.75 adults, $2 senior citizens and children 13–18, $1.75 children under 13. 1-hr. group tours cost $2.25 per person. Open weekdays 9:30–4, weekends and holidays noon–5.*

Montgomery's Inn. This restored inn—one of the few attractions in the west end of Toronto—was built in the early 1830s by an Irish immigrant, and it is a good example of the Loyalist architecture of the time. Costumed staff go about quilting, rug hooking, and cooking traditional foods. There are many tours, and a daily afternoon tea, 2–4:15. *4709 Dundas St., brief walk from Islington subway stop; tel. 416/394–8113. Admission: $2.50 adults, $1.50 students and senior citizens, $1 children, $6 maximum per family. Open weekdays 9:30–4:30, weekends 1–5.*

Old City Hall/New City Hall. *See* Tour 2, *above*.

Queen's Park. *See* Tour 3, *above*.

Spadina. Pronounced spa-*dee*-na, as the avenue should be but never is, it is filled with arts and artifacts of a prominent Toronto family. First built in 1866, it is now a glorious living tribute to the Victorian and Edwardian eras, featuring French porcelain vases, handsome furniture, crystal chandeliers burning softly with natural gas, fine paintings, and magnificent gardens. *285 Spadina Ave., next to Casa Loma; tel. 416/392–6910. Admission: $4.75 adults, $3 senior citizens and children 13–18, $2.75 children 6–12. Slight discount for those with Casa Loma receipt. Open Jan.–May 31, weekdays 9:30–4, weekends noon–5; summer, Mon.–Sat. 9:30–5, Sun. and holidays noon–5; Sept.–Dec. 31, weekdays 9:30–5, weekends and holidays noon–5.*

Todmorden Mills Historic Site. A number of the city's oldest buildings have been restored on their original sites, all in open parkland that is a marvelous place to picnic. The name Todmorden Mills comes from England, as did the settlers who built these structures. There are two pioneer houses, a brewery (1821), a paper mill (1825), and the old Don Train Station, built in 1891 to serve two once-great railroads, the Canadian National and Canadian Pacific. *67 Pottery Rd., just off the Bayview Ave. Extension; tel. 416/425–2250. Admission: $2.25 adults, $1.75 students and senior citizens, $1.25 children 5–12. Open May–Dec., Tues.–Fri. 10–5; weekends and holidays noon–5.*

Union Station. *See* Tour 1, *above*.

Museums and Observatories As befits the largest city in Canada, as well as the capital of the province of Ontario, Metro Toronto has many major museums. These range from one of the world's great museums—the Royal Ontario Museum—to the superb Ontario Science Centre to the tiny but fascinating Museum of the History of Medicine.

Art Gallery of Ontario. *See* Tour 2, *above*.

An astonishing museum, **The Bata Shoe Museum Collection,** opened in May 1992 on the east side of University, across the street from the Royal Ontario Museum. Created by Sonja Bata, the wife of the genius who built Bata Shoes into a billion-dollar world-wide conglomerate, this new museum contains more than 8,500 shoes, ranging from wooden thongs from 2500 BC to Queen Victoria's favorite footwear, and much more. Hours will be vague until 1994, when the collection moves into permanent headquarters on Bloor and St. George streets, a few blocks west. *The Colonnade, 131 Bloor St. W, tel. 416/924–7463.*

Bell Canada Building. Just north of the Old City Hall is a modest display of early telephones that go back to the time of Alexander Graham Bell, who actually invented the darned thing in a town just west of Toronto. You may enjoy seeing the phone book of 1879, which listed 30 houses in Toronto, as well as the offices of 18 doctors and a single dentist. *483 Bay St., in basement; tel. 416/581–4050. Admission free. Open weekdays 9–5.*

Beth Tzedec Museum. Located within an attractive Conservative synagogue of the same name, it is the only museum of Jewish artifacts in Toronto. It has special exhibits, as well as fine regular displays of ancient coins and glass, silver coins from ancient Greece and Rome, medieval Sabbath spice boxes, and even a centuries-old chair on which infant boys would be circumcised. Tours can be arranged. *1700 Bathurst St., about 4 blocks south of Eglinton or 3 mi northwest of Royal Ontario Museum; tel. 416/781–3511. Admission free. Open Mon., Wed., Thurs., 11–5, Sun. 10–1.*

David Dunlap Observatory. Constructed in 1935, this is both a museum of photos of sunspots, nebulae, and galaxies and the largest observatory in all of Canada—and it is only 15 miles north of downtown! Visitors are admitted only in large groups on Saturday nights, from mid-April to early October, but individuals or small groups who call for reservations may join the next tour that has space. Visitors climb a ladder and peek through the 25-ton telescope at the planet, star, or moon that is "playing" that night. It can get extremely chilly under the unheated dome, even in midsummer, so dress warmly for your close encounter. *3 km (1.8 mi) north of Hwy. 7, along Yonge St. Drive past large white dome on right, and turn right on Hillsview Dr. By public transit, take Yonge St. subway to Finch Ave., and then Yonge St. GO bus north. Tel. 416/884–2112. Admission free.*

H.M.C.S. *Haida*. On the grounds of Ontario Place, across from the Canadian National Exhibition, this World War II destroyer is now a floating museum. It is irresistible for children of all ages. *Tel. 416/965–6331. A small charge. Open summers 10–7.*

Hockey Hall of Fame and Museum. Open since 1961, this shrine has everything from the original Stanley Cup, donated in 1893, to displays of goalie masks, skate and stick collections, jerseys of the great players, and video displays of big games. If you wish to see Wayne Gretzky's feet cast in bronze, this is the place to catch them. *Exhibition Place, CNE grounds, tel. 416/595–1345.* In the spring of 1993 it will move to the old Bank of Montreal building, incorporated into the new **BCE Place** at the northwest corner of Yonge and Front streets. *Admission: $3.25 adults, $2.25 students and senior citizens. Open mid-May–mid-Aug., Tues.–Sun. 10–7, Mon. 10–5. During the CNE in Aug. and early Sept., open daily 10–5. Other months, open Tues.–Sun. 10–4:30.*

Lakeview Generating Station. A living museum located in the west end, this giant thermal-electric station produces more power than Niagara Falls' stations. Visitors see coal converted to energy in furnaces towering 17 stories overhead. *Lakeshore and Dixie Rds., a 15-min drive west of downtown; tel. 416/222–2571. Tours weekdays 9:30–4:30. Children should be over 10.*

Marine Museum of Upper Canada. Exhibits cover the War of 1812, fur-trade exploration, and so on. On display are canoes, a diving suit, relics from sunken ships, and a wireless room from the 1930s. Outside the museum is a 1932 steam tugboat in dry dock. *Located inside Exhibition Place on the CNE grounds, near Dufferin St. and Lakeshore Blvd.; tel. 416/392–6827. Take Bathurst St. #511 streetcar from Bathurst/Bloor subway* *stop. Admission: $3.25 adults, $2.50 senior citizens and children 13–18, $2.25 children under 13. Open Jan. 1–Mar. 31, weekends noon–5; Apr. 1–Dec. 31, weekdays 9:30–4, weekends and holidays noon–5.*

McMichael Canadian Collection. Though 20 miles northwest of Toronto, this popular art gallery attracts more than 300,000 visitors a year. The building, constructed from native stone and hand-hewn timber, houses the art of the Group of Seven painters and some of their contemporaries. These talented young men turned to the Canadian landscape for inspiration in the early decades of this century. At a time when 19th-century British styles were still holding the colonies in an artistic stranglehold, this struggle to capture the passion and fury of the raw and powerful Canadian landscape was a great leap forward. In addition to seeing the paintings, you won't want to ignore the 100 acres of river valley around the gallery buildings—an ideal spot for picnics. *Drive west on Hwy. 401 to Hwy. 400, then north to Kleinburg exit; tel. 416/893–1121. Admission: $5 adults, $2.50 senior citizens and children, $8.55 maximum for families. Free to senior citizens on Wed. Open winter Tues.– Sun. 11–4:30; Apr. 1–Oct. 31, daily 10–5 (call to confirm hours).*

Metro Toronto Police Museum and Discovery Centre. Highlights are a replica of a 19th-century police station, an exhibit of counterfeit money, a display of techniques for taking identifications, a wide selection of firearms, and displays of some of the city's most infamous crimes. It will also have many interactive displays, one involving putting together composite drawings with computers. The museum, in the main foyer of the new police headquarters, should be completed by February 1993. *40 College St., a half block west of Yonge; tel. 416/324–6201. Admission free. Open 24 hours a day.*

Museum of the History of Medicine. This is one of the most interesting little museums in Toronto. Founded in 1907, and part of the University of Toronto's Academy of Medicine, it has hundreds of objects on display, including an Egyptian mummy and the record of the recently performed autopsy on it, 300-year-old nursing bottles with chamois nipples, an English wheelchair from 1910, and a North American bleeding bowl from the 1780s. Everything from magical and religious artifacts to prints and photographs shows how people have practiced medicine for thousands of years. *288 Bloor St. W, a few minutes' walk west of the Royal Ontario Museum; tel. 416/922–0564. Admission: $4 adults, $2.50 university students and senior citizens; children free; nominal charge for guided group tours (minimum 10 people). Open weekdays 9:30–4.*

Ontario Science Centre. It has been called a museum of the 21st century, but it's much more than that. Where else can one stand at the edge of a black hole, work hand-in-clamp with a robot, or land on the moon? Even the building itself is extraordinary. Three linked pavilions float gracefully down the side of a ravine at Eglinton Avenue East, near the Don Valley Parkway, and each overflows with exhibits that make space, technology, communications, and life itself irresistible. Early 1992 brought a marvelous new space exhibit called "Challenger." A dozen minitheaters show films that bring the natural world to life. Live demonstrations—of lasers, glassblowing, papermaking, electricity, etc.—take place regularly throughout the day, so check the schedule when you arrive at the center, and plan your time accordingly.

You need at least two hours to scratch the surface; you may want to spend an entire day. Children will love this place, probably more than any other in Toronto, but adults will be enthralled, too. There is a cafeteria, a restaurant, and a gift store with a cornucopia of books and scientific doodads. *770 Don Mills Rd., about 11 km (7 mi) from downtown. By car, head west from Eglinton Ave. exit of Don Valley Pkwy. By public transportation, take Yonge St. subway from downtown to Eglinton station, and transfer to Eglinton E bus. Get off at Don Mills Pkwy. stop. Tel. 416/696–3127 (for recording), 416/ 429–4100 (for further information). Admission (more crazy GST prices): $5.89 adults, $4.82 children 13–17, $2.14 children 5–12, senior citizens and children under 5 free. There's a family rate of $14.98, for up to two adults and six children. Parking is $2. Weekdays are less crowded. Open daily 10–6, Fri. 10–9; free daily after 5 PM.*

Puppet Centre. *See* What to See and Do with Children, above.

Redpath Sugar Museum. Located on the waterfront, a few blocks east of where the ferries depart for the Toronto Island, this museum has displays of sugar harvesting, vintage sugar tools, and an enjoyable 20-minute film, *Raising Cane*. The curator is available to answer questions. *95 Queen's Quay E, by the water; tel. 416/597–0286. Admission free. Open weekdays 10–noon and 1–3.*

Royal Ontario Museum. This spectacular collection is described at length in Tour 3, above, as are its siblings, the **McLaughlin Planetarium,** the **Sigmund Samuel Canadiana Collection,** and the **George R. Gardiner Museum of Ceramic Art.**

Sports Hall of Fame. This is right next door to the hockey museum and honors every other sport known to man, woman, and child, from rowing to running. *Tel. 416/595–1046. Admission free.*

Art Galleries Toronto is a highly cosmopolitan art center, second only to New York in North America. Over 300 commercial art galleries are listed in the Yellow Pages, offering every kind of art for viewing and sale, from Picasso to Warhol, from representational to abstract, from Inuit to Indian. The following is a list of some of the best and most respected galleries. The entertainment section of the Saturday *Globe and Mail* has several pages of listings and reviews of current shows. Most galleries have free copies of the monthly booklet *Slate*, which includes a gallery guide to Toronto. Visitors may want to stroll from gallery to gallery in either of two major districts—the Yorkville area, and the Queen Street area, west of University Avenue. Most galleries are open Tuesdays through Saturdays, 10–5:30 or 6.

Yorkville. In the Yorkville area, just behind the exclusive Hazelton Lanes complex, one can find many important galleries.

Sable–Castelli Gallery (33 Hazelton Ave., tel. 416/961–0011) is the result of the Jared Sable gallery's amalgamation in 1974 with the renowned Castelli galleries of Manhattan. Since then, he has exhibited established American artists such as Warhol, Oldenburg, Johns, and Rosenquist, as well as innovative young Canadian artists who use strong expressive imagery.

Miriam Shiell Fine Art Ltd., located in the same building as Sable–Castelli (tel. 416/925–2461), is a wittily designed space for displaying expensive work from the United States and abroad, as well as that of several established Canadians. One can see Dufy and Matisse, Noland and Olitski, as well as Inuit art.

Mira Godard Gallery (22 Hazelton Ave., tel. 416/964–8197), which came from Montreal to Toronto in 1972, carries such major French-Canadian artists as Borduas and Riopelle, as well as established Canadian artists like Alex Colville, Kenneth Lochhead, David Milne, Jean-Paul Lemieux, and Christopher Pratt.

Nancy Poole's Studio (16 Hazelton Ave., tel. 416/964–9050) is a small, intimate space, almost exclusively exhibiting Canadian contemporary painting and sculpture, generally representational. The artists include Jack Chambers, the astonishing Canadian Indian stone-carver Joe Jacobs, and the fine contemporary painter John Boyle.

Gallery Dresdnere (12 Hazelton Ave., tel. 416/923–4662), created by an ex-Montrealer, shows a fine selection of Canadian abstract and conceptual paintings, as well as graphics and wall hangings.

Glass Art Gallery is the only gallery of its kind in Canada. It is a thrilling showroom of stained glass, laminated and crystal sculpture, and other avant-garde work. *21 Hazelton Ave., tel. 416/968–1823. Open 11–6.*

Gallery One, on the next block (121 Scollard St., tel. 416/929–3103), is one of the mainstays for large-format abstract expressionists in Canada and the United States, as well as for representational landscape art from western Ontario and Inuit art. Color-field painters, from Larry Poons to Jules Olitski, are exhibited here.

Gallery Moos, on Yorkville Avenue, just a block down, was opened by German-born Walter Moos 30 years ago to promote Canadian art. He is a discerning, reliable dealer, whose gallery has Picassos, Chagalls, Miros, and Dufys, as well as such internationally admired Canadians as Gershon Iskowitz, Ken Danby, Sorel Etrog, and Jean-Paul Riopelle. *136 Yorkville Ave., tel. 416/922–6612. Open 11–6.*

The **Inuit Gallery of Eskimo Art** was started by the respected Av Isaacs to showcase fine art and crafts produced in the Canadian Arctic. It is the finest gallery of its kind anywhere. Prints, drawings, sculpture, wall hangings, and antiquities are all beautifully displayed. *9 Prince Arthur Ave., tel. 416/921–9985. One of the rare galleries to remain open on Mon. (10–6).*

Prime Canadian Crafts has crafts from across Canada, including avant-garde ceramics, functional teapots, wall sculpture, and jewelry. *229 Queen St. W, tel. 416/593–5750. Open Mon.–Sat. 11–6.*

Ydessa Hendeles Art Foundation, recently moved to King Street, near Bathurst, is now, more than ever, a wonderful, major showcase for contemporary international art. *778 King St., 2 blocks west of Bathurst St., tel. 416/941–9400. Open Wed.–Sat. 1–5.*

Klonaridis, Inc., is run by a young dealer of discerning taste who displays local talent and imports some of the newest and best from New York and elsewhere south of the border. A must place for those interested in new, exciting art. *80 Spadina Ave., near King St., tel. 416/360–7800. Open Tues.–Sat. 11–5.*

Jane Corkin Photographic Gallery (179 John St. off Queen St., tel. 416/979–1980) has proven that photography is a major art form. Featuring everyone from André Kertesz to Richard Avedon, this gallery is one of the most fascinating in town, showing hand-painted photos, documentary photos, and fashion photography.

Olga Korper (17 Morrow Ave. N off Dundas, a half mile west of Dufferin St., tel. 416/538–8220) is one of the most accessible and knowledgeable dealers in Toronto, and she is a trailblazer who has discovered many important artists. This is a fine place for beginning collectors to visit.

Wynick-Tuck Gallery (80 Spadina Ave., tel. 416/364–8716) represents contemporary Canadian artists whose work expresses a wide range of untrendy, often imagistic concerns. Many of them have become well established, attesting to the gallery's influence.

Bau-Xi Gallery, across the street from the Art Gallery of Ontario (340 Dundas St. W, tel. 416/977–0600), was founded by Paul Wong, an artist and dealer from Vancouver. It provides a window on contemporary Canadian West Coast art (some from Ontario, as well), much of it affordable.

The Drabinsky Gallery (86 Scollard St., tel. 416/324–5766) was created by the man who runs the Pantages, where the *Phantom of the Opera* plays eternally, as well as the North York Performing Arts Centre, opening in late 1993. With its attractive, rosy-maple floors and such major artists as Harold Town and Alex Colville, this is an important new addition to the Yorkville art scene.

The Textile Museum (55 Centre Ave., attached to the Chestnut Park, tel. 416/599–5515) has five floors of remarkable textiles.

Thomson Gallery (on the 9th floor of The Bay's Tower, just south of the Eaton Centre) houses the impressive collection of the billionaire who owns Simpsons, The Bay, and three dozen newspapers, including the *Globe and Mail.*

S. L. Simpson Gallery (515 Queen St. W, tel. 416/362–3738) has new Canadian paintings, and mixed media.

Open Studio Printmaking (520 King St. W, 3rd floor, tel. 416/368–8238) shows original prints of modern Canadian artists.

Parks and Gardens Toronto was originally a series of little villages, each one treasuring its tiny common or park. The metro area now has some 3 million souls, but residents still think in the old village way, saving from development as much parkland as is possible. The parks are more than just grass; they are great places to jog, bike, picnic, see flowers, even bird-watch. Some have skating rinks, tennis courts, and playing fields.

Edwards Gardens. Thirty-five acres of beautiful hillside gardens flow into one of the city's most popular ravines. Paths wind along colorful floral displays and exquisite rock gardens. Refreshments and picnic facilities are available, but no pets are allowed.

The great ravine walk begins at Edwards Gardens (entrance on the southwest corner of Leslie St. and Lawrence Ave. E). Head south through **Wilket Creek Park** and through the winding Don River valley. Pass beneath the Don Valley Parkway and continue along Massey Creek. After hours of walking (or biking, or jogging) through almost uninterrupted parkland, you'll end up at the southern tip of **Taylor Creek Park** on Victoria Park Avenue, just north of the Danforth. From here you can catch a subway train back to your hotel.

High Park. Toronto's equivalent of London's Hyde Park or Manhattan's Central Park (but with no political ranting and few muggings) is 3 or 4 miles from downtown, but it is certainly worth a visit—especially in the summer, when there are many special events, including free productions of Shakespeare. One of the highlights is **Grenadier Pond,** a small lake in the southwest corner. Named after the British soldiers who used to drill on its frozen surface in the last century, it is home today to thousands of migrating birds. You can fish in its well- stocked waters, either from the shore or from a rented rowboat. There are Sunday afternoon concerts in summer and supervised skating in winter. The **High Park Zoo** is a far cry from the Metro Zoo, but it's a lot closer, and it's free. It's modest enough that even young children won't tire walking among the deer, Barbary sheep, peacocks, rabbits, and the only truly native Torontonians extant—raccoons. Other highlights of the park are a large swimming pool, tennis courts, fitness trails, and hillside gardens with roses and sculpted hedges.

Take the Bloor Street subway west to the High Park station, or the College Street streetcar to the eastern end of the park. There's limited parking along Bloor Street, just north of the park, and along the side streets on the eastern side.

Highland Creek ravines. Since these are almost in their natural state, they are considered the most beautiful in Toronto—ideal for cross-country skiing, biking, and jogging. There are two parks that follow Highland Creek, **Colonel Danforth Park** and **Morningside Park.** The Colonel Danforth trail begins south of Kingston Road, on the east side of Highland Creek bridge. Morningside Park is accessible off Morningside Avenue, between Kingston Road and Ellesmere Avenue. Both parks can be entered from the grounds of Scarborough College, 1265 Military Trail, in Scarborough. The **Toronto Field Naturalists** (tel. 416/968–6255) lead over 150 outings every year, mainly within these ravine systems.

Humber Valley. This parkland in Toronto's west end is well worth a hiking/jogging/biking tour. It stretches along the Humber River ravine, from north of the city limits (Steeles Ave.) all the way down to where the Humber flows quietly into Lake Ontario.

James Gardens, a lovely formal garden, can be reached from Edenbridge Drive, east of Royal York Road. Adjoining it to the south is **Scarlet Mills Park,** one of North America's only wildflower reserves. Both parks are open daily until sunset, with lots of free parking.

Nordheimer Ravine. This can be approached from a path leading from Boulton Drive, in the shadow of Casa Loma. On your right is a view of the great mansions of Forest Hill; on your left is Casa Loma, rising above a steep bank of trees. The ravine eventually opens up like a flower, and you are soon at **Churchill Park,** which, as we've noted, has the best tobogganing in the city.

Queen's Park. This small, lovely park in the heart of the downtown area is discussed in Tour 3, above. It's not worth a special trip, but it's certainly worth remembering after a day of shopping or museum-hopping.

The **Rosedale ravines** are only a few minutes' walk from the shopping mecca of Yonge and Bloor streets, in the very heart of the city. They are a series of peaceful ravines that cut through the luxurious, heavily wooded neighborhood of Rosedale. Walk north from the Castle Frank subway station along Castle Frank Road to **Hawthorn Gardens.** There you will find a short footpath to **Craigleigh Gardens.** Suddenly, this tiny, quiet park gives way to a ravine, and paths wind steeply down through a tangle of underbrush. From here you can go west, up Balfour Creek, across Mount Pleasant Road, and through **David Balfour Park** to St. Clair Avenue. Or you can walk northeast, past the Don Valley brickworks to **Chorley Park** and Mount Pleasant Cemetery, by way of the still-undeveloped Moore Park marshes. These marshes remain an excellent breeding ground for wildlife, though they lie within the core of a bustling city. Another way to explore this ravine is to start at Yonge Street and St. Clair Avenue. Walk east along St. Clair Avenue a few blocks, until you come to a bridge. On the north side of the street is a sign marked "nature trail." Believe it.

Scarborough Bluffs. This is the most scenic park along Lake Ontario, with breathtaking views from the high lakeside cliffs. **Cathedral Bluffs Park,** at the foot of Midland Avenue, also offers dramatic views.

Sherwood Park. Farther north, near Lawrence Avenue East and Mount Pleasant Road, is one of the best-kept secrets in Toronto. Sherwood Park has one of the finest children's playgrounds in the city, a lovely wading pool, and a hill that seems to go on forever. Head up Mount Pleasant Road, north of Eglinton Avenue, until you see a little street called Sherwood on the right. Go east a long block, and you're there. A ravine begins at the bottom of the hill. You can follow it across Blythwood Road, all the way to Yonge Street and Lawrence Avenue. There, subways and buses await you—and so do the beautiful rose gardens in **Alexander Muir Park.**

Sir Casimir Gzowski Park. Enjoy marvelous views of the Toronto Islands, Ontario Place, and the downtown skyline, and swim at nearby **Sunnyside Park.** Both lakefront parks are only a few blocks east of Bathurst Street, easily accessible by streetcar.

Sir Winston Churchill Park. Winter visitors—especially those with children—should try not to miss this park, located at Spadina Avenue, only a short walk from Casa Loma. In summer there's a sweet playground, a sandbox, a jogging track, and tennis courts. In winter there's a serious hill offering the most terrifying toboggan run in the city.

Tommy Thompson Park. This interesting place, known until 1985 as the **Leslie Street Spit,** is a peninsula that juts 5 kilometers (3 miles) into Lake Ontario. It was created from the sand dredged for a new port entry and the landfill of a hundred skyscrapers. (These Canadians don't waste a thing.) It has quickly become one of the best areas in the city for cycling, jogging, walking, sailing, photography, and bird-watching.

This strange, man-made peninsula immediately became the home (or stopover) for the largest colony of ring-billed seagulls in the world and for dozens of species of terns, ducks, geese, and snowy egrets.

No private vehicles are permitted, but on weekends, mid-May to mid-October, two vans operate free of charge from the parking lot. In summer, a city bus travels through the park from the corner of Queen Street and Berkshire Avenue.

If you drive, go east along Queen Street to Leslie Street, then south to the lake. The park is open weekends and holidays 9–6.

The Toronto Islands. *See* Tour 1, above.

Theme Parks and Amusement Areas

African Lion Safari. This fabulous drive-through wildlife park is a full hour's drive from Toronto, but it should be considered by anyone with children and access to a car.

If the idea of a giraffe sticking its head into your back seat does not warm your heart, there are air-conditioned trams that carry as many as 3,000 visitors a day over a 6-mile safari trail. Lions, tigers, cheetah, black bears, elephants, white rhinos, and zebras make this astonishingly uncommercial park truly special.

In addition to six large game reserves, there's a birds of prey flying demonstration, a parrot show, an elephant roundup, and even an *African Queen*–style boat that cruises past birds and primates. *Near Cambridge, Ont., due west of Toronto. Take Hwy. 401 west to Hwy. 6. Drive south to Safari Rd., and turn right. The trip takes about an hour. Tel. 519/623–2620. Admission, including boat and railway cruises: about $13 adults (not including 15% provincial taxes and GST), $11 senior citizens and children 13–17, $9 children 3–12. You may want to pack a picnic, but food is available. Open Apr.– late Oct. 10–4, 10–5 on weekends and holidays. July and Aug., daily 10–5:30.*

Black Creek Pioneer Village. This re-creation of a 19th-century Ontario community is a joyous outing for the entire family. *See* Historic Buildings and Sites, *above*.

Canada's Wonderland. Yogi Bear, Fred Flintstone, Scooby Doo, and other Canadian cultural heroes are part of a $160 million theme park overflowing with games, rides, restaurants, and shops. The entertainment ranges from Broadway-style productions to pop and rock performances to dolphin shows. Canada's first world-class theme park lacks the warm evocativeness of Disneyland; and because it's here in the Frozen North, its season runs only from late April to early October. Yet the park is remarkably close to Toronto—barely 30 minutes from downtown, and only 15 minutes from the airport—and a visit here can easily be combined with a trip to Black Creek Pioneer Village.

Children will love it here, but adults should stay away unless they've been longing for brassy entertainment, stomach-churning rides, and eateries such as Yee Ribb Pytt, which serves French Fryes and Shrymps. Indeed, families should consider packing a picnic lunch and eating at the few tables (reluctantly) provided, just outside the park.

Teens and many adults will be delighted to know that on the grounds of Canada's Wonderland is the high-quality **Kingswood Music Theatre** (tel. 416/832–8131), which has excellent pop and rock acts through the summer, which cost less than $10 above the park admission. The open-air facility has 5,200 reserved seats under a covered pavilion and 8,800 additional seats on the sloping lawn.

Low-cost GO express buses leave regularly from Yorkdale and York Mills subway stations. By car, take Hwy. 401 to Hwy. 400; drive north about 10 mins. to Rutherford Rd., and follow signs. Tel. 416/832–7000. Admission: around $25 adults, $13 senior citizens over 60 and children 3–6. Grounds admission alone, which does not include rides, is $14.95 adults. Those who plan to return several times should consider an individual season pass, about $42; a family season pass, around $125; about $32 for each additional person. These prices invariably go up 10% each year. Check newspapers, chain stores, and hotels for half-price tickets. Open spring and fall weekends 10–8; late June–Labor Day, daily 10–10.

The Canadian National Exhibition (the CNE or "the Ex"), at the foot of Dufferin Street and Lakeshore Boulevard, attracts over 3 million people each year. It began back in 1879 as an agricultural show, and remnants of that tradition can still be found in the livestock exhibits. But in its second century, the Ex is a noisy, crowded, often entertaining collection of carnies pushing $5 balloons, tummy-turning midway rides, sexist beauty contests, live bands, horticultural and technological exhibits, and (sometimes) topnotch happenings.

Parades, dog swims, horse shows, grandstand shows with such talent as Bill Cosby, Kenny Rogers, and Whitney Houston— the Exhibition has something for all. It's often vulgar and brassy, the snacks overpriced and greasy, the rides too short and too expensive. But it can also be an enjoyable way to spend an afternoon—after all, the world's largest annual exhibition must have *something* still going for it! *Lakeshore Blvd. W at Strachan ("strawn") Ave. or off Dufferin St., just south of King St., tel. 416/393–6000. In 1993, the CNE will run Aug. 18–Sept. 6. Open daily 8 AM–1 AM; buildings, open 10–10. Admission: about $9 adults, senior citizens free until noon and around $2 thereafter, $2.50 children under 14. Tickets to grandstand shows available from box office or through Ticketmaster (tel. 416/872–1111). Check local newspapers for special daily events. Never take a car to the Ex; the parking is insufficient and always terribly overpriced. Many buses and streetcars labeled "Exhibition" travel across the city into the CNE grounds.*

Centreville. *See* Tour 1, *above.*

Harbourfront Centre. *See* Tour 1, *above.*

Marineland, a park full of quality rides and dolphin/killer whale shows, is about 90 minutes southwest of Toronto (*see* Chapter 8).

Ontario Place. Highlights of this waterfront complex, built on three man-made islands, include the **Cinesphere** (a dome with a six-story movie screen enclosed); several interesting shows in pods that float above the waters of Lake Ontario; the *Haida,* a destroyer from the Second World War that is fun to explore; and, best of all, the outdoor **Forum,** where nightly performances by a fabulous singer or rock group (or orchestra or ballet corps) take place, for astonishingly low prices that range between $8 and $15. Here, too, you will find the **Children's Village**—complete with water games, towering tube slides, and a moon walk. This is one of the most creative playgrounds in the world, and a must for children 3–14. Children's theater, puppet shows, clowns, and magicians are also included with admission. The eateries are uneven, and the Imax films at the massive Cinesphere tend to be all medium and no message (though still a thrill). But Ontario Place is still a major summer draw to the waterfront, and irresistible to those in their early teens and younger. *South of Lakeshore Blvd., across from CNE grounds. Tel. 416/965–7711. Open daily mid-May–mid-Sept. 10 AM–1 AM. Admission free. Bumper boats, pedal boats, miniature golf, Cinesphere, and some other attractions have nominal additional charges.*

Throughout much of the winter, the Cinesphere has been offering 70 mm films such as ET. *Check daily newspapers for times, and remember that one has not truly lived until one has seen* Indiana Jones *surrounded by snakes on a 60 ft. by 80 ft. screen.*

Canada's Wild Water Kingdom. *See* What to See and Do with Children, *above.*

Libraries and Special Collections **Boys and Girls House.** When it opened in 1922, this was the first library in the British Empire that was devoted entirely to children's books. It's still one of the best (40 St. George St., tel. 416/393–7746). **The Osborne and Smith Collections of Early Children's Books,** located in the same building, is a world-renowned collection of children's literature. Dr. Edgar Osborne, a British librarian, presented his private collection of about 2,000 children's books to the Toronto Public Library in 1949; today there are more than 21,000. The collection includes letters written and illustrated by Beatrix Potter, and the oldest book is a fairy tale printed in 1476. There are regular lectures and changing exhibits on everything from fairy tales to Christmas customs of the Victorians. *Tel. 416/393–7753. Open weekdays 10–6, Sat. 9–5.*

Metropolitan Toronto Library is one of the most beautiful and accessible public libraries in the world (*see* Tour 3, *above*).

The Merril Collection of Science Fiction, Speculation and Fantasy. Formerly the **Spaced Out Library,** this is the largest public collection of science-fiction material in the world. Although only a small percentage of the volumes is allowed to circulate, the collection includes more than 20,000 books, many of them in foreign languages, and close to 10,000 magazines, including a complete collection of *Galaxy. 40 St. George St., on 2nd floor of Boys and Girls House; tel. 416/393–7748. Open weekdays 10–6, Sat. 9–5.*

Thomas Fisher Rare Books Library. Scholars and lovers of antique books may find this place of particular interest. Part of the University of Toronto, it has tomes and manuscripts going back to the early Middle Ages. *120 St. George St., a few blocks west of University Ave. and Royal Ontario Museum and just south of Bloor St.; tel. 416/978–5285. Open weekdays 9–4:45.*

3   Shopping

Toronto prides itself on having some of the finest shopping in North America; and, indeed, most of the world's name boutiques can be found here, especially along the Bloor Street strip (between Yonge St. and Avenue Rd.) and in the Yorkville area, which covers the three streets immediately north of and parallel to the Bloor Street strip.

Although some Canadians have traditionally frowned on the concept of discount stores as vulgar and beneath them, there are many moderately priced stores around the city and a lively off-price clothing trade. Because of the weakness of the Canadian dollar, visitors obtain what amounts to an immediate discount on any purchase.

Toronto has a large artistic and crafts community, with many art galleries, custom jewelers, clothing designers, and artisans. From sophisticated glass sculpture to native and Inuit art, the many beautiful objects you'll find are ideal for gifts or for your own home. Among traditional crafts, available at antiques and specialty stores, are quilts, wood carvings, and pine furniture.

Food items that are fairly easy to transport as gifts include wild rice, available in bulk or in gift packages, and maple syrup in jars or cans.

Fur coats and hats are popular purchases with visitors from outside Canada. You can buy from a high-fashion outlet such as Creed's (on Bloor St. west of Yonge St.) or directly from a furrier in the Spadina Avenue garment district. Beaded Indian slippers and moccasins are also popular souvenirs. Distinctive **Hudson Bay** wool blankets, available only at The Bay, are an enduring Canadian tradition. The unique Tilley hat, sold by mail order or in the **Tilley Endurables** boutique at Queen's Quay Terminal, is an ideal present for sailors and adventurers: It's advertised as having been retrieved intact after being eaten by an elephant, and comes with a lifetime guarantee and owner's manual.

The better record stores stock a good selection of Canadian musicians, from Maureen Forrester and Liona Boyd to Anne Murray, Leonard Cohen, Kate and Anna McGarrigle, the Nylons, and Stringband, as well as French-Canadian stars like Robert Charlebois. Similarly, good bookstores will introduce you to Canadian authors such as Margaret Atwood, Robertson Davies, Timothy Findley, Margaret Laurence, Alice Munro, and popular historian Pierre Berton.

Most stores accept MasterCard and Visa without minimums, though if you charge a purchase under $5 you won't be too popular. Major stores also accept American Express. You'll find American cash generally accepted, although not always at the most favorable rate of exchange.

Most stores are open late on Thursdays; some, like the Eaton Centre and The Bay downtown, are open late every weekday. Liquor stores are unlikely to be open late more than one night a week, perhaps Friday, although beer stores stay open later.

The biggest sale day of the year is Boxing Day, the first business day after Christmas, when nearly everything in the city, including furs, is half price. In fact, clothing prices tend to drop even further as winter fades. Summer sales start in late June and continue through August.

Shopping Districts

The **Yorkville Avenue/Bloor Street area** is where you'll find the big fashion names, fine leather goods, important jewelers, some of the top private art galleries, upscale shoe stores, and discount china and glassware. Streets to explore include Yorkville Avenue, Cumberland Street, and Scollard Street, all running parallel to Bloor Street, and Hazelton Avenue, running north from Yorkville Avenue near Avenue Road. Hazelton Lanes, between Hazelton Avenue and Avenue Road, and the adjacent York Square are among the most chichi shopping areas in Canada, and they are headquarters for café society during the brief annual spell of warm weather. Back in the 1960s, Yorkville was Canada's hippie headquarters, a mecca for potheads, runaways, and folk musicians. Goodbye Dylan, hello Gucci.

On **Bloor Street** you'll find **Holt Renfrew,** a very high-end clothing store (Holt's has men's and children's departments as well), and Harry Rosen for men, Georg Jensen, and shoe shops like Boutique Quinto and David's.

The **Eaton Centre** is a very large galleria-style shopping center downtown, on Yonge Street between Queen and Dundas streets. With scores of large and small stores and restaurants, all sheltered from the weather, it's one of the city's major tourist attractions. Generally speaking, the lower levels are lower priced and the higher levels are more expensive. In the immediate area are Sam the Record Man, probably Toronto's most comprehensive record/CD store; The Bay department store; a smaller shopping center called **The Atrium on Bay,** which is immediately north of the Eaton Centre and not tremendously interesting; and an assortment of cut-price consumer electronics stores on Yonge Street.

Queen Street West, starting just west of University Avenue and continuing past Spadina Avenue, creeping ever westward past Bathurst Street, is a trendy area near the Ontario College of Art. Here you'll find young, hip designers; stores that stock new and used books; vintage clothes; two comic book stores, including the biggest in North America (**Silver Snail,** #367; see also Dragon Lady Comic Shop at #200); and the more progressive private galleries. People-watching is fun here, too. The action is spreading onto John Street and other cross streets, and there's a rather interesting assortment of shops in **Village by the Grange,** a development on McCaul Street south of Dundas Street, across from the Art Gallery of Ontario.

Harbourfront Centre includes an antiques market that's Canada's biggest on Sundays, when there are around 200 dealers (390 Queen's Quay W, tel. 416/340–8377. Open Tues.–Fri., 11–6, Sat. 10–6, Sun. 8–6). The **Queen's Quay Terminal** is a renovated warehouse that now houses a collection of unique boutiques, craft stalls, patisseries, and so on; it's a great place to buy gifts. There's a free shuttle bus from Union Station, but it's a fairly easy walk. Parking is expensive.

Mirvish Village, a one-block assortment of bookstores, antiques shops, and boutiques, on Markham Street south of Bloor Street, has the advantage of being open Sundays. (Harbourfront Centre is, too.) If you're in Mirvish Village on any other day, though (preferably not Saturday, which is unbearably

Toronto Shopping

crowded), check out **Honest Ed's** bargain house at Bathurst and Bloor streets, the truly silly deep-discount store that financed the revival of London's Old Vic theater. It's a good place to buy film for your camera, by the way. The strip of Bloor Street running east from Honest Ed's to Spadina Avenue is a vibrant mix of discount bookstores, casual clothing and health-food shops, pubs frequented by students from the University of Toronto, cafés, and Hungarian restaurants; it makes a delightful walk, particularly in the evening.

Another good bet for summer Sundays is **The Beaches,** on Queen Street East, starting at Woodbine Avenue. Here you'll find lots of casual clothing stores, gift and antiques shops, and bars and restaurants, all with a resort atmosphere: A boardwalk along the lake is just to the south. Take the Queen Street streetcar; parking can be a hassle.

Spadina Avenue, from Wellington Street north to College Street, has plenty of low-price clothing for the whole family, as well as fur and leather factory outlets. **Winner's,** south of King Street, is a good discount outlet for women and children. **Evex Luggage Centre**, at 369 Spadina Avenue, south of College Street, has good discount luggage, handbags, and leather accessories.

Downtown Toronto has a vast underground maze of shopping warrens that burrow in between and underneath the office towers. The tenants of the **Underground City** are mostly the usual assortment of chain stores, and the shopping is rather dull; also, directions are poorly marked. The network runs roughly from the Royal York Hotel near Union Station north to the Eaton Centre.

If you're venturing to the suburbs, there's a large shopping center at **Yorkdale,** easily reached by subway but pointless if you've been to the Eaton Centre. The area also has a number of off-price outlets within driving distance; check ads in the *Toronto Star.*

For the visitor with time to explore outside the central area, **Little Italy,** on St. Clair Avenue West (roughly between Lansdowne and Westmount streets), has some high-fashion Milanese clothing stores like Christian Boutique (#1236), LaScala Men's Wear (#1190), Gente Boutique (#1228), and the more casual Cheeky (#1180).

Department Stores

The major department stores have branches around the city and flagship stores downtown. They accept major credit cards and have liberal return policies. However, service tends to be very slow and uninformed compared with that of boutiques, and the stores generally lack the cachet of American chains like Bloomingdale's or Macy's. The big names are **Eaton's,** in the Eaton Centre, and **The Bay** (The Hudson Bay Company), at Yonge and Bloor streets.

Specialty Shops

Antiques and Galleries Yorkville is the headquarters of the establishment antiques dealers, including **Navarro Gallery** (33 Hazelton Ave., tel. 416/921–0031). There are several other pockets around town, including a strip along Queen Street East, roughly between Sherbourne Street and George Street.

The Allery (322½ Queen St. W, tel. 416/593–0853) specializes in antique prints and maps.

Art Metropole (788 King St. W, tel. 416/367–2304) specializes in limited-edition, small-press, or self-published artists' books from around the world. These works often hover between visual arts and literature. There's also a range of serious art periodicals and ephemera. It's a fascinating destination for those interested in what's happening on the fringes of the artistic community.

Ballenford Architectural Books (98 Scollard St., tel. 416/960–0055) has Canada's largest selection of architecture titles and a gallery with usually interesting exhibits of architectural drawings and related work.

Jane Corkin Gallery (179 John St., north of Queen St.; tel. 416/979–1980) specializes in photography. The more avant-garde galleries include **Cold City** (30 Duncan St.), **YYZ** (1087 Queen St. W), and **Mercer Union** (333 Adelaide St. W). Also check out **Toronto Photographers Workshop** and the other galleries at 80 Spadina Avenue, where you'll usually find at least one opening on a Saturday afternoon.

Glass Art Gallery (21 Hazelton Ave., tel. 416/968–1823) often has interesting Canadian and international exhibitions.

Prime Canadian Crafts (229 Queen St. W, tel. 416/593–5750) has an ever-changing array of merchandise.

Quasi Modo (789 Queen St. W, next door to Dufflet Pastries; tel. 416/366–8370) has a quirky collection of 20th-century furniture and design. You never know what will be on display: vintage bicycles, Noguchi lamps, a corrugated cardboard table by Frank Gehry. They will order any (available) lamp for you.

Sawtooth Borders (5 Macpherson Ave., tel. 416/961–8187) sells good-quality antique quilts.

20th Century (23 Beverley St., just north of Queen St.; tel. 416/598–2172) is for serious collectors of 20th-century design, particularly furniture, lamps, jewelry, and decorative arts. Many of the pieces are museum quality, and the owners are extremely erudite.

Auctions   **Christie's Auctioneers** (94 Cumberland Ave., tel. 416/960–2063).

Sotheby's (Canada) Inc. (9 Hazelton Ave., tel. 416/926–1774).

Books   Toronto is rich in bookstores selling new books, used books, best-sellers, and remainders. If you need a current magazine or a paperback for the plane, there are the ubiquitous chains—Coles, Classic Bookshops, and W.H. Smith. Otherwise, we recommend:

The **Albert Britnell Book Shop** (765 Yonge St., just north of Bloor St.; tel. 416/924–3321) has been a Toronto legend since 1893. The shop is now run by the third generation of the family. It has a superb search service that is getting rare. Its customers receive solicitous attention from the staff and its marvelous, British-like ambience makes for great browsing.

The **Book Cellar** (1560 Yonge St., above St. Clair Ave., tel. 416/967–5577; 142 Yorkville Ave., near Avenue Rd., tel. 416/925–9955) offers a fine choice of classical records, as well as international political and intellectual journals.

Book City has three locations (501 Bloor St. W, near Honest Ed's; Carrot Common, 348 Danforth Ave., near Chester Station; 2350 Bloor St. W, in "Bloor Village," 2 blocks east of Jane St.). It's strong on good remaindered books, has a knowledgeable staff, and offers a fine choice of magazines. It is usually open late into the evening.

The **Children's Bookstore** (604 Markham St., in Mirvish Village; tel. 416/535–7011) is simply magical: beautiful, large, with readings and concerts—the best-stocked bookstore of its kind on this child-obsessed globe. The staff knows and loves children and the literature they long for and need. It also has a superior collection of children's records, many of them Canadian.

David Mirvish Books/Books on Art is just down the block (596 Markham St., tel. 416/531–9975): A gorgeous place, it overflows with quality books and many remainders; it has the best price in town for the Sunday *New York Times*.

Edward's Books and Art is now at four locations (356 Queen St. W, near Spadina Ave.; 2179 Queen St. E, in The Beaches; in the Park Plaza Hotel, 4 Avenue Rd., at the northwest corner of Bloor St. W; and 2200 Yonge St., south of Eglinton Ave.). All are open Sundays. This is one of the loveliest minichains in the city. It advertises huge discounts on best-sellers and remainders in every Saturday's *Globe and Mail*, as does David Mirvish.

Lichtman's News and Books is at several locations (144 Yonge St. near Adelaide St.; the Atrium on Bay St., near Dundas St.; and 1430 Yonge St., south of St. Clair Ave.). There's a good selection of books, but Lichtman's is best known for its selection of magazines and its newspapers from around the world, often only a day old.

Longhouse Book Shop (recently relocated to 497 Bloor St. W, just west of Bathurst St., tel. 416/921–9995) stocks only Canadian titles, more than 20,000 back titles and new publications, handsomely shelved or piled high on pine tables. The respect and love for Canadian writers and writing is palpable here.

Bob Miller Book Room (180 Bloor St. W, just northwest of the Royal Ontario Museum; tel. 416/922–3557) has the best literature section in the city and a staff that has been with Bob for decades.

Pages Books and Magazines (256 Queen St. W, tel. 416/598–1447) has a wide selection of international and small-press literature; fashion and design books and magazines; and books on film, art, and literary criticism.

Old Favourites Bookshop (250 Adelaide St., west of University Ave.; tel. 416/977–2944) has over a quarter-million used books, magazines, and journals at fair prices.

This Ain't the Rosedale Library (483 Church St., south of Wellesley Ave.; tel. 416/929–9912) stocks the largest selection of baseball books in Canada, as well as a good selection of fiction, poetry, photography, design, rock, and jazz books. The staff is well read and can offer intelligent advice when asked.

Writers & Co. (2005 Yonge St. near Davisville Ave., a few blocks south of Eglinton Ave.; tel. 416/481–8432) is arguably Canada's finest literary bookstore, with hard-to-find poets, essayists, and world novelists. If you have been looking for a rare Caribbean poetry collection, a Swedish play in translation, or an Asian novella, this is the one to visit. It's a marvelous place, and they'll be happy to order any book for you.

Special-Interest Bookstores **Bakka Science Fiction Book Shoppe** (282 Queen St. W, tel. 416/596–8161) is the largest sci-fi and fantasy bookstore in the country (8,000 new and 3,000 used titles), with rare books and posters as well.

Can-Do Bookstore (311 Queen St. W, tel. 416/977–2351) stocks over 17,000 how-to titles for the mad, obsessed do-it-yourselfer.

The **Cookbook Store** (850 Yonge St., north of Bloor St.; tel. 416/920–2665) has the city's largest selection of books and magazines on cooking and wine.

Glad Day Bookshop (598a Yonge St., tel. 416/961–4161) is Toronto's leading gay book store.

Open Air Books and Maps (25 Toronto St., just east of Yonge and King Sts.; tel. 416/363–0719) offers over 10,000 travel guides, oodles of atlases and road maps, specialized travel books, and titles on nature and food.

Sleuth of Baker Street (1595 Bayview Ave., south of Eglinton Ave.; tel. 416/483–3111) is the best place for mysteries and detective fiction.

Theatrebooks (25 Bloor St. W, tel. 416/922–7175) has an astounding collection of plays from around the world and large sections on every other theatrical topic.

Toronto Women's Bookstore (73 Harbord St., near Spadina Ave.; tel. 416/922–8744) carries the latest feminist works on women's political and legal issues, divorce, childbirth, etc. A reading lounge is upstairs.

China, Flatware, and Crystal There are a few well-known outlets, but the best-known discounter, and bride's best friend, is **William Ashley** (50 Bloor St. W, just off Yonge St.; tel. 416/964–2900). They will ship anywhere.

Clothing **Atomic Age** (350 Queen St. W, tel. 416/977–1296) features the hottest young Toronto designers. (Also in the neighborhood are other stores for the young and zany: **Fab** at #274, **290 Ion** at #290, **B Scene** at #352, **Fashion Crimes** at #395, **Strange** at #319, **Boomer** for men at #309, **Metropolis** at #265 and **I.X.L.** at #198.)

Brown's (1975 Avenue Rd., south of Hwy. 401; tel. 416/489–1975) provides classic clothing for short men and women. There is also a store for men only (545 Queen St. W, tel. 416/368–5937). An offshoot is **Muskat & Brown** (2528 Yonge St., tel. 416/489–4005) for petite women.

Clotheslines (50 Bloor St. W, 2nd floor; tel. 416/920–9340) features designs by owners Shelley Wickabrod and Bernard McGee.

Fetoun (97 Scollard St., tel. 416/923–3434) is one of the latest high-fashion emporiums for the nouveau riche. If you go to a lot of charity balls, this is the place to shop.

La Mode de Vija (601 Markham St., in Mirvish Village; tel. 416/534–6711) sells discount designer clothing with names like Anne Klein at good prices.

Sportables (Queen's Quay Terminal, tel. 416/360–6540) offers a good assortment of well-made casual wear in natural fibers.

Sublime (156 Cumberland Ave., tel. 416/962–7303) attracts the keenest fashion buyers in Toronto with its usually excellent assortment of zany hats and avant-garde designs for men and women, from New York, Milan, and Toronto. Service is attentive and friendly, as it should be at these prices.

Vintage Furs (39a Charles St. W, at Bloor and Bay Sts.; tel. 416/960–5020) sells second-hand furs for men and women.

Willie Wonderful has several suburban locations. It's a reliable source for discounted clothing for women and children. Check the large ads in the Thursday *Toronto Star*.

Food Markets **Kensington Market** (northwest of Dundas St. and Spadina Ave.) is an outdoor market with a vibrant ethnic mix. This is where you'll find delightful and exotic Caribbean foods; great cheese, coffee, nuts, and spices; natural foods; South American delicacies; Portuguese bakeries; and charming restaurants. Saturday is the best day to go, preferably by public transit, as parking is difficult.

St. Lawrence Market (Front St. and Jarvis St., tel. 416/392–7219) is best early on Saturdays, when, in addition to the permanent indoor market on the south side of Front Street, there's a farmer's market in the building on the north side. The historic south market was once Toronto's city hall, and it fronted the lake before extensive landfill projects were undertaken.

Specialty Food Shops **David Wood Food Shop** (1110 Yonge St., tel. 416/968–6967) is Toronto's mini–Fortnum and Mason and is the neighborhood grocer to Toronto's old money.

The Big Carrot (on Danforth Ave., near Chester subway station; tel. 416/466–2129) is a new and pricey health-food supermarket, complete with organic butcher shop.

Just Game (1386 Bayview Ave., near Moore Ave.; tel. 416/481–1616) stocks a wide variety of game.

All the Best Breads and All the Best Cheese (1099 and 1097 Yonge St., tel. 416/928–3330) are just what it says.

Footwear **Boutique Quinto** (110 Bloor St. W, tel. 416/928–0954) has the wildest shoes in town for men and women.

David's (66 Bloor St. W, at Bay St.; tel. 416/920–1000) has a somewhat more subdued but always elegant collection.

Brown's (Hazelton Lanes, Simpson's downtown, and other locations, tel. 416/968–1806) has an excellent selection of well-made shoes, handbags, and boots.

Marek, the Best of Europe (110 Bloor St. W, tel. 416/923–5100), is located in a lane running between Cumberland Street and Yorkville Avenue. It has an interesting assortment of shoes, as well as belts and other leather goods; it also has shirts, an outstanding selection of men's ties, and other wearing apparel.

Gift Ideas **The Back Store** (2111 Yonge, south of Eglinton Ave., tel. 416/482-0426) has everything for a friend with an aching spine.

Early Learning (387 Queen St. W, tel. 416/598-2135) sells European and Japanese playthings.

Filigree (1210 Yonge St., tel. 415/961-5223) has a good assortment of linens, as well as drawer liners, silver frames, and other Victorian pleasures. In the neighborhood are other gift shops selling fine glass and antiques.

Bragg (446 Queen St., west of Spadina Ave.; tel. 416/366-6717) has an amusing assortment of vintage bric-a-brac, china, cards, and jewelry.

Jewelry **Secrett Jewel Salon** (150 Bloor St. W, tel. 416/967-7500) is a reputable source of unusual gemstones and fine new and estate jewelry; local gemologists consider it the best in town.

Time Out Here are a few suggestions for places to rest your feet while shopping:

Eaton Centre area. If the Centre's restaurants and fast-food joints don't appeal to you, walk two blocks north to *The Bangkok Garden* (18 Elm St.) for delicious Thai food in a luxurious atmosphere. The related bar, *The Brass Flamingo*, offers less expensive light meals, all of which are good. For an inexpensive meal, get a fabulous home-style burger at *Lick's* (Yonge St. at Dundas Sq., opposite the Eaton Centre); there's also one in The Beaches, and at Yonge Street and Eglinton Avenue. Kids will enjoy the singing counter help.

Queen Street West. We recommend *The BamBoo* (#312), a unique Thai-Caribbean experience with courtyard service in summer; *The Queen Mother* (#206), a neighborhood favorite with wholesome meals and fabulous desserts, all at reasonable prices; *The Peter Pan* (#373, at Peter St.); and the *Parrot Express* (#254), for gourmet pizza and other goodies to stay or go.

Bloor Street/Yorkville. *The Copenhagen Room* (corner of Bloor St. and St. Thomas St., near Georg Jensen) is a Toronto stalwart, if you like Danish open-faced sandwiches. Next door, in the Windsor Arms Hotel (St. Thomas St.), is *The Courtyard Cafe*, a popular hangout for visiting movie stars. For Canadian ingredients interestingly prepared, try *Metropolis* (838 Yonge St., north of Bloor St.).

Spadina Avenue. For spicy Chinese food, it's *The Great Wall* (444 Spadina Ave., south of College St.). For falafel and gingery Jamaica sweet-potato pudding, check out *Tiger's Coconut Grove* (12 Kensington Ave., in the market).

Bargaining

Toronto is *not* the Middle East, but one might haggle at flea markets, including the Harbourfront Antique Market, and perhaps in the Chinatown and Kensington Market/Spadina Avenue areas.

Refund Information

Visitors, including Canadians from other provinces, can receive a refund on the 8% Ontario sales tax for purchases over $100, as well as on the 5% sales tax on hotel and motel bills, provided they leave within 30 days. It's worthwhile if you do a significant amount of shopping. There's a form to be sent in with your receipts after you leave Ontario. You can get the form at Pearson Airport, at visitors' information booths like the one outside the Eaton Centre, at Traveller's Aid in Union Station, or from the merchants themselves.

Visitors to Canada may be surprised to encounter a new 7% federal tax on all merchandise, services, and accommodations—the infamous GST (Goods and Services Tax). Since January 1, 1991, it has replaced Canada's earlier, 13½% tax on manufactured goods and covers many more items.

On leaving Canada, tourists are eligible for a refund of taxes paid on all accommodations, and goods purchased for export. Goods consumed or used in Canada, such as meals in restaurants or ski tickets, are not exempt from this tax.

Please remember: Reimbursement (in Canadian dollars, in this case) is immediate at all duty-free shops in airports and at border crossings, where forms are available. But returning travelers may also mail in their forms if they wish to receive a refund check in U.S. dollars. Again, tourists must spend at least $100 (Canadian) to receive the rebate—with families combining expenditures, if desired. A new pamphlet explaining this tax is available at all border crossings and at most U.S. airports.

4 Sports and Fitness

Participant Sports

A wide range of sports is available for each of Toronto's four distinct seasons. From Lake Ontario to the skiing hills just outside the city and the beautiful lakes and parks beyond, a thousand sports and recreational activities are available.

Contact the Ministry of Tourism and Recreation (Queen's Park, Toronto, Ont. M7A 2R2) for pamphlets on various activities. For information on sports activities in the province, phone 800/268–3735 from anywhere in the continental United States and Canada (except the Northwest Territories and the Yukon). In Toronto, contact Ontario Travel (tel. 416/965–4008).

A number of fine **conservation areas** circle the Metro Toronto area, many less than a half-hour from downtown. Most have large swimming areas, sledding, and cross-country skiing, as well as skating, fishing, and boating. Contact the Metro Conservation Authority (tel. 416/661–6600) and ask for the pamphlet.

Bicycling There are over 18 miles of street bike routes cutting across the city and dozens more along safer paths through Toronto's many parks (*see* Sightseeing Checklists in Chapter 2). Bikes can be rented on the Toronto Islands. The **Martin Goodman Trail** is a 12–mile strip that runs along the waterfront all the way from the Balmy Beach Club in the east end, out past the western beaches southwest of High Park. Phone the *Toronto Star* (tel. 416/367–2000) for a map.

Metro Parks Department (tel. 416/392–8186) has maps that show bike (and jogging) routes that run through Toronto parkland. **Ontario Cycling** (tel. 416/495–4141) has maps, booklets, and information.

Boardsailing Equipment can be rented in various areas of the waterfront. Try along Bloor Street West, near the High Park subway station.

Boating Grenadier Pond in High Park, Centre Island, Ontario Place, Harbourfront Centre, and most of the Conservation Areas surrounding Metro Toronto rent canoes, punts, and/or sailboats.

Bowling Don't laugh; Toronto has 5-pin, a marvelous tradition unknown to most Americans. This sport of rolling a tiny ball down an alley at five fat pins—each with a different numerical value, for a possible (impossible) score of 450—is perfect for children, even as young as 3 or 4. **Bowlerama** has lanes all over the city; look in the Yellow Pages for locations. This can provide an entertaining few hours on a rainy day.

Fishing One does not have to go very far from downtown Toronto to catch trout, perch, bass, walleye, salmon, muskie, pike, and whitefish. Contact Communication Services, Wildlife Information, Ministry of Natural Resources (Queen's Park, Toronto M7A 1W3, tel. 416/965–4251).

Within Metro Toronto itself, fishing is permitted in the trout pond at Hanlon's Point on Toronto Island, as well as in Grenadier Pond in High Park. And the salmon fishing just off the Scarborough Bluffs, in Toronto's east end, is extraordinary! Every summer there is a Great Salmon Hunt, with cash prizes. Check the *Toronto Star*, which sponsors it, for details.

There are over 100 charter boats on Lake Ontario (about $60 for a half-day). Contact **Ontario Travel** (tel. 416/965–4008). Be warned, though: Some fish caught in this province have such high levels of mercury in them that you can take your temperature at the same time that you eat them. It's sad, but water pollution (including acid rain) has taken its toll upon the edibility of many fish in Ontario.

Golf The season lasts only from April to late October. The top course is **Glen Abbey** (tel. 416/844–1800), where the Canadian Open Championships is held. Cart and green fees go up to $75 on weekends, but this course is a real beauty.

Less challenging courses—and much closer to the heart of the city—include the **Don Valley Golf Course,** just south of Highway 401 (Yonge St., tel. 416/392–2465); and the **Flemingdon Park Golf Club** (Don Mills Rd. and Eglinton Ave., tel. 416/429–1740). For other courses, contact Metro Parks (tel. 416/367–8186) or Ontario Travel (tel. 416/965–4008).

Horseback Riding There are two stables within the city limits. **Central Don Stables,** in Sunnybrook Park (Leslie St. and Eglinton Ave., tel. 416/444–4044), has an indoor arena, an outdoor ring, and nearly 12 miles of bridle trails through the Don Valley. **Eglinton Equestrian Club** (near Don Mills Rd. and John St., tel. 416/889–6375) has two indoor arenas.

Just north of the city, in Richmond Hill, the **Rocking Horse Ranch** (tel. 416/884–3292) offers scenic western trail rides year-round. For booklets detailing riding establishments across the province, call **Ontario Travel** (tel. 416/965–4008) or **Equestrian Ontario** (tel. 416/495–4125). People with disabilities will be pleased to hear of the **Community Association for Riding for the Disabled** (tel. 416/667–8600), which offers riding in a park near Black Creek Pioneer Village. Children as young as 4 years old can ride here, thanks to the **Variety Club** (tel. 416/961–7300).

Hunting There is little hunting within a few hours' drive of Toronto, and even that is limited to the fall: deer, moose, and black bear. The waterfowl season is longer, extending from fall into the winter. Contact Public Information Centre, Room 1640, Ministry of Natural Resources (Queen's Park, Toronto M7A 1W3, tel. 416/965–4251), or write the Ontario Federation of Anglers and Hunters (Box 1269, Campbellford, Ontario).

Ice Skating Toronto operates some 30 outdoor artificial rinks and 100 natural-ice rinks—and all are free! Among the most popular are in Nathan Phillips Square, in front of the New City Hall, at Queen and Bay streets; down at Harbourfront Centre (which has Canada's largest outdoor artificial ice rink); College Park, at Yonge and College streets; Grenadier Pond, within High Park, at Bloor and Keele streets; and inside Hazelton Lanes, that classy shopping mall on the edge of Yorkville, on Avenue Road, just above Bloor Street. For details on city rinks, call 416/392–1111.

Jogging The **Martin Goodman Trail** (*see above*) is ideal. Also try the boardwalk of The Beaches in the east end; High Park in the west end; the Toronto Islands; or any of Toronto's parks.

Sailing This can be a breeze, especially between April and October. Contact the Ontario Sailing Association (tel. 416/495–4240).

Skiing
Cross-country Try Toronto's parks and ravines; High Park; the lakefront along the southern edge of the city; Tommy Thompson Park; Toronto Islands; and, perhaps best of all, the inspired concept of Zooski, out at the stunning Metro Toronto Zoo, where one can ski past lions, leopards, and other furry friends. Check the Yellow Pages for ski-equipment rentals; there are many places. Only Zooski charges a fee; all other places are free.

Downhill Although there are a few places where one can get a taste of this sport within Metro Toronto, such as **Earl Bales Park,** on Bathurst Street, just south of Sheppard Avenue, and **Centennial Park Ski Hill** in Etobicoke (tel. 416/394–8754), the *best* alpine hills are 30–60 minutes north of the city. These include **Blue Mountain Resorts** in Collingwood, Ontario (tel. 416/869–3799), the **Caledon Ski Club** in Caledon (tel. 416/453–7404), **Glen Eden Ski Area** in Milton (tel. 416/878–5011), **Hidden Valley** in Huntsville (tel. 705/789–2301), **Hockley Valley Resort** in Orangeville (tel. 519/942–0754), and **Horseshoe Valley** (tel. 705/835–2790) and **Snow Valley Ski Resort** both just outside Barrie (tel. 416/283–2439, a number that can be called directly from Toronto). Phone 416/963–2992 for lift and surface conditions.

Sleigh Riding and
Tobogganing **Black Creek Pioneer Village** (tel. 416/661–6610 or 416/661–6600), north of 401 along Highway 400, at Steeles Avenue, is open winter weekends 10-4 for skating, tobogganing, and horse-drawn sleigh rides. The best parks for tobogganing include **High Park,** in the west end, and our favorite, **Winston Churchill Park,** at Spadina Avenue and St. Clair Avenue, just two blocks from Casa Loma. It is sheer terror.

Swimming The beaches of Lake Ontario are studies in extremes: The water can be bitter cold, even through the summer, while the sand can raise blisters on the hottest days of the year. Many beaches are too polluted for safe swimming; phone the city's public health department (tel. 416/392–7466) for the latest report.

In the east end, **Beaches Park,** south of Queen Street and east of Coxwell Avenue, is lovely, thanks to the lengthy boardwalk, local canoe club, public washrooms, and tennis courts. Even closer to downtown—only a 20-minute streetcar-ride away, along Queen Street—are **Woodbine Beach Park** and **Ashbridges Bay Park,** both fine for sunbathing and boat-watching. To the west of downtown, another fine area, **Sunnyside Beach,** has a pool, snack bar, Jungle Gym, and washrooms.

The most pleasing beaches—and certainly the ones with the best views—are on the **Toronto Islands** (*see* Tour 1 in Chapter 2). Remember, though, Lake Ontario is rarely warm enough for sustained swimming, except in late August.

Public swimming is available in 16 indoor pools, 12 outdoor pools, and 15 community recreation centers; call the Toronto Department of Parks and Recreation (tel. 416/392–7259).

Tennis The city provides dozens of courts, all free, many of them floodlighted. Parks with courts open from 7 AM to 11 PM, in season, include the famous High Park in the west end; Stanley Park, on King Street West, three blocks west of Bathurst Street; and Eglinton Park, on Eglinton Avenue West, just east of Avenue Road. Call the Ontario Tennis Association (tel. 416/495–4215).

Hotel Health
Facilities Nearly every major hotel in the Metro Toronto area has a decent indoor swimming pool; some even have indoor/outdoor swimming pools. The best include the **Sheraton Centre,** at

Queen and Bay streets, and the **Inn on the Park,** at Eglinton Avenue near Leslie Street. Many also have health clubs.

Spectator Sports

Toronto has always been an exciting sports city, but since the Toronto Blue Jays made their debut—in a snowstorm!—in 1977, the place has gone wild. (Indeed, while the Blue Jays lolled about in the basement of the American League for their first five years, nearly 8 million fans poured into the ugly, uncomfortable Exhibition Stadium, down at the CNE grounds.) With the June 1989 opening of the extraordinary new SkyDome, you can just imagine how revved up the city is.

Auto Racing For the past several years, the **Molson Indy** (tel. 416/595–5445) has been roaring around the Canadian National Exhibition grounds, including the major thoroughfare of Lakeshore Boulevard, for three days in mid-July. You'll pay more than $85 for a three-day "red" reserved seat, but general admission for the qualification rounds, the practice rounds, and the Indy itself, can be as cheap as $10–$20, depending upon the day.

Then, there is **Mosport,** about 60 miles northeast of Toronto, where motorcycle and formula racing are held. *Take 401 east to Exit 75, then drive north to track. Tel. 416/665–6665.*

Less than a half-hour drive away is the **Cayuga International Speedway** (tel. 416/765–4461), where international stock-car races are held from May through September.

Baseball As noted, the **Toronto Blue Jays** have developed into one of baseball's most dynamic teams, and are all the more popular since their move into the SkyDome in the summer of 1989. The Jays have the most costly tickets in the Major Leagues, ranging from rotten $4 seats (near heaven) to seats for over $17. And they usually sell out *nearly every single home game,* so plan *way ahead* of your visit. There are nearly always dozens of scalpers hawking tickets to that day's game just outside the SkyDome. *A hot tip:* Arrive a bit late, say, in the second or third inning, and they will often unload their tickets at a fraction of what they would have asked a half-hour earlier. *For ticket information, tel. 416/341–1111/341–1234.*

Canoeing and Rowing The world's largest **canoeing and rowing regatta** is held every July 1, as it has been for over a century, on Toronto Island's Long Pond. *Canoe Ontario, tel. 416/495–4180.*

Football Although the Canadian Football League has been teetering on the brink of dissolution, the **Toronto Argonauts** have, in recent years, developed into annual contenders. Since the Argos were bought by a consortium of new owners—including the Canadian hockey star Wayne Gretzky and the Canadian comic actor John Candy—in 1991, the team has gone from strength to strength, capturing both its division and the revered Grey Cup that year. Americans might find the three downs and 110-yard field to be rather quaint, but the game is much like their own. *Tel. 416/595–1131 for tickets and information.*

Golf The permanent site of the **Canadian Open** golf championship is Glen Abbey, a course designed by Jack Nicklaus. This tournament is one of golf's Big Five and is always played in late summer. *Less than a 45-min drive west, along the Queen Elizabeth Way (QEW). Tel. 416/844–1800.*

Hockey The **Toronto Maple Leafs** play 40 home games each season (Oct.–Apr.), usually on Wednesday and Saturday nights, in the big, ugly Maple Leaf Gardens. Tickets are always available at each game—at least from scalpers in front of the stadium on Carlton Street, a half-block east of the corner of Yonge and College streets. Call the office (tel. 416/977–1641) at 9 AM sharp on the day of the game. Be warned: Over the past two decades, the "Maple Griefs" have turned into a laughing stock and are usually the worst or semiworst in the National Hockey League. But who cares about winning? Not our Leafs!

Horse Racing
Harness Racing The **Greenwood** track, built in 1874, is where the best trotters and pacers do their stuff, at three annual meetings. *Tel. 416/675–6110. Spring gathering, Jan.–mid-Mar.; summer meeting, late May–Sept.; winter meeting, last two weeks in Dec.*

Thoroughbred Racing Four major racetracks are handled by the Ontario Jockey Club (tel. 416/675–6110): two in the Toronto area; one down in Fort Erie, near Buffalo; and another about 24 miles west of Toronto.

Greenwood Race Track is one of the premier harness tracks in North America and is the home of many of Canada's greatest trotting and pacing events, including the North American Cup. It is located in the city's east end, a 10-minute streetcar ride from downtown, at Woodbine Avenue and Queen Street East, near the lakeshore. *Tel. 416/698–3131. Winter meeting runs late Oct.–early Dec.; spring meeting runs mid-Mar.–late Apr.*

Woodbine Race Track is the showplace of Thoroughbreds in Canada. *30-min northeast of downtown, near airport, at Hwy. 27 and Rexdale Blvd.; tel. 416/675–6110. Races late Apr.–late Oct.*

Mohawk is in the heart of Ontario's Standardbred breeding country, and it features a glass-enclosed, climate-controlled grandstand and other attractive facilities. *A 30-min. drive west of Toronto, along Hwy. 401, past Milton; tel. 416/854–2255.*

Fort Erie, in the Niagara tourist region, is one of the most picturesque racetracks in the world, with willows, manicured hedges, and flower-bordered infield lakes. It has racing on the dirt as well as on grass, with the year's highlight being the Prince of Wales Stakes, the second jewel in Canada's Triple Crown of Racing. *Tel. 416/871–3200 from Toronto, 716/856–0293 from Buffalo.*

Royal Horse Show This highlight of Canada's equestrian season is part of the Royal Winter Fair each November. *The CNE grounds, Dufferin St., by the waterfront; tel. 416/393–6400.*

Ice Canoe Racing Every January, five-man/woman teams haul canoes across the ice floes off Harbourfront Centre.

Soccer Although Toronto keeps getting and losing and getting a professional soccer team, one can catch this exciting sport, as well as collegiate football, in the very handy **Varsity Stadium.** *Bloor St. W at Bedford, a block west of Royal Ontario Museum and University Ave; tel. 416/979–2186.*

Tennis The finest players in the world gather at the tennis complex on the York University campus, near Finch Avenue and Keele Street, each summer, for the **Player's International Canadian Open.** *For tickets, phone Tennis Canada, tel. 416/665–9777, or Ticketron outlets, tel. 416/872–1212.*

You've Let Your Imagination Go, Now Get Up And Follow Your Dreams.

For The Vacation You're Dreaming Of, Call American Express® Travel Agency At 1-800-YES-AMEX.*

American Express will send more than your imagination soaring. We'll fly you, sail you, drive you to any Fodor's destination and beyond. Because American Express believes the best vacations happen from Europe to the Orient, Walt Disney® World to Hawaii and everywhere in between.

For dependable service, expert advice, and value wherever your dreams take you, call on American Express. After all, the best traveling companion is a trustworthy friend.

It's easy to recognize a good place when you see one.

American Express Cardmembers have been doing it for years.

The secret? Instead of just relying on what they see in the window, they look at the door. If there's an American Express Blue Box on it, they know they've found an establishment that cares about high standards.

Whether it's a place to eat, to sleep, to shop, or simply meet, they know they will be warmly welcomed.

So much so, they're rarely taken in by anything else.

Always a good sign.

5 Dining

by Joanne Kates

Restaurant critic for the Toronto Globe and Mail, *Joanne Kates in 1988 won both the best restaurant critic and best food writer awards in the Canadian food writing association. She is the author of five books, including her own cookbook and a Toronto restaurant guide.*

Updated by Mary Adachi

A decade ago visitors to Toronto enjoyed a varied mix of ethnic restaurants, but good food could not be found in the middle ground of gastronomy—between the Italian sandwiches and the Dover sole. Today Toronto is a city of bistros.

The "bistroization" of Toronto is due in part to a new generation of chefs, the first wave of young people who are just now fanning out across the city, opening neighborhood restaurants that are a little cheaper, slightly less ambitious, and thus more accessible than those of their teachers. There are Mark McEwan at North 44, Bob Bermann at The Avocado Club, and Susur Lee, who was influenced by Stadtlander, at Lotus restaurant.

What the bistros serve is another matter. That old tired imitation Continental menu, which Toronto's upper crust dined out on since before the Beatles, is finally dead. We are no longer stuck eating less than perfect imitations of what they do in Paris and Rome. The new bistros are eclectic, as likely to borrow from Bangkok as they are from Los Angeles. Furthermore, their clever mentors have taught the new generation of young chefs to do things that have heretofore been forbidden in kitchens; think for themselves; create dishes based on what dazzles them in the morning market; and use local ingredients and spontaneity of approach.

As a result, we are beginning to enjoy a Toronto cuisine that is based on the present rather than the past. The food is becoming simple. Sauces, if they exist at all, are quietly elemental; they sit under the main event and do not obscure it. Toronto eats more and more grilled foods, because the more frequently people eat out (which Torontonians do more than any other Canadians), the more healthful they want it. Hence the turn to stripped-down plates: grilled fish or meat and vegetable, a little garlic or fresh thyme for excitement. Toronto restaurants' great strength is this simplicity—what home cooking should be but so rarely is. Twenty years ago the nuclear family was Toronto's haven in a heartless world. Today it's our favorite bistro.

Highly recommended restaurants in each category are indicated with a star ★.

Category	Cost*
Very Expensive	over $40
Expensive	$30–$40
Moderate	$20–$30
Inexpensive	under $20

per person without tax, tip, or drinks

Bistros

Expensive **Bistro 990.** This is a gorgeous homage to a French provincial
★ bistro. Owner Tom Kristenbrun studied hard to come up with the right idea. Chef Jeff Dueck excels at country cooking *à la française*. There is magret de canard, confit, duck terrine, hearty stews, sweet french fries, kidneys, and fresh and buttery desserts. This is Gallic bistro bliss. *990 Bay St., tel. 416/*

921–9990. Reservations recommended. Dress: informal. AE, MC, V. Closed Sun.

★ **Brownes Bistro.** In one night, you can count a dozen mink coats. Full-length dark ranch. What does a person who spends $17,000 on a coat want in a restaurant? Apparently she wants an impeccable bistro that avoids the tarted-up Paris look. Everything at Brownes is breathtakingly simple, from the white paper on the tables to the small black-and-white ceramic tiles. The monochromatic room is colored only by dark wood paneling and one fuchsia azalea at the bar. Lack of pretension is elevated to art. Former Cordon Bleu cooking teacher Beverly Burge had a reputation for strictest adherence to *la cuisine classique*. Breeding tells. Brownes's pizza may be the best in Toronto. The gnocchi are unexceptional. The bouillabaisse has perfect, sweet little fresh scallops, but a blandness of broth. There are seven main courses, and three of them are lamb. Brownes gives full glory to lamb's heretofore neglected parts, such as shanks (braised till they soften like butter and served in their own heartwarming broth, slightly blanched, with fennel, potatoes, and carrots). A lemon curd and a darkly dense chocolate cake, served with crème fraîche and chocolate sauce, are both fine. The price of under $70 for two, with wine—a real bargain—makes Brownes the hottest show in town. *4 Woodlawn Ave. E, tel. 416/924–8132. Reservations required. Tie and jacket optional. AE, DC, MC, V. No lunch Sun.*

Joso's. Because properly cooked fish is hard to find in Toronto, you put up with certain annoyances at Joso's, the city's best seafood restaurant. Joso Spralja exhibits tasteless sculpture throughout his restaurant. But his Adriatic way with fish is dazzling: a drizzle of extra-virgin olive oil, a fast trip on a hot grill. Sweet little squids come hot and golden; sea bass is thick and firm, never overcooked; seafood salad is incredibly tender and fragrant from its olive-oil bath. Joso even dares, and succeeds, at risotto. For all this pleasure, tacky decor and insouciant service are a small price to pay. *202 Davenport Rd., tel 416/925–1903. Reservations recommended. Dress: informal. AE, MC, V. Closed Sun.*

Moderate **Avocado Club.** A sun-splashed fun spot, serving casual food
★ that is also of the highest quality, the Avocado Club exerts its light-hearted ambience from the minute you walk through the door. Bright and sassy colors are everywhere. The Devil's Avocado, the restaurant's most popular starter, is warmed avocado with scallops and shrimps in a black bean chili sauce with Japanese cooking sake. Other appetizers refer, but always with chef Bob Bermann's light touch, to Thailand, Vietnam, and India, such as satay skewers and sweet/hot curried mussel salad. These days this type of cooking is as common as mosquitoes in a swamp, but rarely are so many culinary influences collected with such a gentle touch. *165 John St., tel. 416/598–4656. Reservations advised. Dress: informal. AE, MC, V. No lunch Sat.; closed Sun.*

★ **BamBoo.** Inside a funky little inner courtyard decorated by a bohemian hand—fishnets on the walls, a stand of Muskoka bamboo, fading signs, all bordered by a thatch roof, à la South Pacific—is a relentlessly low-tech club cum restaurant that rebukes glitz-crazed Toronto with a smile up its sleeve. More and more ordinary people are going to the BamBoo for one purpose only: to eat food that joyously caresses the tongue. You can eat in the club area (240 seats, barnlike but warm) or in the small

Metropolitan Toronto Dining

Arlequin, **10**
Astoria Shish
Kabob, **19**
Brownes Bistro, **17**
Camarra's, **2**
Centre Street Deli, **1**

Centro, **15**
Chiado, **3**
Dufflet Pastries, **4**
Ellas, **21**
Filippo's Gourmet
Pizzeria, **5**
Grano, **18**

Jerusalem, **7**
Joso's, **11**
North 44, **16**
New World, **23**
Ouzeri, **22**
Patachou Patisserie, **6**

Pearl Court, **20**
Scaramouche, **9**
Sisi Trattoria, **12**
Thai Magic, **13**
Tipplers, **14**
United Bakers, **8**

Earl Bales Park

401

York Mills Rd.

M

ve.

M

Leslie St.

Avenue Rd.

Yonge St.

Lawrence Ave. E.

8

Allen Expwy.

2

Don Mills Rd.

Wigmore Park

15 16

Eglinton Ave. E.

Oakwood Ave.

7 6

18

Laird Dr.

Sunnybrook Park

Don Valley Pkwy.

5

Mount Pleasant Rd.

9

Taylor Creek Park

Davenport Rd.

EAST YORK

17

404

O'Connor Dr.

Dupont St.

14

Greenwood Ave.

Coxwell Ave.

Woodbine Ave.

St.

Bathurst St.

10 11

13

Bayview Ext.

Broadview Ave.

Pape Ave.

12

M M M M M M M M M M M M M M M M

19 22 21

Danforth Ave.

DOWNTOWN

St.

Gerrard St. E.

3

Parliament St.

2

Dundas St. W.

20

Leslie St. E.

4

Dundas St. E.

Queen St. E.

Eastern Ave.

King St. W.

2

Lake Shore Blvd. E.

23

0   1 mile

0   1500 meters

funky dining room off to the right. On weekends guests line up for both the food and the live reggae, African, funk, and Latin music, which starts at 10 PM. Much of the food is spicy. The *callalloo*, a creamed spinach and coconut soup, is the very weapon that blocked sinuses require. BamBoo's single most popular dish, Thai spicy noodles, comes in three modes, mild, medium, and wow! Mild is a superlative ungreasy wok fry of rice noodles with peanuts, bean sprouts, chicken, shrimp, tofu, egg, Vietnamese fish sauce, chilies, sugar, garlic, and fresh lime juice. Chicken wings are marinated overnight in ginger, mustard, soy sauce, oyster sauce, sesame oil, pepper, and paprika; deep-fried into hot juicy submission; and served with a pretty spectacular garlic chili vinegar dipping sauce. This is not artistic Thai cooking; things are more casual and more multi-ethnic—but portions are large, the flavors assertive, and the cooking rather like the best of fresh home cooking. *312 Queen St. W, tel. 416/593–5771. No reservations. Dress: informal. AE, MC, V. Closed Sun.*

Tipplers. Right in midtown, this charmer sells more than 30 wines by the glass, including Chateauneuf-du-Pape, Bourgogne Aligote, decent Chablis, and Meursault. But there's more than wine: Tipplers' chef, a disciple of Susur Lee (the wizard of the restaurant Lotus), drives himself to ever greater flights of nouvelle fancy. There are tempura scallops floating in the corn chowder, and chili soya glaze on the seared tuna. For dessert lichee fruits appear in the cheesecake, and Ice wine (a sweet dessert wine) in your glass. *1276 Yonge St., near Summerhill Ave.; tel. 416/967–9463. Reservations recommended. Jacket optional. AE, DC, MC, V. No lunch weekends.*

Brunch

Moderate   **Kensington Kitchen.** Its clientele is the self-consciously unchic
★   University of Toronto people who live in the area and appreciate the ask-nothing ambience. The reigning sensibility belongs to Said Mukhayesh, who leans heavily toward the healthy, so his interpretation of Middle East cooking includes whole-wheat pita; and if there's rice, it's brown. But none of this prevents Mukhayesh from serving wickedly wonderful spinach-and-cheese ravioli in a dense cream sauce. Ingredients are fresh and always prepared with affection and care. Where else do you get velvety *baba ghannoush* (puréed broiled eggplant flavored with garlic and lemon juice), *lubya* (green beans in a thick sauce of cinnamon and cardamom), divinely garlicky fried eggplant, and assertive cream soups? The *tabbouleh* (cracked wheat salad with parsley, tomato, and cucumber) is delicate, and the falafel in pita is a class act. Two people could lunch splendidly for $10. *124 Harbord St., south of Bloor St.; tel. 416/961–3404. Reservations not necessary. Dress: informal. MC, V.*

Inexpensive   **The Boulevard Cafe.** Don't worry about being underdressed; the neighbors are countercultural, but charming. The tables are made out of hand-painted ceramic tiles; wall hangings from South America announce the Peruvian theme. Brunch varies from week to week, but there are always Peruvian specialties, ranging from scrambled eggs with hot peppers to more exotic fare. There is also French toast or other simple egg dishes, plus a titillating collection of coffees: Borgia, Colombian, Peruvian, etc. *161 Harbord St., tel. 416/961–7676. Reservations not necessary. Dress: informal. AE, MC, V. Summer outdoor dining.*

Cafés

Inexpensive **The Amsterdam.** This is everything you would expect a good dining room not to be: It's rowdy, noisy, a symphony of heavy metal, a deliberately down-scale barn of a place. But like a Maserati in overdrive, it goes. It serves home-smoked meats and fish, as well as such dishes as pickerel baked in parchment paper, mussels steamed in home-brewed beer with curried cream sauce, and spicy Thai beef salad with baby greens. Breads and desserts are baked in the traditional Dutch fashion in a nearby sister restaurant. The dining room is part of a popular combination brewery and pub that serves about 100 brands of beer (four of which are brewed on the premises). The prices are astonishingly reasonable, too. *133 John St., near Queen St. and University Ave.; tel. 416/595–8201. Reservations recommended. Dress: informal. AE, MC, V.*

L'Express Café. Just across from the charming Parrot bistro on Queen Street West is a café that since the fall of 1987 has been serving good casual food with some dispatch. For under $6, it takes the ordinary (chicken salad, ham and cheese) and anoints it with goat cheese or roasted red peppers in oil, laid lovingly between slices of impeccable Italian bread. The pizzas and savory tarts are enough to justify its existence. (The former are simple and robust; the latter, a texture of gossamer, thanks to the 35% cream.) The leek and *chèvre* tart with a touch of curry is one of the most inventive dishes. *254 Queen St. W, within walking distance of New City Hall; tel. 416/596–0205. No reservations. Dress: informal. V for orders over $10. Brunch only Sun.*

Cajun

Moderate **Southern Accent.** When the cooks here blacken something they
★ do not aim to compete with the fossil kingdom. Blackened here means spiced and seared, melting in the middle and its sensuousness ensured by lemony beurre blanc on top. The appetizers are dazzling—light but strong daily soups, often sweet and hot and sour. There are crunchy hush puppies (deep-fried corn fritters), and lovely greens with toasted pecans and citrus-scented vinaigrette. The gumbo is a dream from the bayou—highly flavored *andouille* (pork sausage) and other meats in a strong, dark *roux jambalaya.* This roux is the major statement of Louisiana cooking, and is rice based, with andouille, smoked ham, beef, chicken, bacon, vegetables, and shrimp, in Cajun spices. Southern Accent does it proud. *595 Markham St., tel. 416/536–3211. Reservations recommended. Dress: informal. AE, DC, MC, V. No lunch.*

Chinese

Moderate **Champion House.** In our never-ending quest for the perfect Peking duck, we tried this popular Toronto restaurant. A brass gong is hit when your duck enters the dining room, inspiring expressions of delight from those at the table: The combination of the sweet, crackling duck skin with sharp onions and jazzy sauce is the ultimate fulfillment of the pleasure principle. Then comes the refreshing and light duck salad, the pungent duck in a hot sauce full of ginger, star anise, and chilies, and the duck soup. "Ants climbing up a tree" (alias bean starch noodles and minced pork in brown sauce) and scallops with chilies and peanuts are both first rate. Order the Peking duck (for 4) in advance. *478 Dundas St. W, at Spadina Ave.; tel. 416/977–8282. Reservations recommended. Dress: informal. AE, DC, MC, V.*

New World. There is probably very little that could induce you to penetrate the wilds of Scarborough on a wintry night, but this place can. Again and again and again. Do not miss the New World's *shui kow* soup—a sea of fine stock afloat with freshly made dumplings of chopped shrimp, Chinese mushrooms, and barbecued pork—and the fresh abalone that comes in its shell accompanied by one pristine broccoli floret in a translucent sauce made from beef stock reduced with oyster sauce. It's not on the menu, but the password is, "Kam Wong said we could have it." New World is frankly Cantonese. There is a lick and a promise in the direction of Szechuan, but the cook's heart is on the sea. Big fat indelicate West Coast oysters come properly (barely) cooked in their own shells, dressed up with black beans, fresh coriander, and chives. Chicken cubes and scallops in phoenix nest are not to be missed. And I have never tasted fish so fresh in hot pots, nor eaten a hot pot dish crowned with soft-shell crab and oyster. No reservations are taken for the hot-pot tables, so go early. This place is a treasure. *3600 Victoria Park Ave., tel. 416/498–1818. Reservations recommended on weekends. Dress: informal. AE, MC, V.*

Young Lok. Upwardly mobile and still serving delicious food, this is a handsome restaurant in the very attractive Village by the Grange. The menu is biblical in scope, ranging from old tired Cantonese clichés to the fiery stars of the Szechuan kitchen. The clear soups are great; the panfried pancakes with scallions is a bargain appetizer and wonderful: cheap, greasy, and oniony. The main courses are almost all terrific: Sautéed shrimp with ginger and scallion is crunchy on the outside, sweetly juicy on the inside. Fresh lobster in black bean sauce is a perfect juxtaposition of sweet flesh and salty beans. Vegetarians' hodgepodge, a Young Lok classic, has a variety of crunchy vegetables. Mandarin crispy duck is for all unrepentant grease lovers. *122 St. Patrick St., at Dundas St., just south of the Art Gallery; tel. 416/593–9819. Reservations recommended. Dress: informal. AE, MC, V. Dim sum weekends 10:30 AM–3 PM. Summer outdoor dining.*

Inexpensive **Eating Counter.** After you've visited the Art Gallery of Ontario, drop in for some glorious Chinese seafood. This spot is the darling of the cognoscenti of Cantonese cuisine, who line up on weekends for the food, not for the Formica-table-Pepsi-sign ambience, you can be sure. The delights include the extremely fresh lobster with ginger and green onions, a variety of sizzling hot-plate dishes with barely cooked vegetables, and sweet and tangy barbecued specialties. Most of the items described by Chinese characters on the wall are not listed in English, so ask the waiter what's fresh that day. *23 Baldwin St., near Dundas St., tel. 416/977–7028. Reservations recommended. Dress: informal. MC, V.*

Lee Garden. From October till May, it has a Mongolian fire pot on every table, with people dipping bounteous piles of fish, meat, and morsels in raw egg. With the summer, it switches to Szechuan and Hakka dishes, ideal for the heat. This place is better and cheaper, and has lighter and more inventive food, than most other Szechuan places on Spadina Avenue. The soups are excellent, and the Hakka dish—shrimp with eggplant—is pretty and very original. The pièce de résistance is baked shrimp with pepper. The decor is dreadful, the food, scrumptious. *358 Spadina Ave., south of College St.; tel. 416/ 593-9524. Reservations accepted at door. Dress: informal. MC, V. No lunch.*

★ **Pearl Court.** In 1991, Pearl Court made a lot of Sinophiles happy: It moved from cramped and dingy quarters to a two-story, postmodern dusty-rose and pale-green Chinese heaven. And the quality of the food suffered not a whit. The lobsters in ginger and green onion are still seductive, and the scallops in black-bean sauce on a hot iron plate are fat and fresh. There are also barely cooked, fat, fresh oysters sizzling on a hot iron plate with black pepper and green onion. Or fresh kiwi clams, each one steamed with a half-teaspoon of minced garlic. Garlic is a central theme here. So is fresh coriander. Lemon grass accents the oxtail in a fine citrusy stew pot. Chicken in paper is a platter of little paper packets, each holding a little morsel of pink tender chicken steamed in soy with five-spice powder. Skip the soups, which are bland, and consider the oysters. *663 Gerrard St. E, tel. 416/463-8773. Dress: informal. V.*

Delis

Inexpensive **Centre Street Deli.** Owners Cheryl Morantz and Sam Agelopoulos came from Montréal's Snowdon Deli, which Cheryl's dad has owned for 45 years. Centre Street imports smoked meat from Montreal and hand-slices it, for juicy, spicy sandwiches, tasty enough to make corned beef seem like eating a sponge. Add their rich homemade cabbage soup the way Grandma makes it, and fresh-cut french fries—it's deli heaven, and well worth the short drive north. *1102 Centre St., Thornhill, tel. 416/731-8037. No reservations. Dress: informal. MC, V.*

★ **United Bakers.** For nearly seven decades, this noisy, crowded, Formica restaurant served the Jews of Spadina—and all other nationalities with the wisdom to head for the old needle-trade area—with great Jewish food. Just a few years ago, it sadly closed its doors, but not before the third generation of Ladovskys—Philip and Ruth—opened a branch in a small plaza, a few miles northwest of downtown Toronto. The soups are wonderful, with the cabbage soup and the barley bean soup among the best. The cheese blintzes, sweet and sour pike, gefilte fish, whitefish and carp, toasted bagels with lox and cream cheese—all are superb. Don't miss the vegetarian chopped liver—this is, after all, a dairy restaurant. *In Lawrence Plaza, corner of Bathurst St. and Lawrence Ave. W; tel. 416/789-0519. No reservations. Dress: informal. MC, V.*

French

Expensive **Scaramouche.** This is Toronto's most luxurious French restaurant, with a stunning view of downtown Toronto, gorgeous ambience, and delicious food. The superb service, the tasteful luxury of the room, the amazing wines, and the carefully prepared food all add up to understated elegance. No particular dish dazzles and none disappoints. Your guinea fowl will be juicy, your salmon perfectly cooked, your lamb pink, and your sauces limpid. New money seeks Thai/Italian/Californian taste

treats—old money dines at Scaramouche. *1 Benevenuto Pl.,
tel. 416/961–8011. Reservations recommended. Jacket optional. Valet parking. AE, DC, MC, V. No lunch; closed Sun. and
Mon.*

Moderate–Expensive
★ **Le Bistingo.** Certain gifts from Chef Claude Bouillet's kitchen
are among the finest flavors Toronto can offer: His open ravioli
filled with shrimp and scallops is astonishing—toothsome pasta sheets laid over and under with soft, sweet seafood, all
bathed in the lightest of beurres blancs thinned with fish stock.
The house signature appetizer, duck liver sautéed until just
pink and soft and zapped with a very tart raisin sauce, is fabulous. Among main courses the fish dishes shine. A perfectly
cooked fat red snapper sits on a wondrously astringent bed of
stewed endive, surrounded by beurre blanc cleverly thinned
with vermouth. Those in the know order a hot dessert with dinner, and are thus seduced by fresh-from-the-oven buttery puff
pastry cradling caramelized apples, then bathed in a foam of
Calvados sabayon. As if that were not enough, there are sau-
ternes by the glass (or real champagne) to wash it all down. *349
Queen St. W, tel. 416/598–3490. Reservations required. Tie
and jacket optional. AE, DC, MC, V.*

Moderate **Arlequin.** There are no velvet banquettes or chandeliers here;
merely a very clever small dining room with a gently stated
theme: the harlequin. The waiter brings garlic toast and
tapenade (a purée of olives, olive oil, capers, and anchovies)—
the Provençal spread. The menu changes seasonally; you might
find chicken baked in bread dough with prosciutto and chicken
livers, fresh grouper with a strong anchovy sauce, or tender
rabbit, thyme-scented on a bed of basil and spinach. The desserts are among the best in Toronto. *134 Avenue Rd., near
Davenport Rd.; tel. 416/928–9521. Reservations recommended
for dinner. Jacket optional. AE, DC, MC, V. Closed Mon.*

Greek

Moderate **Astoria Shish Kabob House.** Out in Greektown, a 10-minute
★ subway ride east from Bloor and Yonge streets, are some superior ethnic restaurants. This one is a delightful Danforth Avenue escape (Bloor St. changes its name east of the Don Valley
Pkwy.), where hardly anything is served but terrific Greek-
style charcoal-barbecued foods, the best of which are the barbecued quails, the sweet little birds prepared with a hint of
lemon. They're so tender you can eat the bones. Also try the
calamari and Greek salad with a baklava chaser. *390 Danforth
Ave., near Chester Ave.; tel. 416/463–2838. No reservations.
Dress: informal. AE, MC, V.*

Inexpensive **Ellas.** You can get informal, delicious Greek food here, making
your choices from the steaming food on the stove. The fish is
always flaky and sweet, the roast lamb fork-tender, the potatoes moist. A good place to take the kids: It's noisy and informal, and the service is fast. For Mom and Dad, Ellas can
provide *dolmas* (stuffed grape leaves), *taramasalata* (salted
fish roe with onion and lemon juice), shish kebab, *spanakopita*
(phyllo pastry filled with spinach and cheddar cheese), and feta
salads. *702 Pape Ave., at Danforth Ave.; tel. 416/463–0334.
Reservations recommended. Dress: informal. AE, MC, V.*
Ouzeri. Salads, appetizers, and small meals are served to
standing-room-only crowds. This is nouvelle Greek—a little

lighter than the real thing. The dips are grand, the grilled octopus is superb, as are the savory phyllo pies and the garlicky lamb kebabs. The room is huge, noisy, and colorful. Bring your earplugs. *500 Danforth Ave., tel. 416/778-0500. Reservations not necessary. Dress: informal. AE, DC, MC, V.*

Italian

Expensive **Barolo.** For 14 years Michael Pagliaro worked under Luigi
★ Orgera of La Fenice (*see below*), learning everything the master had to teach. And he learned it well. Barolo serves the nouvelle Italian cooking that grills scallops just until their fat and juicy hearts run sweet, that puts plump capers and red pepper purée on tuna, that lovingly prepares wild mushrooms in the fall, gilding them in the sauté pan, then bedding them down on a splendid variety of garden greens. With every dessert there are enough fresh berries and fine butterfat to bring strong epicures to their knees. *193 Carlton St., tel. 416/961-4747. Reservations advised. Jacket optional. AE, DC, MC, V. No lunch Sat.; closed Sun.*

★ **Centro.** Franco Prevedello spent blood, sweat, and $2 million on dreamlike art deco lighting, etched glass, 18-foot ceilings with fat white columns, oxblood leather armchairs, Rosenthal china worth $45 a plate, and the most exciting Italian wine cellar in Toronto. The food can be heavy and overcomplicated—*agnolotti* (chopped-meat-and-vegetable–filled ravioli in the shape of small turnovers) with too much cream; overcooked poached salmon—but every day it moves closer to inspired Italian country style, with such specialties as poached skate in a mustardy coriander vinaigrette, and a fat juicy roasted capon breast garnished with fresh pecans and lemon-pepper garlic mayonnaise. *2472 Yonge St., tel. 416/483-2211. Reservations recommended. Jacket optional. AE, DC, MC, V. No lunch; closed Sun.*

★ **La Fenice.** This is the most authentic Italian restaurant in Toronto. Luigi Orgera is a wonder to behold in the kitchen, the Nureyev of the grill. Who else in Toronto has fresh porcini mushrooms in October? Who else grates heavenly slivers of fresh white truffle on pasta? The antipasto trolley is more Rome than Toronto: mint-scented grilled eggplant; roasted zucchini; tangy salad of shrimps and squid; roasted sweet red peppers anointed in extra-virgin olive oil; and more. His *risotto al mare* is a tiny perfect stew of clams and mussels; the spaghetti is tossed with sweet chunks of sun-dried tomatoes, southern Italy incarnate. In fish, one can expect red and white snapper, yellowtail, and porgy, all as fresh as fish can be in this city. In 1990 La Fenice added a basement pasta bar. It's small and noisy and the chairs are uncomfortable, but for an inexpensive version of the Orgera alchemy, a little suffering goes a long way. *319 King St. W, near John St.; tel. 416/585-2377. Reservations required. Dress: informal. AE, DC, MC, V. No lunch Sat.; closed Sun.*

★ **Splendido.** Thanks to lighting as fun sculpture, glorious huge painted flowers, and a kitchen full of chefs in painter's hats, all behind a glass wall splashed with colors, Splendido is sophisticated fun. It is Toronto's answer to the Cal/Ital aesthetic: homemade lamb sausage with silken polenta and a fresh rosemary sauce; perfectly cooked juicy quails with pasta in tomato sauce; competent pizzas with the usual new-age toppings; nice light gnocchi; rich strong soups with nary a hint of powdered

base. The wood-roasted chicken on sourdough-bread salad,
Italian style via Zuni in San Francisco, is wondrously crisp.
Rabbit is served in classic Italian style, with creamy porcini
fettucine, kale, and rapini. Avoid the nouvelle items; they sink
like stones. Splendido is so fashionable and pretty that the true
nature and strength of the food are obscured: It's the ultimate
trattoria. Prices are like those in Italy, too, more's the pity. *88
Harbord St., tel. 416/929–7788. Reservations advised. Dress:
casual, but chic. AE, MC, V. No lunch.*

Moderate–Expensive   **Sisi Trattoria.** A proper trattoria—just 42 seats and unpreten-
tious in the extreme. The ceiling is low, the pipes are exposed
(not on purpose). The only thing that's high is the price—$100
for two with wine and the essential etceteras. The only decor is
a few glued-on plaster ornaments. But I am drawn back again
and again to Sisi's hot-blooded kitchen, her chorus of oil and
wine, lemon and garlic, her gifts from the sea. Fresh sardines
sit fragrant on the mesquite grill, sweet and earthy. Sisi's hus-
band, Leo Schipani, grills fresh succulent oyster mushrooms
and a slice of slightly aged *romanelle* cheese (from Italy) till
they both crunch and explode in the mouth. His spaghetti Pa-
lermo is a carnival of anchovies, capers, black olives, tomato,
parsley, and *pecorino* cheese. His linguine Saraceni is superior
as well. The cuisine is southern Italian, a rarity in Canada.
*116A Avenue Rd., above Bloor St.; tel. 416/962–0011. Reserva-
tions required. Jacket optional. AE, V. No lunch; closed Sun.*

Inexpensive   **Camarra's.** Pizza heaven, in northwest Toronto. The dough
here has always been high and soft, with the delightful bite of
leavening. And on top are only good ingredients—real Italian
plum tomatoes, not the canned tomato sauce of too many Toronto pizzerias. Very casual. *2899 Dufferin St., 1 mi south of Hwy.
401; tel. 416/789–3222. Reservations not necessary. Dress: informal. AE, MC, V. No lunch Sun.; closed Tues.*

Filippo's Gourmet Pizzeria. Pizza is the fast food that was supposedly invented by prescient Neapolitan cooks who antici-
pated the two-income family with no time to cook. It is best
kept simple. Resist Filippo's designer pizza called La Yuppie
(with salmon and goat cheese). The normal pizzas, such as the
Calabrese, with huge green olives, roasted red peppers, spicy
soprossata sausage, mozzarella, and tomato sauce, are excellent—crunchy on the outside, softhearted on the inside. Salads
are large and crispy. You can eat in or take out. *744 Clair Ave.
W, tel. 416/658–0568. Reservations not necessary. Dress: informal. AE, MC, V.*

Japanese

Expensive   **Ema-Tei.** One could survive on a parade of appetizers at Ema-
Tei, with sushi for dessert. There is *ohitashi*, a small salad of
emerald spinach topped with a great flurry of dried shaved bo-
nito fish. *Beef yanagawa* is a miniature flat earthenware casse-
role holding tender steamed beef (or eel) mixed with burdock
root, and slightly scrambled, barely cooked egg. The *nasu
dengaku* here makes the nasu dengakus of yesteryear seem like
gooey mistakes. It is small thin Chinese eggplant smeared with
quality miso. Plump fresh shiitake mushrooms are steamed
with soy sauce and a little butter. Tiny clams are steamed with
sake and served in the resulting broth, which is at once subtle
and strong. Newcomers to Japanese cuisine would do well to
put themselves in the chef's hands and order his fixed price $45

dinner, a waltz through Japan's most important cooking techniques, or variations on a fish theme. *30 St. Patrick St., tel. 416/ 340–0472. Reservations recommended. Dress: informal. AE, DC, MC, V. No lunch Sat.; closed Sun.*

★ **Nami.** Just steps from the Eaton Centre sits this very fine restaurant, with a beautiful, spare Japanese ambience. Here, you will find *robata:* fish or vegetables, cooked on a gas grill (sushi is served, too). Lunches are less carefully prepared; this solid restaurant is for long, slow, relaxing evenings in the tatami rooms. *55 Adelaide St. E, near Yonge St.; tel. 416/362–7373. Reservations recommended for lunch and weekends. Dress: informal. AE, DC, MC, V. No lunch Sat.; closed Sun.*

Mexican

Inexpensive **Santa Fe Bar & Grill.** You wouldn't be able to find Santa Fe if
★ you didn't know it was there. The only clue to its presence is a big turquoise lizard on the roof. The interior has all the southwestern elements—adobe walls, cowhide tub chairs, wooden chairs painted with a Georgia O'Keeffe palette, southwestern rugs on the walls. The kitchen has troubled itself to stock the staples of casual Mexican cuisine: *chipotles* (smoked jalapeños), *jicamas* (sweet crunchy white tubers), blue corn chips, corn husks, flour tortillas, and black beans. It's fun food. Sip a blue margarita in a huge highball glass with a little pizza or a platter of blue and gold corn chips. The more proper Mexican cooking is done with the right chilies and generosity of spirit. *129 Peter St., tel. 416/345–9345. Reservations advised. Dress: informal. AE, DC, MC, V. Closed Sun.*

Nouvelle

Expensive **China Blues.** Chef Greg Couillard, Toronto's spicemeister, has moved on, but many of his signature dishes, with seasonings of India, Thailand, and the Caribbean, are still on the menu. You'll find tandoori salmon (baked with coconut, lime leaf, and coriander butter) and the popular "jump-up soup," an artful balance on the knife's edge of hot and sweet, thanks to hot and sweet peppers, coconut, allspice, ginger, lime, and jerk-chicken fragments. When you order a salad, it's so long romaine and bibb, hello organic greens, Chinese vegetables, green mango, and passion fruit–honey vinaigrette. A number of the dishes are spicy and you may not recognize some of the ingredients; others are more conventional. This generally satisfying menu is a globe-trotter from Italy to the Far East. *125 King St. E, tel. 416/366–2556. Reservations required. Dress: informal. AE, MC, V. No lunch Sat.; closed Sun.*

Lotus. This tiny homemade room, with no decor to speak of, is hotter than Szechuan garlic eggplant. Chef Susur Lee, who apprenticed in classical French cuisine at Hong Kong's Peninsula Hotel and a number of better Toronto eateries, calls the shots here, with every plate bearing his signature. One night, a thick, gutsy hot-and-sour soup with the favorite undertone of the late '80s: coriander. Another night, a fresh, sweet duck liver fried barely unto pinkness, dressed in pumpkin-seed oil and plum wine, and garnished with poached pear and Japanese basil. Lee buys as much organic meat and vegetables as is possible, and no factory chicken could ever taste as strong and real as his free-range bird stuffed with fresh apricots, raisins, and ginger, in black cherry sauce. Desserts include homemade tropical ice creams, baked fruits atop limpid coconut custards, and buttery pastries made from whole-wheat flour. This is French Chinese cooking, a true hybrid. *96 Tecumseth St. at King St., west of Bathurst St.; tel. 416/368-7620. Reservations recommended. Jacket optional. AE, MC, V. No lunch; closed Sun. and Mon.*

★ **North 44.** North 44, Toronto's longitude, is the restaurant's logo and an oft-repeated visual refrain. Everywhere you look there is another design statement. The message is metallic and modern; even the washrooms have the designer touch. Chef Mark McEwan is one of the five best cooks in Toronto; his theme is southwest cuisine with a southeast Asian undertone, all afloat on a sea of beurre blanc and executed with finesse. McEwan dips fresh oysters in cornmeal, fries them crisp on the outside, melting on the inside, and sits them on a chili cream sauce. He pats together corn, potato and shrimp fragments into a pancake and fries it. Order the huge barely roasted scallops and you get grilled bok choy and creamed peppers. The fried rock snapper comes with gingered plum tomatoes and a McEwan introduction—french-fried leeks, sophisticated kissin' cousin to onion rings. *2537 Yonge St., tel. 416/487-4897. Reservations advised. Jacket optional. AE, DC, MC, V. No lunch; brunch only Sun.*

Patisseries

Inexpensive **Dufflet Pastries.** For the best desserts in Toronto, bar none, check this one out. Dufflet Rosenberg has been supplying her inspired creations to dozens of the city's restaurants since 1974, but you can buy direct—it's cheaper and fresher. The chocolate orange Bavarian, the cranapple pie, the Linzer torte, the chocolate oatmeal cookies, the hazelnut chocolate balls and hazelnut cheesecake: All could give a diet doctor heart failure. And her chocolate mud cake (a deep, dark cake spiked with bourbon and coffee and iced with even darker semisweet chocolate) is one of the cakes that made Dufflet famous. Don't miss her two other classics: the toasted almond meringue torte and the chocolate fudge cake. *787 Queen St. W, near Bathurst St.; tel. 416/368-1812. Reservations not necessary. Dress: informal. AE, DC, MC, V. Closed Sun. and Mon.*

Patachou Patisserie. Up in a tiny plaza at Bathurst Street and Eglinton Avenue is this little place that feels like a neighborhood café on the Right Bank in Paris. (And there's a more central branch on Yonge St., several blocks south of St. Clair Ave.) The brioches are as light and as buttery as any in Paris; the croissants and *pain au raisin* will make you long for France (you can eat them here or take them out). The *salade niçoise* is fine, and the *salade composée* at lunchtime is a treat—choose from three delicious salads. The Diplomate Pudding is superb, the Sacher torte good, the assorted fruit tarts a visual symphony that tastes as good as it looks. And the apple butter tart—quite incredible. *875 Eglinton Ave. W, tel. 416/782-1322; 1097 Yonge St., tel. 416/927-1105. Reservations not necessary. Dress: informal. No credit cards. Closed Sun. at Eglinton Ave. W location only.*

Quick Meals

Moderate **Studio Café.** This is the coffee shop of the Four Seasons Hotel, but it's no ordinary coffee shop. The decor is eye-catchingly chic, with lots of chrome, designer furniture, and designer fabrics. Art is everywhere—paintings by Canadian artists hang on the walls, and handmade glass art is beautifully displayed in illuminated showcases (the glass art is for sale). The breakfast menu includes traditional fare as well as a Japanese breakfast of miso soup, grilled salmon, and rice. The lunch and dinner menus offer a wide selection ranging from pizzas and pastas to halibut burgers and "crunchy whole quail," which tastes much better than it sounds. *21 Avenue Rd., just north of Bloor St.; tel. 416/964–0411. Reservations recommended. Jacket optional. AE, DC, MC, V.*

Senator. This is a remake of the diner of yesteryear. It is distinguished from other such efforts by a commitment to using the honest ingredients of the good old days, not the mass-produced pap favored by most modern pseudo-diners. Senator serves thick shakes and great fizzy sodas, huge sandwiches on first-class bread, lovely burgers, and fresh-made fries. *253 Victoria St., tel. 416/364–7517. Reservations not necessary. Dress: informal. AE, MC, V.*

Inexpensive **Grano.** Franco Prevedello has served as godfather to a winner, helping a young couple, the Martellas, create a basic café—southern Italian style—the prettiest and busiest café in Toronto. The soups and antipasti are dreams come true, the soups thick and strong, with fresh thyme and good stock. And some of the antipasti are as good as what you'd get in Bologna: Strips of zucchini are marinated with sweet oregano; a hint of caraway flavors the thin chewy strips of eggplant in oil. Grano's pizzas are so attractive because bread is the secret love at Grano (which means grain). All day the baker toils in the cellar under the café, and all day the breads come upstairs, fragrant and warm: The two most wonderful are the *foccaccia* and the oatmeal buttermilk bread. Avoid the steam-table stuff. *2035 Yonge St., below Eglinton Ave., tel. 416/440–1986. No reservations. Dress: informal. AE, MC, V. Closed Sun.*

★ **Jerusalem.** This is the ultimate family restaurant: the broadloom is dark red with a brown pattern, so accidents by children can go practically unnoticed. Service is fast. The bustle and noise are enough to camouflage the most unruly youngsters. And the food will not deliver a crisis to the taste buds. Jerusalem serves a rich variety of wonderful Middle Eastern foods—the most tender falafel in town, rich fried tomatoes with garlic, *sam bousek* (a deep-fried dough packet of ground meat and pine nuts), very sweet charcoal-grilled shish kebab, and ungooey baklava. *955 Eglinton Ave. W, tel. 416/783–6494. No reservations. Dress: informal. AE, MC, V.*

Portuguese

Moderate **Chiado.** Located in west-end Toronto, Chiado stands out from its neighboring restaurants by its upscale look. There is a luxurious warmth to the decor, with its cushy velvet armchairs, wood paneling, oil paintings, and skylights—an unusual mix of the traditional and the contemporary. But what really makes this place special is the homespun food—especially the Portuguese dishes. This means a practiced hand with fresh fish, kind attention to potatoes; in fact, compassion for all vegetables. It all adds up to a rustic, hearty menu with some spirited spicing. A whole fresh squid is turned tender and sweet on the grill. A fish stew is laden with mussels, chunks of grouper, and loads of flavor in a light broth with a slightly spicy undertow. A gener-

ous fillet of salt cod is seared, baked, and served with new potatoes. Rabbit is braised and glazed with Madeira; the meat soft
and well seasoned, the glaze a nice foil to the savory. If you have
room for dessert, order the fresh peach and coconut pie, or settle for a light meringue dessert of caramelized sugar and egg
whites. An unusual feature is the wine list; it's exclusively Portuguese. *864 College St., tel. 416/538–1910. Reservations recommended. Dress: informal. AE, DC, MC, V.*

Thai

Moderate–Expensive
★ **Thai Magic.** Consistency and competence are the bywords
here: The food is neither greasy nor too sweet. But chiliphobes
beware: The divine Thai Magic mussels, steamed with curry
sauce and unctuous coconut cream, are mouth-burners, as is
the otherwise lovely chicken coconut soup, Thailand's national
soup, which is an amalgam of smooth coconut and sharp *kha* (a
gingerlike root). Barbecued foods, a piece of Thai magic served
with sweet/spicy peanut sauce, are short on chilies and long on
charm. Even the satay is very good, as far as satay goes (which
is not very far, considering the relative banality of meat on a
stick). *1118 Yonge St., tel. 416/968–7366. Reservations recommended on weekends. Dress: informal. AE, MC, V. Closed
Sun. and for lunch.*

Inexpensive
Young Thailand. This modest-looking restaurant in a slightly
offbeat location is worth searching out. The dining room is open
and airy, its plainness tempered with a few Thai decorative
touches. Chef and owner Wandee Young is well known from her
days at the BamBoo, and here she displays her skills at combin-
ing the fresh herbs and flavors that are characteristically Thai.
The food is fresh and varied and includes the popular *phad thai*
(a noodle dish with shrimp, slivers of chicken, egg, bean
sprouts, and a squeeze of lime). The green-mango salad is de-
lightfully fresh, with shrimp, chicken, and red onion. The
soups can be searing, most notably the *tom yum goong*, which
includes a few tiger shrimp, lemon grass, lime juice, mushrooms, and some vicious red chilies. Not all dishes are hot:
Some have a sweetness reminiscent of Cantonese food. *111
Gerrard St. E, tel. 416/599–9099. Reservations recommended.
Dress: informal. MC, V. No lunch weekends.*

Vegetarian

Inexpensive
Renaissance Cafe. This is a modest restaurant with a limited
but cosmopolitan menu—the likes of ratatouille and curries.
The daily buffet lunches are pleasant. *509 Bloor St. W, near
Bathurst St.; tel. 416/968–6639. Reservations recommended.
Dress: informal. AE, DC, MC, V.*
The Vegetarian Restaurant. For the uninitiated, there are lovely soups and salads; for the adventuresome, soyburgers and
tofu Bourguignon. Dine in a cheerfully renovated Victorian
house, with cafeteria-style service. *4 Dundonald St., just east
of Yonge St.; tel. 416/961–9522. No reservations. Dress: informal. DC, MC, V. No lunch Sun.*

6 Lodging

Places to stay in this cosmopolitan city range, as one might expect, from luxurious hotels to budget motels to a handful of bed-and-breakfasts in private homes.

Prices are cut nearly in half over weekends and during special times of the year (many Toronto hotels drop their rates a full 50% in January and February).

If you are traveling with children or are planning to do a good deal of sightseeing, you should consider staying in the downtown area (south of Bloor St., east of Bathurst St., west of Jarvis St.). This is where you will find Harbourfront Centre, the CN Tower, Eaton Centre, the Toronto Islands, the SkyDome, Chinatown, and most of the finest shopping and restaurants. If you are staying only a day or two, and are mainly interested in visiting the zoo, the Ontario Science Centre, and Canada's Wonderland, then look into some of the places listed below as Off the Beaten Track or along the airport strip.

Accommodation Toronto (tel. 416/596–7117), a service of the Hotel Association of Toronto, is an excellent source for finding the room and price you want. Don't forget to ask about family deals and special packages.

Highly recommended properties in each category are indicated with a star ★.

Category	Cost*
Very Expensive	over $175
Expensive	$125–$174
Moderate	$70–$124
Inexpensive	under $70

All prices are for a standard double room, excluding 7% GST (Goods and Services Tax).

Downtown

Very Expensive ★ **Four Seasons Toronto.** It's hard to imagine a lovelier or more exclusive hotel than the Four Seasons, which is usually rated among the top two dozen hotels in the world and one of the top three in North America. The location is one of the most ideal in the city: on the edge of Yorkville, a few meters from the Royal Ontario Museum. The 380 units are tastefully appointed. Maids come twice a day, and there are comfortable bathrobes, oversize towels, fresh flowers, and a fine indoor/outdoor pool. Even the special family rates, however, will not drop the cost much below $200 a night. Yet, during such slow months as January through March, sometimes into April, rooms on weekends have been offered for less than $150 per night (per person), and even in high season, weekend specials can drop the price to around $170 per night, over a hundred dollars less than normal. Ask for upper rooms with views facing downtown and the lake. The Studio Café is one of the best business breakfast, lunch, or dinner spots in town. Other restaurants include the Lobby Bar, La Serre, and Truffles, the formal dining room. *21 Avenue Rd., M5R 2G1, a block north of Bloor St.; tel. 416/964–0411 or 800/ 332–3442. AE, DC, MC, V.*

King Edward Hotel. After too many years of neglect, this Ed-

wardian classic was finally purchased and thoroughly renovated by a group of local investors. Some of the restorations
were less than sensitive; the kitschy platform with pergola in
Chiaro's, the formal dining room, desecrates one of Toronto's
great interiors. Still, it's a treat having this splendid structure
restored to its pink marble grandeur, and, under the British
Trusthouse Forte group, again attracting the well-heeled clientele it so manifestly deserves. What other hotel gives you not
only bathrobes and hairdryers, but even umbrellas? There's a
nonsmoker's floor, and family and weekend rates are available.
Facilities include a health club. The 315-room King Edward
also has Cafe Victoria (open all day), the Consort Bar, and the
Lobby Lounge for afternoon tea on weekends. *37 King St. E,
M5C 1E9, tel. 416/863–9700 or 800/225–5843. AE, DC, MC, V.*
Park Plaza Hotel. It may lack a pool, but it has one of the best
locations in the city: a short distance from the Royal Ontario
Museum, Queen's Park, and Yorkville (one of the city's great
shopping areas). As of 1990, the first phase of its massive reno-
vation was completed in the South Tower, which has the great
views of downtown Toronto. The newer North Tower is finally
open. The ground floor now consists of upscale retail shops,
while the 64 guest rooms (of which 20 are suites) are done in the
finest residential/traditional, yet updated style: cornice mold-
ings in the rooms; peachy pink with white trim wood; antique
vanity tables. The Roof Restaurant was once described by novelist Mordecai Richler as "the only civilized place in Toronto."
For a business breakfast or lunch, you cannot do better than the
very comfortable Prince Arthur Room. Additions include a
550-seat ballroom, a business center, a palm court, and a restaurant in the lobby, all designed by Zeidler Roberts Partner-
ship, the same architects who were responsible for the Eaton
Centre and Ontario Place. This is très New York Park Avenue.
Moderately priced weekend packages are sometimes available.
*4 Avenue Rd., M5R 2E8, at corner of Bloor St. W; tel. 416/924–
5471 or 800/268–4927. AE, DC, MC, V.*
Radisson Plaza Hotel Admiral. This small, intimate hotel is exquisitely situated on the edge of Lake Ontario, overlooking
Harbourfront Centre. It has only 157 rooms and 17 handsomely
furnished suites, as well as a main dining room, the Gallery
Café, and a bar. The lacquered wood shines and the polished
brass gleams in the stunning lobby. The Promenade Deck on
the fifth level, surrounding the outdoor heated swimming pool,
allows for fabulous views of the bustling harbor. There's frequent courtesy shuttle bus service for the downtown area.
Weekend rates can be as low as $160, which includes free park-
ing and breakfast for one, but this hotel will usually run closer
to $200 for a double. *249 Queen's Quay W, M5J 2N5, tel. 416/
364–5444. AE, D, DC, MC, V.*
Renaissance. This relatively small, modern, 256-room hotel is
one that Torontonians tend to forget. It's part of the Hudson
Bay complex, near the busy intersection of Yonge and Bloor
streets. Facilities include a pool and a sauna, a restaurant, and
a lounge (which is being renovated). Weekend rates at this
Ramada hotel can be as low as $140 a night. *90 Bloor St. E,
M4W 1A7, tel. 416/961–8000 or 800/323–7500. AE, D, DC, MC,
V.*
Sutton Place Hotel. This 33-story tower, located close to the
various ministries of the Ontario provincial government, is a
favorite of lobbyists, lawyers, and the like. Service is more per-

Toronto Lodging

Moss Park

Queen St. E.

Richmond St. E.

Front St. E.

Wilton St.

Jarvis St.

Church St.

Berti St.

Victoria St.

Lombard St.

Adelaide St. E.   **25**

King St. E.

Toronto St.

Leader La.

Colborne St.

Wellington St. E.

Front St. E.

Scott St.

The Esplanade

22

19

Yonge St.

Temperance St.

Bay St.

Sheppard St.

Nathan Phillips Square

St.

AE

AE

12

10

York St.

University Ave.

Simcoe St.

Duncan St.

Nelson St.

Pearl St.

John St.

Widmer St.

Peter St.

Mercer St.

Wellington St. W.

Windsor St.

Piper St.

Heenan Pl.

11

York St.

Station St.

Renfrew Pl.

Pullan Pl.

Bulwer St.

Spadina Ave.

4

Camden St.

Brant St.

Augusta Ave.

Brant Pl.

Richmond St. W.

Adelaide St. W.

Portland St.

Front St. W.

King St. W.

Wellington St. W.

Wolseley St.

Queen St. W.

Tecumseth St.

Bathurst St.

Fleet St.

Queen's Quay W.

Lake Shore Blvd. W.

7

Lake Shore Blvd. W.

Gardiner Expwy.

Lake Shore Blvd. E.

Queen's Quay E.

Cooper St.

Freeland St.

16

440 yards

400 meters

0

0

KEY

AE American Express Office

Best Western/
Chestnut Park, **13**
Bristol Place, **1**
Brownstone Hotel, **20**
Delta Chelsea Inn, **17**
ETA Suites Inc., **14**

Four Seasons
Toronto, **9**
Glen Rouge Park
camping, **27**
Guild Inn, **26**
Harbour Castle
Westin, **16**

Holiday Inn on
King, **4**
Hotel Ibis, **24**
Inn on the Park, **18**
InterContinental
Toronto, **6**

Journey's End
Hotel, **5, 25**
Journey's End
Suites, **3**
King Edward, **22**

Neill-Wycik College-
Hotel, **23**
Novotel Toronto
Centre, **19**
Park Plaza, **8**
Radisson Plaza Hotel
Admiral, **7**
Regal Constellation, **2**

Renaissance, **21**
Royal York, **11**
Sheraton Centre, **12**
Sutton Place
Hotel, **15**
Toronto Hilton
International, **10**

sonal than you would think, because many of the floors have luxury apartments, not hotel rooms. Being next to Wellesley Street means that it's within walking distance of Queen's Park, the Royal Ontario Museum, and many other midtown attractions. Facilities include a pool, health club, 24-hour room service, special floors for nonsmokers, and a stunning restaurant Sanssouci, serving three meals. Family and weekend rates are available. *955 Bay St., M5S 2A2, tel. 416/924–9221. 280 rooms. AE, DC, MC, V.*

Expensive **Best Western/Chestnut Park Hotel.** One of the newest—and biggest—additions to Toronto's hotel scene, this handsome 16-floor hotel with glass-enclosed atrium lobby could hardly be more convenient: just steps behind City Hall and a few short blocks from Eaton Centre. The 522 guest rooms, which include 21 for the disabled, are all well decorated, with finely crafted furniture and desks; many have queen- and king-size beds. The Tapestry restaurant is open from 6 AM until 1 AM. Recreational facilities include a large heated indoor pool, sauna, Jacuzzi, health club and gymnasium, and a children's creative center. In addition, the Chestnut Hill is now connected by a walkway from the mezzanine level to a Museum of Textiles, where some 15,000 textiles from around the world are displayed—the only museum of its kind in Canada. *108 Chestnut St., M5G 1R3, just north of Nathan Phillips Sq.; tel. 416/977–5000. AE, D, DC, MC, V.*

Delta Chelsea Inn. The 977 rooms on the south side of Gerrard Street began as a budget hotel. Prices have crept up, but they're still reasonable by downtown standards. The Chelsea is much favored by tour operators, and the elevators, which were meant to serve the apartment building this was originally intended to be, can be hard to catch when all the buses are leaving at once. On the positive side, the hotel has a creative, supervised day-care service for children ages 3–8, open from 9:30 AM to 10 PM. Facilities include a pool and sauna, and two restaurants (The Market Garden, and The Wittles). As of late 1992, the hotel was up to 1,600 rooms, with weekend specials as low as $100 per night. Ask for the southeast and southwest rooms in the south wing, overlooking downtown and the lake; many rooms are for the disabled. *33 Gerrard St., M5G 1Z5, at the corner of Yonge St.; tel. 416/595–1975 or 800/268–1133. AE, D, DC, MC, V.*

Harbour Castle Westin. This was a Hilton International hotel until 1987, when Westin and Hilton suddenly switched ownership of their major downtown Toronto hotels. A favorite of conventioners, it's located just steps from Harbourfront Centre and the Toronto Island ferry. It's a bit inconvenient to the city's amenities except for those directly on the lakeshore, but it enjoys the best views of any hotel in the city. There's a shuttle bus service to downtown business and shopping, and the swimming pool, squash courts, and health club are among the best in town. The Regatta restaurant is open all day; the revolving Lighthouse restaurant, perched atop the 37th floor, is open for lunch and dinner. And what a view! Its 900 rooms are well appointed and tastefully modern, and the frequent family and weekend rates help bring its regular price down by as much as a third. All rooms have a lake view, but you may wish to ask for a corner one, which also looks up to the glittering bank and office towers just to the north. The North Tower was recently entirely renovated. *1 Harbour Sq., M5J 1A6, tel. 416/869–1600 or 800/228–3000. AE, DC, MC, V.*

InterContinental Toronto. This handsome high rise, part of the respected international chain, is just a half-block west of the major intersection of Bloor Street, Avenue Road, and University Avenue, making it a two-minute walk to the Royal Ontario Museum and the Yorkville shopping area. With 213 rooms (including a dozen suites), a fully equipped fitness center with indoor swimming pool and sauna, and two restaurants (The Signatures and The Harmony Lounge), it's a welcome addition to this prime area. The rooms are spacious and well appointed; the service—especially the superb Executive Business Centre and secretarial service—is topnotch. *220 Bloor St. W, M5S 1T8, tel. 416/960–5200. AE, DC, MC, V.*

Novotel Toronto Centre. This once moderately priced hotel—part of a popular French chain—opened in December 1987. There are 266 modest, modern rooms on nine floors in the heart of downtown, in walking distance of Harbourfront and the CN Tower. Facilities include an indoor pool, whirlpool, exercise room, and sauna. The Café Nicole is open all day. *45 The Esplanade, M5E 1W2, tel. 416/367–8900 or 800/221–4542. AE, DC, MC, V.*

Royal York. Although no longer the largest hotel in the British Commonwealth (after decades with this title, the Delta Chelsea Inn, above, is now bigger), the Royal York has 1,438 completely renovated rooms, 100 of which are studio suites, and 13 restaurants and lounges; it's certainly still a monster of a place. The service is necessarily impersonal, and there's always a convention of some sort going on. Still, it's venerable, comfortable, close to the financial core of the city, and rarely booked solid. *100 Front St. W, M5J 1E3, tel. 416/368–2511 or 800/828–7447. AE, D, DC, MC, V.*

Sheraton Centre. This 1,430-room conventioneer's tower is located across from the New City Hall, just a block from Eaton Centre. As of 1992, $47 million had been spent on renovations, with completely refurbished guest rooms and bathrooms, six new floors in the exclusive Sheraton Towers, and 15 new automated check-in and cashier stations. The below-ground level is part of Toronto's labyrinth of shop-lined corridors, and there are more shops on the ground floor and second floor. The restaurants' reach seems to exceed their grasp, but the Long Bar, overlooking Nathan Phillips Square, is a great place to meet friends for a drink. All views are marvelous; to the south is the CN Tower and SkyDome; to the north, both city halls. Weekday specials can drop to under $140, even less in winter. Facilities include a huge indoor/outdoor pool, hot tub, sauna, and workout room. *123 Queen St. W, M5H 2M9, tel. 416/361–1000 or 800/325–3535. AE, DC, MC, V.*

Toronto Hilton International. As noted above, this hotel, located in the financial district, recently switched ownership with the Westin. The 600 rooms have been renovated, and its nearness to the financial district, New City Hall, the CN Tower, and more makes it a convenient base for most visitors. The indoor/outdoor pool is modest, but the view of the city from the glass-enclosed elevators is a thrill. The Garden Court restaurant in the lobby is open all day; Trader Vic's, on the Convention Level, is open for lunch and dinner. There are family plans and weekend rates, as always, and children can stay free. Although on the top end of the Expensive scale, specials throughout the week can drop the price of a single or a double to the $125 range. *145 Richmond St. W and University Ave., M5H 3M6, tel. 416/869–3456. AE, DC, MC, V.*

Moderate **Brownstone Hotel.** This intimate hotel—110 units in all—has some of the charm of a private club. You could not be closer to the center of town and still get a quiet night's sleep. Ask for one of the recently renovated rooms; there is no additional charge for children under 14. Pralines restaurant is open all day for meals and snacks. During the summer of 1992 there were double rooms available for $90; in winter prices drop to as low as $70. Some packages include Continental breakfast. *15 Charles St. E, M4Y 1S1, tel. 416/924–7381 or 800/263–8967. AE, DC, MC, V.*

Holiday Inn on King. This new addition in the heart of the fashion district is just three blocks north of the Metro Toronto Convention Centre, SkyDome, and the CN Tower. Although the structure is 20 floors high, half of that is office space; the hotel takes up the 9th–20th floors only. Two restaurants—one of them Japanese—and a deli provide for the 426 rooms. The swimming pool is tiny, but the fitness center is good, and one can request views of either Lake Ontario, the downtown skyline, or SkyDome. Executive suites have whirlpool bathtubs. Being a Holiday Inn, there are no surprises. *370 King St. W, M5V 1J9, tel. 416/599–4000. AE, D, DC, MC, V.*

Inexpensive **Hotel Ibis.** This recently opened hotel belongs to one of Europe's leading chains. It is centrally located, just a few blocks from the New City Hall and Eaton Centre. As it proudly declares, "No bellhops, doormen, or concierges. No gushing fountains. And no room service with fancy silver trays." What it does have are 294 comfortable rooms with bare necessities (as well as 10 others specially designed and equipped for the disabled). There's no pool, and the nearby-health-club hook is long past, but there is a lounge (called The Bar) and a restaurant (Le Restaurant). *240 Jarvis St., M5B 2B8, tel. 416/593–9400. AE, DC, MC, V.*

Journey's End Hotel. Rooms are clean and spartan in this 16-story chain hotel located in the downtown core area, a 10-minute walk from Eaton Centre. There are no pools, saunas, or convention rooms, but prices (less than $110 a night for doubles, and only about $60 during winter weekends in 1992) are reasonable. And businesspeople might be charmed by its offering of free phone calls and less than $50 for a 9–4 "Traveler's Day," which includes free papers and coffee. The Lombard Street location has The Vogue Bistro, and the Bloor Street hotel has Obie's, a fast-food eatery open from 7 AM until 1 AM. *111 Lombard St., M5C 2T9, and 280 Bloor St. W, M5S 1V8, tel. 800/ 668–4200. 196 rooms. AE, DC, MC, V.*

Neill-Wycik College-Hotel. This is an attractive alternative for young people or families on a tight budget. From early May through late August, the college residence becomes Toronto's best hotel value. Rooms are private, but guests must share facilities with five or six other hotel guests. A cafeteria serves breakfast 6:30–11:30. There's a great view of the city from the cedar roof deck. Prices have edged up to the high $30s for a single, mid-40s for a small double, and close to $50 for a couple/ family, but that's still pretty astonishing. *96 Gerrard St. E, M5B 1G7, tel. 416/977–2320. 265 rooms. MC, V.*

Toronto Bed & Breakfast. More than two dozen private homes are affiliated with this service, most of them scattered across metro Toronto. Singles range from the low $40s to the low $60s; doubles from the low $50s to the mid-$80s. *Tel. 416/961–3676.*

Off the Beaten Track

Very Expensive   **Inn on the Park.** This is another classy member of the Four Seasons chain. It is located across the street from the Ontario Science Centre, just off Don Valley Parkway, only a 10-minute drive from downtown Toronto. The only resort in the city, it offers 600 acres of parkland, miles of cross-country ski trails, swimming, biking, jogging, and access to tennis, racquetball, squash, and horseback riding. Children ages 5–12 can disappear all day into a supervised program, complete with swimming, arts and crafts, and other activities. Its two restaurants are the formal Seasons, for lunch and dinner, as well as a lavish Sunday brunch, and the family-style Harvest Room, open daily 6:30 AM–nearly midnight. There are 568 modern rooms and 11 suites. The more expensive rooms are in the 22-story tower, where you should ask for south views, toward downtown and the lake. But the smaller back rooms in the main building (sans vue) can cost as little as $80–$90 for winter weekends and about $100 for the rest of the year. *1100 Eglinton Ave. E, M3C 1H8, tel. 416/444–2561 or 800/332–3442. AE, DC, MC, V.*

Moderate   **Guild Inn.** Modern units are built around a 1930s country inn on some 90 acres of forest, gardens, and woodland trails, a 20- to 30-minute drive from downtown Toronto. Facilities include a heated outdoor pool, a tennis court, and dining room. Guests have a choice of 13 traditional rooms in the original building or 67 modern rooms in the newer wing. Weekend rates can be as low as $59 for one night, $99 for two, and $150 for three—extraordinary for a gorgeous and unique resort! *201 Guildwood Pkwy., Scarborough M1E 1P6, tel. 416/261–3331. AE, MC, V.*

The Airport Strip

Few hotels along the airport strip offer anything more than your standard, no-surprises rooms and meals. Most have pools, pay TV, and weekend rates, and their prices vary greatly.

Expensive   **Bristol Place.** This has long been considered the ritziest of all the hotels along the airport strip, and, thanks to a $2 million face-lift in 1987, it is more attractive than ever. All 287 bedrooms and suites have been redone. Bedrooms have mahogany armoires, tables, desks, and minibars. Zachary's, the main dining room, is open for lunch and dinner, and Le Café is open every day from 7 AM until midnight. Call its special airport bus from the arrival level when you have your bags; it's only two minutes away. And, for an airport hotel, it's fairly quiet; rooms that face east are the quietest of all. Rates verge on the very expensive, but weekend specials (which run a generous Thursday, Friday, Saturday, and Sunday) in the $100 range are available all year round. *950 Dixon Rd., M9W 5N4, next to airport; tel. 416/675–9444. Facilities: indoor and outdoor pools, saunas, health club with exercise equipment, children's play area. AE, DC, MC, V.*

Moderate–Expensive   **Regal Constellation.** Now part of the Regal chain out of Hong Kong, the former Constellation continues to be one of the bright lights at the airport, and one of its classiest members. There is a stunning, seven-story, glass-enclosed lobby; a fully equipped health club, including saunas and a delightful indoor/outdoor swimming pool; quality dining; and very impressive service. The south wing has minisuites, all of them larger than the other rooms. The Burgundy, the main dining room, is open for lunch and dinner, and the Atrium Restaurant is open daily from 5 AM until midnight. One nice touch: By law, airplanes cannot fly on the north side of Dixon, making this a very quiet hotel. Don't miss the weekend rates of under $100, which actually includes a $20 breakfast for one, for free! *900 Dixon Rd., M9W 1J7, tel. 416/675–1500. 900 rooms. AE, DC, MC, V.*

Inexpensive **Journey's End Suites.** This is one of the most successful budget motel/hotel chains in Canada, and its new-suites concept near the airport is an irresistible combination: king-size beds, living areas, a large table and even four chairs for business meetings. There's no pool or any health club access, but there's a restaurant, and a courtesy bus runs to/from the airport every half hour. And, like its downtown hotel, J.E.S. provides free papers, free local phone calls, and a Traveler's Day Rate of under $50, for a 9–4 day, a superb deal, especially for executives on a budget. *262 Carlingview Dr., Etobicoke, ON M9W 5G1, tel. 416/674–8442; 800/668–4200. 258 suites. AE, DC, MC, V.*

Executive Apartments

Moderate–Expensive **Executive Travel Apartment Suites Inc.** Since 1977 this concern (formerly ETA Suites) has been supplying corporate clients with short-term rates (as little as one night, cheaper by the week or month) for nicely appointed apartment suites in many cities across North America and Europe. It has 10 town houses in Burlington, a half-hour drive southwest of Toronto (on the way to Buffalo), an additional 18 in nearby Oakville, dozens near the corner of Bay and Bloor streets, and two dozen more in such fine neighborhoods as Rosedale, Forest Hill, and the Annex. These quality miniapartments have fully equipped kitchens and vastly greater space and privacy than conventional hotel rooms. They might be particularly attractive to business travelers who are in the city for several days or even weeks, and who find most hotel rooms claustrophobic. *40 St. Mary St., M4Y 2S8, tel. 416/923–3000. All suites. AE, D, MC, V.*

Family Farms

It's daring and different, but families with children might find it exciting to stay on a farm, not far from the city of Toronto. Including bed-and-breakfast, rates range from as low as $35 to $60 a night for two on weekends, to about $200 per person for a week. For further information on family farm vacations—in both summer and winter—write, enclosing a big envelope and a 60¢ stamp, to **Ontario Vacation Farm Association** (R.R. 2, Alma, Ont., N0B 1A0; tel. 519/846–9788).

Camping

This is a very citified area; the only location offering tent and trailer camping within Metro Toronto is **Glen Rouge Park,** 25 acres in the city's northeast end. Its attractions include nature trails, horseback riding, and proximity to the city's fabulous zoo. For a list of licensed private campgrounds and trailer parks, write to Travel Information, Ministry of Industry and Tourism, Third Floor, Hearst Block, Queen's Park, Toronto M7A 2E5. A list of provincial parks and recreation and conservation areas is available from Provincial Parks Information, Whitney Block, Queen's Park, Toronto M7A 1W3.

7 The Arts and Nightlife

The Arts

Toronto is the capital of the lively arts in Canada. True, Winnipeg has a very fine ballet, and Montreal's orchestra is superb. But in nearly every aspect of music, opera, dance, and theater, Toronto is truly the New York City of the North.

It was not always this way; before 1950—four decades ago—Toronto had no opera company, no ballet, and very little theater worthy of the title "professional." Then came the Massey Report on the Arts, one of those government-sponsored studies that usually helps put sensitive subjects on the back burner for several more years, but in this case, all Heaven broke loose: Money began to come from a variety of government grants; two prominent Canadian millionaires passed to their reward, and their death taxes were put toward the creation of a Canada Council, which doled out more money; the Canadian Opera Company, CBC television, and the National Ballet of Canada were born; and a number of little theaters began to pop up, culminating in an artistic explosion throughout the 1970s, in every aspect of the arts.

The reasons for this explosion were many: massive immigration from more culturally nourished countries of Eastern and Central Europe, as well as from England; a growing sense of independence from the mother country; a recognition that if Canada was not to develop its own arts, then the damned Yankees would do it for them; and, in general, a growing civic and cultural maturity.

Some of Toronto's impressive growth in the lively arts was sheer chance; after all, who can explain the miracle of pianist Glenn Gould's birth in this city, or the fact that ballet master Baryshnikov decided to defect here and later came often to teach and dance with the National Ballet of Canada?

But it would not be fair to pass it off as simply as that. Toronto was like an awkward, gawky teenager for many decades, it's true, but there were always a number of cultural events happening; the city did not suddenly give birth to art overnight, like Athena bursting out, fully clothed and mature, from the head of Zeus.

The best places to get information on cultural events are in the Friday editions of the *Toronto Star* (its "What's On" section is superlative); the Saturday (weekend) *Globe and Mail* (whose entertainment section is the most critically solid); the free, weekly *Now* and *eye* newspapers, as well as *Toronto Life*. To obtain half-price tickets on the day of a performance, don't forget the **Five Star Tickets booth,** located in the Royal Ontario Museum lobby during the winter and, at other times, at the corner of Yonge Street and Dundas Street, outside the Eaton Centre. The museum booth is open daily noon–6, and Tuesday and Thursday to 7; the Yonge and Dundas booth is open—in good weather—Monday–Saturday, noon–7:30, and Sunday, 11–3. Tickets are sold for cash only, all sales are final, and a small service charge is added to the price of each ticket. The booth outside the Eaton Centre also gives out piles of superb brochures and pamphlets on the city.

Concert Halls and Theaters

The **Roy Thomson Hall** (just below the CN Tower) has become since 1982 the most important concert hall in Toronto.

It was to have been named the New Massey Hall, since it was replacing the much-loved original, which had served Toronto since 1894. But then the family of billionaire newspaper magnate Lord Thomson of Fleet gave the largest single donation ($4.5 million of its $43 million cost) and gave his name to the hall instead. Critics were silenced by the beauty of the hall's design and the sensitivity of its acoustics. It is the home today of the Toronto Symphony and the Toronto Mendelssohn Choir, one of the world's finest choral groups. It also hosts orchestras from around the world and popular entertainers from Liza Minelli to Anne Murray. *60 Simcoe St., at corner of King Street W., a block west of University Ave.; tel. 416/593-4828. Tickets $20–$60 (best seats rows H and J in Orchestra and row L upstairs). Rush seats ($10) sold day of performance, beginning two hours before show time. Daily tours, highlighting the acoustic and architectural features of the stunning structure, take place Mon.–Sat., 12:30 PM (cost: $3). Call to confirm; tours subject to cancellation (tel. 416/593-4822, ext. 363). There are also tours of its impressive organ on Wed. at 12:30 (cost: $5).*

Massey Hall has always been cramped and dingy, but its near-perfect acoustics and its handsome, U-shape tiers sloping down to the stage have made it a happy place to hear the Toronto Symphony, or almost anyone else in the world of music, for nearly a century. The nearly 2,800 seats are not terribly comfortable, and a small number are blocked by pillars that hold up the ancient structure, but it remains a venerable place to catch the greats and near-greats of the music world. *178 Victoria St. at Shuster St., just a block north of Queen St. and a few feet east of Eaton Centre; tel. 416/593-4828. Best seats are rows G–M, center, and in balcony, rows 32–50.*

The **Edward Johnson Building,** in the Bloor Street/University Avenue area, houses the **MacMillan Theatre,** and it is an important place to hear avant-garde artists and the stars of the future. Because it's run by the faculty of music of the University of Toronto, the academic year also brings serious jazz trios and baroque chamber works—at little or no cost. The U of T newspaper, *The Varsity,* found across campus, often lists concerts planned for this special place. *Behind McLaughlin Planetarium, just south of Royal Ontario Museum subway exit; tel. 416/978-3744.*

The **O'Keefe Centre** has become the home of the Canadian Opera Company and the National Ballet of Canada. It is also home to visiting comedians, pre-Broadway musicals, rock stars, and almost anyone else who can fill it. When it was built in 1960, its 3,167 seats made it the largest concert hall on the continent. The acoustics leave much to be desired, and its cavernous nature makes almost anything but the most lavish opera or musical seem dwarfed, but you will still feel as if you were attending a cultural event. The city owns the building now and offers half-price seats to students and senior citizens for many of its shows. *1 Front St. E, a block east of Union Station; tel. 416/872-2262. Tickets $25–$60. Try for seats close to A47–48; avoid very front rows, such as AA, BB, etc.*

About 50 yards east of the O'Keefe is the **St. Lawrence Centre for the Arts.** Since 1970, it has been presenting everything from live theater to string quartets and forums on city issues. The main hall, the luxuriously appointed **Bluma Appel Theatre,** hosts the often brilliant productions of the **Canadian Stage Company** and **Theatre Plus.** Classical and contemporary plays are often on a level with the best of Broadway and London's West End. *Front St. at the corner of Scott St., a block east of Yonge St., two blocks from Union Station; tel. 416/366–7723. Tickets $15–$35. Try for rows E–N, seats 1–10.*

The other important theater in the city is the **Royal Alexandra,** which has been the place to be seen in Toronto since its opening in 1907. The plush red seats, gold brocade, and baroque swirls and curlicues all make theater-going a refined experience. It's astonishing to recall that all this magnificence was about to be torn down in the 1960s but was rescued by none other than "Honest Ed" Mirvish of discount-store fame. He not only restored the theater to its former glory but also made it profitable. *Les Misérables* ran from March 1989 through May 1990, and returned in the summer of 1991, after a full year crisscrossing Canada. It's a marvelous production. *260 King St. W, a few blocks west of University Ave., two blocks southwest of CN Tower; tel. 416/872–3333. Tickets $30–$60. Student tickets can be as low as $12. Avoid rows A and B; try for rows C–L center. For musicals, try first rows of first balcony.*

Since the summer of 1989, the gigantic **SkyDome** has been opening its doors (and roof, in good weather). Although its expressed purpose is for baseball and football, its 70,000 seats are often used for concerts—more than likely rock. *Located on the south side of Front St., just west of CN Tower; tel. 416/341–3663.*

The most exciting new theater is the **Pantages,** a 1920 vaudeville theater, which was turned into a complex of half a dozen movie theaters. In 1988-89, the Cineplex/Odeon people poured some $18 million into refurbishing the theater as a majestic work of art. In the fall of 1989, a Canadian company of *Phantom of the Opera* opened, and the show should run well into the 1990s. Tickets can be ordered through Ticketmaster. Tickets are $56, $67, $78, and $91, and most audiences seem to believe that only the most expensive seats have decent sightlines and are worth the money. The Lloyd Webber score is only so-so, and the book is unimpressive, in spite of its world-wide success. Still, the production is first-class, with a wonderful set, fabulous costumes, and superior singing. And the theater itself is one of the most beautiful in the world. *263 Yonge St., just a half-block south of Dundas St., across from Eaton Centre; tel. 416/872–2222. Performances Tues.–Sat. 8 PM; Wed. 2 PM, Sun. 3 PM.*

The other major concert/theater halls in the Toronto area are in **Stratford** and **Niagara-on-the-Lake** (*see* Chapter 8).

Classical Concerts

The Toronto Symphony, now over 65 years old, is not about to retire. Since 1922, with conductors of the quality of Seiji Ozawa, Walter Susskind, Sir Thomas Beecham, and Andrew Davis, it has achieved world acclaim. Its music director in 1991, briefly, was Maestro Gunther Helbig. When the TS is home, it presents about three concerts weekly from September to May

> This trip
> we found a
> road less
> traveled.
> And the
> perfect way
> to see it.

Vacation Cars. Vacation Prices. Wherever you travel, Budget offers you a wide selection of quality cars – from economy models to roomy minivans and even convertibles. You'll find them all at competitively low rates that include unlimited mileage. At over 1500 locations in the U.S. and Canada. For information and reservations, call your travel consultant or Budget at **800-527-0700**. In Canada, call **800-268-8900**.

Budget

THE SMART MONEY IS ON BUDGET.®

We feature Lincoln-Mercury and other fine cars.   *A system of corporate and licensee owned locations.*

2½ Hours
VHS-C

2½ Hours
8mm

SONY

PACK WISELY.

Given a choice, the seasoned traveler always carries less.
Case in point: Sony Handycam® camcorders, America's most
popular. They record up to 2½ hours on a single tape.
VHS-C tapes record only 30 minutes.* And why carry five tapes
when you can record everything on one? Which brings us
to the first rule of traveling: pack a Sony Handycam camcorder.

American Express offers Travelers Cheques built for two.

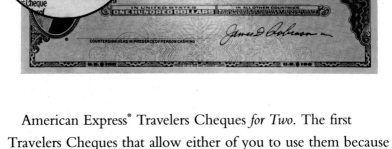

American Express® Travelers Cheques *for Two*. The first Travelers Cheques that allow either of you to use them because both of you have signed them. And only one of you needs to be present to purchase them.

Cheques *for Two* are accepted anywhere regular American Express Travelers Cheques are, which is just about everywhere. So stop by before your next trip and ask for Cheques *for Two*.

Travelers Cheques

in Roy Thomson Hall and a miniseason each summer at Ontario Place. *60 Simcoe St., on King St., just west of University Ave.; tel. 416/593–4828. Tickets $16–$35.*

The **Toronto Mendelssohn Choir** often guests with the Toronto Symphony. This 180-singer group, going since 1894, has been applauded worldwide, and its *Messiah* is handeled well every Christmas (no, we couldn't resist that). *For program information, tel. 416/598–0422; for tickets, Roy Thomson Hall, tel. 416/ 593–4828.*

The **Elmer Isler Singers,** a fine group of nearly two dozen members, has also performed around the globe, and is a respected Toronto choir. *Tel. 416/482–1664.*

The **Orford String Quartet,** another world-class musical group, is based in Toronto at the Edward Johnson Building. *Tel. 416/ 978–3744.*

Tafelmusik ("table music") is a local orchestra that goes for baroque music on original instruments. *St. Paul Centre at Trinity Church, 427 Bloor St. W, near Spadina Ave. subway stop; tel. 416/964–6337.*

Music at Sharon is a marvelous concert series that takes place on weekends every July in the Sharon Temple, located in a small town about a 45-minute drive north of downtown Toronto. The old temple has wonderful acoustics. For over a decade, concerts have ranged from flute offerings and humor in music to Haydn afternoons (and evenings). *Sharon is 4 km north of Newmarket, which is just above Hwy. 9, after taking Don Valley Parkway/Hwy. 404 north from 401. Tel. 416/478–2431, or write to Music at Sharon, Box 331, Sharon, Ont. L0G 1V0.*

Pop and Rock Concerts

Most major international recording companies have offices in Toronto, so it's not by chance that the city is a regular stop for top musical performers of today, including Frank Sinatra, Billy Joel, Whitney Houston, Sting, Michael Jackson, and Bruce Springsteen. Tickets ($15–$40) can usually be booked through **Ticketmaster** (tel. 416/872–1111).

Major venues include the **SkyDome,** just west of the CN Tower, on Front Street, tel. 416/963–3513; **Maple Leaf Gardens,** 60 Carlton Street, a block east of Yonge Street and the College Street subway stop, tel. 416/977–1641; the **O'Keefe Centre,** Yonge and Front streets, tel. 416/872–2262; and **Exhibition Stadium,** at the CNE grounds, tel. 416/393–6000.

Ontario Place (tel. 416/965–7711) has pop, rock, and jazz concerts throughout its summer season at extremely modest prices. This is one of the loveliest and least expensive places to see and hear a concert in all of Toronto.

Kingswood Music Theatre, next to Canada's Wonderland, also has important rock and pop concerts during the warmer months. *Located along Hwy. 400, 10 min north of Hwy. 401; tel. 416/832–8131. Admission usually less than $10 above cost of entry to Canada's Wonderland.*

Superstars Niteclub is a new venue for popular concerts. Opened in May 1989, this 1,700-seat club is the largest in the Metro Toronto area, presenting comedy, pop, rock, jazz, and

more. Shows are Monday–Wednesday, with weekends dedi-
cated to dance. *6487 Dixie Rd., 1 mi. north of Hwy. 401, just
west of airport, tel. 416/670–2211. Open Thurs.–Sun. 7 PM–
1:30 AM; closed Sun., except for "unlicensed" (aka no booze)
events for teens. Shows cost $10–$25, with dance nights in $8–
$10 range.*

Opera

Since its founding in 1950, the **Canadian Opera Company** has
grown into the largest producer of opera in Canada and the
fifth largest company on the continent. From the most popular
operas, such as *Carmen* and *Madama Butterfly*, usually performed in the original language, to more modern or rare works,
such as *Jenufa*, and the erotic success of 1988, *Lady Macbeth of
Mtsensk*, the COC has proven trustworthy and often daring.

Each year, at Toronto's O'Keefe Centre, more than 150,000
people attend its season of seven operas, which have included
such memorable productions as Canada's first presentation of
Benjamin Britten's *Death in Venice*, the North American premiere of Tchaikovsky's *Joan of Arc*, and the continent's second
presentation of the complete three-act *Lulu* by Alban Berg.

Like all important companies, the COC often hosts world-class
performers such as Joan Sutherland, Grace Bumbry, Martina
Arroyo, Marilyn Horne, and Canada's own Louis Quilico and
Maureen Forrester. The company also pioneered the use of
surtitles, which allow the audience to follow the libretto in English in a capsulized translation. The COC also performs mini-
operas in a tent during the summer, down at Harbourfront, on
the shores of Lake Ontario. *Tel. 416/363–8231 or 416/393–7469.*

Dance

The Bolshoi is two centuries old; the **National Ballet of Canada**
can trace itself all the way back to November 12, 1951, when it
made its official debut on the cramped stage of the old Eaton
Auditorium on College Street. In less than four decades, the
company has done some extraordinary things and reaped some
revered awards, with such principal dancers as Karen Kain,
Frank Augustyn, Kevin Pugh, and Owen Montague all wowing
the Russians at the Moscow competitions. Today, Canada's premier dance company has 70 dancers; it is the third largest
troupe in North America and the fifth largest in the world. *Performances Nov., Feb., and May at O'Keefe Centre, at corner of
Front and Yonge Sts.; in summer at Ontario Pl. Office, tel. 416/
362–1041, 416/872–1111 or 416/872–2277; O'Keefe Centre, 416/
872–2262. Tickets $15–$55.*

Toronto Dance Theatre, its roots in the Martha Graham tradition, is the oldest contemporary dance company in the city.
Since its beginnings in the 1960s, it has created close to 100
works, over a third using original scores commissioned from
Canadian composers. It tours Canada and has played major festivals in England, Europe, and the United States. After a decade of steady success, it purchased a beautiful renovated
church, St. Enoch's, built in 1891, and a neighboring hall in the
heart of Cabbagetown. They serve as home for its school and
over three dozen full-time students. *Most performances are in*

the Premiere Dance Theatre, at Harbourfront Centre, 235 Queen's Quay W; tel. 416/869–8444.

Dancemakers is another important Toronto modern-dance company, drawing on everyone from Martha Graham to Jose Limon and Merce Cunningham. It performs at both the Premiere Dance Theatre and Solar Stage (First Canadian Pl., on King St. near Bay St.; tel. 416/368–5135 or 416/535–8880).

Theater

There are over four dozen performing spaces in Toronto; we will mention only a handful of the most prominent.

The **Royal Alexandra**, the **O'Keefe**, and the **St. Lawrence Centre** are described in our Historic Buildings and Sites section, above.

The **Young People's Theatre** is the only theater center in the country devoted solely to children. But unlike purveyors of much of traditional children's fare, this place does not condescend or compromise its dramatic integrity. *165 Front St. E, near Sherbourne St., 8 blocks east of Yonge St. Take Yonge St. subway to King St. and then King St. streetcar east, and walk down one block. Tel. 416/864–9732.*

The **Tarragon Theatre,** located in an unpleasant area of railroad tracks and old factories, is the natural habitat for indigenous Canadian theater. Almost anything worthwhile in this country's drama first saw the light of day here. *30 Bridgman Ave., 1 block east of Bathurst St. and north of Dupont St.; tel. 416/531–1827.*

Le Théâtre Français de Toronto, until recently known as Le Théâtre du P'tit Bonheur, has been providing French-language drama of high quality for many years. Its repertoire has ranged from classical to contemporary, from both France and French Canada. Recently it moved to a marvelous location at Harbourfront, next door to the stunning Queen's Quay Terminal. In 1988, the theater performed a bilingual play, so English-speaking theatergoers could follow along. *The DuMaurier Centre, 231 Queen's Quay W, tel. 416/534–6604.*

Théâtre Passe Muraille, in the unfashionable area of Bathurst and Queen streets, has long been the home of fine collaborative theater—Canadian, good, innovative. *16 Ryerson Ave., running north from Queen St. W, 1 block east of Bathurst St.; tel. 416/363–2416.*

Toronto Free Theatre, although no longer free (and recently joining forces with the major Canadian Stage Company, which operates out of the St. Lawrence Centre), remains freewheeling and fascinating. This space has seen most of Canada's finest performers and playwrights showing their wares. *26 Berkeley St., just south of Front St. and 1 block west of Parliament St.; tel. 416/368–2856.*

The **Elgin** and **Winter Garden Theaters** are two of the newest/oldest jewels in the crown of the Toronto arts scene. Both are old vaudeville places, stacked upon one another (The Elgin, downstairs, has about 1,500 seats, and is more suited for musicals; the Winter Garden, upstairs, is some 500 seats smaller, and more initmate; both are stunningly attractive.) Recently renovated, they have been used for jazz festivals, locally pro-

duced musicals *(The Wizard of Oz)*, and—a pleasant example—
British actor/director Kenneth Branagh's Renaissance Theatre Company's productions of *King Lear* and *A Midsummer
Night's Dream. 189 Yonge St., just north of Queen St., tel. 416/
872–5555.*

Bathurst Street Theatre, almost at the corner of Bathurst and
Bloor streets (another unfashionable address), is a church converted to theater space, but the gods have remained. The
premises are used by dance groups and many of the more interesting theater groups in the city. The pews aren't terribly comfortable, but now they don't stop in the middle of the plays and
pass the hat. *736 Bathurst St., just south of Honest Ed's, and
around the corner from Mirvish Village; tel. 416/535–0591.*

Factory Theatre is another major alternate theater devoted to
original and experimental work. *125 Bathurst St., at Adelaide
St. W; tel. 416/864–9971.*

Hart House Theatre is smack in the middle of the University of
Toronto campus and is the main theater space of the U of T.
Amateur, student, and occasional professional productions
have been presented here for a half century, many of them controversial (and uncommercial). *Just off Queen's Park Crescent
W, about one block west of Parliament buildings, and a few
blocks south of Royal Ontario Museum; tel. 416/978–8668.*

Two interesting new companies, **Nightwood Theatre** (tel. 416/
961–7202), which is a feminist collective, and **Buddies in Bad
Times** (tel. 416/593–0653), which presents poetic, musical, and
often gay productions, both appear frequently around town.
They often use **The Annex,** *730 Bathurst St., just south of Bloor
St. and next door to Bathurst Street Theatre; tel. 416/537–4193.*

Second City, the Toronto version of the famous Chicago company, is the place where the inspired SCTV series had its genesis.
Its revues tend to be the brightest, most reliable comedy in
town. *The Old Firehall Theatre, 110 Lombard St., downtown,
just east of Yonge St; tel. 416/863–1162.*

Two of the most entertaining presentations of the past few
years are free and take place in two major parks each July and
early August: Skylight Theatre and Dream in High Park, the
latter named after its original production of Shakespeare's *A
Midsummer Night's Dream.*

Since the summer of 1988, **Skylight Theatre** has had a new am-
phitheater. And it is well deserved; some of its productions over
the past few years—*The Little Prince, Frankenstein, Twelfth
Night*—have been better than many in Stratford. It is top-
notch theater. *Earl Bales Park, tel. 416/781–4846. Take Bloor
St. subway to Bathurst St., then Bathurst St. bus about a mile
north of Hwy. 401. You enter park at Bainbridge Ave., a few
blocks south of Sheppard Ave. W. Admission free.*

Dream in High Park, now a half-dozen years old, presents quali-
ty productions of Shakespeare (and occasionally a musical) each
July in the heart of Toronto's most glorious area, High Park.
The open-air productions are usually a knockout. *Bloor and
Keele Sts., tel. 416/368–2856. Take Bloor St. subway to High
Park stop, then walk south into park.*

Dinner Theater There are many local productions of Broadway musicals and
comedies presented in Toronto's numerous dinner theaters.

These include **Harper's East** (38 Lombard St., downtown; tel. 416/863–6223) and **Limelight Dinner Theatre** (2026 Yonge St., just below Eglinton Ave.; tel. 416/482–5200). This city just doesn't stop.

Mysteriously Yours . . . should be of special interest to murder-mystery buffs. On Thursday, Friday, and Saturday evenings, a "despicable crime" is perpetrated at the Royal York Hotel. Cocktails begin at 6:30; the mystery begins to unravel during dinner and is solved after dinner, by 10. The complete dinner and mystery costs $50–$60 per person, including tax and tip. Call Brian Caws at 416/486–7469 or 800/NOT–DEAD.

Film

Every September since 1976, Toronto has been holding a world-class film festival, called—with no great modesty—**The Festival of Festivals** (tel. 416/967–7371). Whether retrospectives consist of the films of Marguerite Duras, Jean-Luc Godard, and Max Ophuls, or tributes to the careers of Martin Scorsese, Robert Duvall, and John Schlesinger, this is the time for lovers of film.

Toronto is one of the film capitals of the world, and you can often catch a movie here that is not showing anywhere else—or even available on video. The Cineplex concept, which now has over 1,500 screens across North America, was created in Toronto; the multiscreened one in Eaton Centre was its genesis. Foreigners will be either delighted or disappointed to discover that Toronto is still subject to the strange machinations of a provincial—in more ways than one—censor board, and therefore has no friendly neighborhood porno movies.

Fox Beaches (2236 Queen St. E, tel. 416/691–7330) is an old-style movie house that will flood anyone over 40 with warm nostalgia.

Reg Hartt Presents is one of the more delightful traditions of underground film in the city. On various days each month, in the Grapevine Room of the Diamond Club (410 Sherbourne St. north of Carlton), this movie-maniac maven will show such films as *The History of Animation* and *The Uncensored History of Warner Brothers Looney Tunes & Merrie Melodies*. ("Warning: Many of these cartoons are sexist, racist, and as violent as a two-by-four in the face!" read his ads.) *Admission: $7–$10. Tel. 416/964–2739.*

Carlton Cinemas, part of the Cineplex chain, shows rare, important films from around the world in nearly a dozen screening rooms. *20 Carlton St., just steps east of College St. subway; tel. 416/296–FILM.*

Ontario Film Theatre is in the Ontario Science Centre. A provincially funded film house, it is much admired for its foreign art films and retrospectives. *770 Don Mills Rd., near Eglinton Ave. E; tel. 416/429–4100.*

Other places in Toronto with regular showings of important films and film series—often free or close to it—include the **Art Gallery of Ontario** (317 Dundas St. W, tel. 416/977–0414); **Harbourfront Centre** (235 Queen's Quay W, tel. 416/973–4000); the **Metro Toronto Reference Library** (789 Yonge St., tel. 416/393–7141); **Innis Film Society** of the University of Toronto (2

Sussex Ave., tel. 416/588–8940); **Cinesphere,** at Ontario Place (955 Lakeshore Blvd. W, tel. 416/965–7711); and the **Royal Ontario Museum** (100 Queen's Park Crescent, at Bloor St. and University Ave., tel. 416/586–5549).

Nightlife

Jazz Clubs

As recently as the 1991 edition of this guide, we complained that "jazz in Toronto has dried up considerably over the past few years." Not true anymore! In spite of the sad passing of the wonderful **Café des Copains,** a whole slew of new places have opened up across Toronto, providing superior jazz and happy audiences once again.

Top O' The Senator is this city's first club exclusively for jazz, and, sitting right atop the Senator diner, the room has the atmosphere of a between-the-wars jazz lounge. With its long wooden bar and dark-blue, towering ceilings, this is one fabulous 125-seat place. *249 Victoria St., tel. 416/364–7517.*

Bermuda Onion Restaurant and Jazz Club provides endless neon, aluminum tables, and some of the best jazz in Toronto— sitting incongruously on the second floor of The Colonnade, just southeast of the hot corner of Bloor Street and University Avenue. There's even a Sunday jazz brunch! *131 Bloor St. W, tel. 416/925–1470.*

A few blocks east of the Eaton Centre is **George's Spaghetti House** (290 Dundas St. E, corner of Sherbourne St.; tel. 416/ 923–9887), the oldest continuously running jazz club in the city. The music starts at 8:30 PM, with the world-famous Moe Koffman (of Swinging Shepherd Blues fame) performing one week each month. (For Moe, and on weekends, you'll need reservations.) George's has a modest cover charge and a decent Italian menu. *Closed Sun.*

Chick 'n Deli has long been one of the great jazz places in Toronto. A casual atmosphere prevails, and the lack of a dress code helps with the neighborhood-bar ambience. There's a dance floor and dark wood everywhere, giving it a pub-like feel. It's also famous for wings and live music; the former half-price, Mon.–Tues. until 9, the latter playing at 9 PM most nights, and 7:30 on Sundays. Check out the occasional earlier jazz shows, and the Sunday brunch—all you can eat for less than $10. *744 Mount Pleasant Rd., near Eglinton Ave.; tel. 416/489–3363 or 489–7931.*

Meyer's Deli is convenient to downtown and midtown hotels (69 Yorkville Ave., near Bay and Bloor Sts., tel. 416/960–4780). It is an attractive deli with solid, Jewish-style food, cheesecake worth killing or at least maiming for, and some of the better jazz to be experienced in Toronto. Here is where you can hear late-night sets Thursday, 9–1, Friday and Saturday 9:30–2 AM. This being Toronto, there's no alcohol served after 1 AM.

Rock

Since May 1989, **Superstars Niteclub** has been packing 1,700 people nightly into its giant room. Mondays through Wednesdays, it has highly professional acts, on the line of The Fixx and Jerry Seinfeld, with prices ranging from $10 to $25. Thursdays to Saturdays are for dancing, with a cover of around $9. Hamburgers, chicken fingers, etc., provide the fuel. Laws banning liquor from being served on Sundays have freed the owners to use the place for children's and teen's concerts, featuring rap groups. *6487 Dixie Rd., 1 mi. north of Hwy. 401, and just west of airport; tel. 416/670-2211. Open Thurs.–Sun., 7 PM–1:30 AM.*

Upstairs, above the Spadina Hotel, along an unfashionable strip of King Street, is the very popular **Cabana Room.** Paneling recalling the rec room of your youth is combined with crazy red wallpaper—all the better to watch some of the local talent. There's no food, the cover charge varies, and long hair and jeans are worn by all. Everything goes here, from garage bands to country and folk groups. It's an endless party every night but Sunday, from 8 PM on. *460 King St. W, tel. 416/368-0729.*

Along Bloor Street West is **Clinton's Tavern,** which has been described as "the city's best taproom with a stage view." There's only a tiny dance floor, but this is where the brilliant Cowboy Junkies have put on shows. The logs on the walls may be fake, but not the great rock. *693 Bloor St. W, tel. 416/535-1429.*

Not far away is **Cameron Public House,** a small, eclectic kind of place. The music here alternates from jazz to hard rock to new wave; "alternative music," they proudly call it. Because it's close to the Ontario College of Art, the Cameron gets a creative crowd, with many regulars. The suburbanite scene gets heavy on weekends, as do the crowds. *408 Queen St. W, tel. 416/364-0811.*

Pop rock reigns at the famous **Horseshoe Tavern,** also along the Queen Street strip. Good bands perform here, six days a week, with no food but lots of booze and a cover charge. It's a real tavern, with a pool table, lots of flannel-shirt types, mostly blue collar. Rock memorabilia lines the walls, and far more men than women line the bar. On weeknights, the ages range from 25 to 40; on weekends, it's younger. For over four decades, the Horseshoe was known across the city as the tavern with entertainment, especially country music. (Charlie Pride, Tex Ritter, Hank Williams, Loretta Lynn all played here.) There's lots of country-style dancing, but also live roots, blues, and rockabilly: "Conway Twitty meets Chuck Berry," according to one critic. *370 Queen St. W, corner of Spadina Ave.; tel. 416/598-4753. Closed Sun.*

A major showcase for more daring arts in Toronto has long been **The Rivoli,** along the Queen Street "mall." A place for new, local artists not yet established enough to have their own gallery showings, the back room functions as a club, with theater happenings, "new music" (progressive rock and jazz), comedy troupes providing very funny improvisations twice a month, and more. Try to catch the "Poetry Sweatshop" every fourth Wednesday, in which local, nonliterary personalities judge various poets. Dinner for two, without alcohol, runs about $25. *332 Queen St. W, just west of University Ave.; tel. 416/596-1908. No dress code. Cover charge $5–$10. Closed Sun.*

Rhythm and Blues

The undisputed champion of R&B in Toronto is **Club Bluenote,** a few blocks north of the Yorkville area. It's unique, with many world-class musicians and singers frequenting it, and occasionally getting up and doing their stuff. The dance floor's small, but who cares, with so much talent hanging around? The age range is 25–50, and the clientele is upper class. And this is no hit bar; people come here to listen to music in a serious way. When Whitney Houston, Sugar Ray Leonard, et al., are in town, this is where they go. *128 Pears Ave., just north of Davenport Rd. and west of Avenue Rd.; tel. 416/924–8244. Usually closed Sun. Cover charge: $10 range.*

Blues jams don't stop at the very hot **Down Towne Browne's,** just on the edge of the theater district. Here one can enjoy live blues, R&B, and jazz, with three sets nightly, starting at 9:30 PM. The "open-stage blues jams" every Sunday attract enthusiastic crowds. Finger food and light snacks are available. *49 Front St. E, tel. 416/367–4949.*

Albert's Hall has been called one of the top 25 bars in all of North America, in spite of its shabby decor. It features top blues bands. The crowd's older and more laid-back than downstairs, in the Brunswick, but it's still noisy and friendly—and *loud. 481 Bloor St. W, near Spadina Ave., tel. 416/964–2242. Cover charge on weekends; closed Sun.*

Black Swan was an old-time bar for three quarters of a century; today, its 120 customers nightly watch, listen and tap toes to wonderful, live rhythm and blues. Located out in the east end—where Bloor Street turns magically into "The Danforth," on the other side of the Don Valley Parkway—this spot will zap classic R&B lovers back into the 1960s. *154 Danforth Ave., tel. 416/469–0537.*

Chicago's, along the delightful Queen Street West strip, heading west from University Avenue, is a real charmer. Downstairs is a cowboyish bar and good hamburgers; upstairs is where you can see and hear the blues stars of tomorrow, and the day after. Dig the red neon sign in the shape of a beer cap. *335 Queen St. W, tel. 416/598–3301.*

Surrounded by Chinese eateries and discount stores, the old, raunchy **Grossman's Tavern** has the best Saturday afternoons in the city. As one writer has noted, "long established, but never entirely reputable, Grossman's is perhaps a little too elemental for more refined tastes, but it's hard to imagine a more apt home for the blues." *379 Spadina Ave, tel. 416/977–7000.*

Reggae and Caribbean

BamBoo is listed in our restaurant section because its Thai/Caribbean food is remarkably delicious and just as remarkably reasonably priced. But this crazy old building, a one-time commercial laundry hidden behind the popular Queen Street strip, is where to find everything from reggae to calypso, Caribbean to African, and even jazz. The sightlines can be terrible, it's no place for a quiet conversation, but it's wildly popular: great eating, and great music. *312 Queen St. W, tel. 416/593–5771.*

Bars

There is something to be said for the province's liquor laws. Having a legal drinking age of 19 and a police force that regularly stops cars (whether driven suspiciously or not—something unconstitutional in the United States) to check the driver's sobriety with a Breathalyzer has cut down on drunken driving considerably. All the police have to discover is a greater amount than .08% of alcohol in the blood level of a driver and it's jail.

For a European atmosphere and a friendly, relaxed place to meet people, one of the most popular bars is **The Amsterdam.** It was recently voted "the most crowded bar," and although its busiest night is Thursday, it's jammed every business day at 5. Expect a 20- to 60-minute wait Thursday–Saturday evenings. The clientele is Bay Street—up-and-coming stockbrokers and business types. On weekends, suburbanites come out, and the population turns younger. The fixed menu is low ($10–$15), and reservations are a must. The extensive beer list includes three homemade brews. *133 John St., near University Ave. and Queen St.; tel. 416/595–8201. No cover.*

In the middle of the ever-popular Yorkville area is the **Bellair Cafe,** *the* meeting place in Toronto. The outdoor patios are lovely in the summer, and the upstairs lounge has been converted to the Club Bellair, an ever-so-trendy, glitzy dancing spot, with a DJ spinning the top 40. The dress code is "upscale casual to evening attire." It's a moneyed crowd, ages 25–55 and *très* sophisticated; if you wear gray, you might vanish into the ultramodern surroundings. *100 Cumberland St., tel. 416/964–2222. No cover.*

In the unfashionable Bathurst Street/Spadina Avenue area is the ever-popular **Brunswick House,** where "Rocking Irene" has been singing for centuries. Doctors and lawyers keep coming back to visit their old favorite watering hole, to hear the same songstress of their university days. (It's near the University of Toronto.) Irene's repertoire is of the "Roll Out the Barrel" variety, and everyone sings and drinks along. It's loud, raucous, and fun. *481 Bloor St. W, tel. 416/964–2242. No cover.*

One of the most crowded singles' bars in Toronto is **Hemingway's,** also conveniently located in the Yorkville area. Three-quarters are regulars, middle- to upper-class professionals, and not as pretentious as the bar's name. The atmosphere is sort of homey here, and it's less tense than at other Yorkville hangouts. The stand-up bar has a nice and easy atmosphere, and the decor is not glitzy, but literary, with a green interior, comfortable high-back chairs, mirrors, artsy posters, and real, live books lining one wall. As of 1991, this has also become a home to pop, MOR (middle-of-the-road), and blues, with nightly entertainment. Sunday evenings, R&B predominates. And there are even Australian and New Zealand theme nights! Dress is casual—just as Ernest would have wanted. *142 Cumberland St., near Avenue Rd. and Bloor St.; tel. 416/968–2828. No cover.*

Remy's seems to top the list of places for successful people to go in the early 1990s: Being right next door to the elegant Four Seasons Hotel means that Jane Fonda and nearly everyone else filming in Toronto seems to end up here. It's very elegant, so if you see casually attired men at the bar, you can be sure they can afford to look scruffy. The decor is European-inspired, all brass and shiny. There's an outdoor patio, three bars, and a restaurant where two can eat from the Italian menu for $50, including wine. *115 Yorkville Ave.; near Avenue Rd.; tel. 416/968–9429.*

Bemelmans is all chandeliers, mirrors, marble, wood, and great beauty. The patio is lovely, but the real action is the crowded bar, where performers and artists pour in after their shows. (It doesn't hurt to have a 3 AM closing time, a rarity in this once staunchly WASP city.) And just a few hundred feet away from the heart of the city, Bloor and Yonge streets. *83 Bloor St. W., tel. 416/960–0306.*

Comedy Clubs

Second City, just east of the heart of downtown, has been providing some of the best comedy in Toronto—and North America—since its owner Andrew Alexander bought the rights to the name from its Chicago godfather, Bernie Sahlins, for one dollar. Interestingly, Alexander recently bought the original company and has since opened other clubs in London, Ontario, and Los Angeles—Canadian imperialism in action. This converted fire hall has given much to the world, through both *Saturday Night Live* and the inspired *SCTV* series. Among those who have cut their teeth on the Toronto stage are Gilda Radner, Dan Aykroyd, Martin Short, Andrea Martin, Catherine O'Hara, and John Candy. Shows can be seen alone or as part of a dinner-theater package. Try to catch the free improvisations, Monday–Thursday at 10:30 PM, when the troupe works out new material for future shows. *110 Lombard St., corner of Jarvis St., just a few blocks northeast of Front and Yonge Sts.; tel. 416/863–1111.*

Every Wednesday at 8 PM, would-be actors and comics get together for a night of improvisational work at **Theatresports,** down in the Harbourfront area. Two "teams" compete at different exercises, with three judges grading each sketch. Audience participation is the key, because it must dictate the character/situation of the various skits. Sometimes it's wonderfully funny, and you can catch fresh talent before it's discovered. *Water's Edge Cafe, 235 Queen's Quay W, on Lake Ontario; tel. 416/756–2444. Cover charge: $7.*

Next to Second City, **Yuk-Yuk's Komedy Kabaret** has always been the major place for comedy in Toronto. This is where the zany comedian Howie Mandel and the inspired impressionist Jim Carrey got their start, and where such comic luminaries as George Carlin, Rodney Dangerfield, Robin Williams, and Mort Sahl have presented their best routines. Down on Bay Street, Yuk Yuk's has its amateur night on Monday. Up on Yonge Street and Eglinton Avenue, new talent pipes up on Tuesdays. A dinner-show package can run $25 and up per person. *1280 Bay St., just above Bloor St.; 2335 Yonge St., just above Eglinton Ave.; and 5165 Dixie, just above Eglinton; tel. 416/967–6425. No dress code. Cover charge: $8 and up. The Bay and Dixie locations are open Sun.*

Dancing

Berlin quickly became one of the most popular spots in Toronto, within a year of its opening in early 1987. There's no dress code, but people dress up for this upscale, European-styled multilevel club. There is a Continental menu for dining and a seven-piece band for jazz, pop, and R&B. The crowd is 25–35 years old, and very rich, and the club radiates a feeling of exclusivity. A classy cross between the BamBoo and the Imperial Room, Berlin is one very hot/cool place. *2335 Yonge St., north of Eglinton Ave.; tel. 416/489-7777. Open Tues.–Sat., to 2 or 3 AM on weekends. Cover: $6–$12.*

DJs play '60s music (downstairs) and '90s music (upstairs) in a four-story century-old fun house named **Big Bop.** Drinks Wednesday nights cost $2.50; Thursday nights are Ladies' Nights, with no cover for women. The decor is early bizarre and late weird; you walk in and feel as though you've already had two drinks. In rebellion against the New York School of Glitzy, there is no chrome or mirrors—just a deliberate effort to be campy, vibrant, and unpretentious. The clientele is 18–25 years old. It's a true meat market, but it doesn't pretend to be otherwise. Capacity is 800, and jeans are de rigueur. Many international stars walk in, but the owner insists that it's no big deal. (No big deal? Jack Nicholson. William Hurt. Matt Dillon.) One DJ is a grad of the Wolfman Jack School of Strangeness. You can see why the kids love it here. *651 Queen St. W, tel. 416/366-6699. Open weekends to 3 AM.*

An important after-hours club is **Focus,** which is open weekends only for a young crowd that doesn't mind staying up way past its bedtime. Hours are 8 PM–6 AM, Thurs.–Sun. No alcohol is served; music and dancing are the attractions. The music is funk, the crowd is young, and the soda pop flows like water. *11a Joseph St., one block north of Wellesley Ave. and Yonge St.; tel. 416/653-7524. Cover charge: $10 range. Dress casual, but no sneakers or jeans on Sat.*

It's out in the northeast, in the town of Markham, but the **Cotton Club** has become one of the dancing hot spots of Toronto. Here one encounters alternative and underground dance music, with DJs keeping the crowds up and moving every night of the week except Monday. "Coffee House Sunday" has live jams; cover charge on weekends is in the modest $5 range. *7750 Markham Rd., tel. 416/471-4314.*

Right on the edge of the University of Toronto campus is the double-trouble combination of **The Dance Cave,** with wild, live rock groups and dancing (open till 3 AM Fri. and Sat.), and the equally popular **Lee's Palace** downstairs, where rock-and-roll and blues are delivered by local talent. There, jams last from 8 PM on, with varying (low) cover. And dig that crazy, wild decor! *529 Bloor St. W, tel. 416/532-7632; 532-7983.*

Since it's right in the astonishing SkyDome, we mustn't ignore the **Hard Rock Cafe**'s new location. With rock-and-roll memorabilia on the walls, all-star rock jams every Monday at 8 PM, and lots of dancing to DJs (until 1 AM every night), this is one très hot spot. *Gate 1 of SkyDome, 277 Front St. W, tel. 416/341-2388. (You can't miss it; it's the only retractable dome in the world.)*

Earl's Tin Palace has been described as the star attraction of the Yonge/Eglinton/Mt. Pleasant singles scene, and it does its job well: The fashionable, affluent people have made this place their home, and many arrive in groups. The decor is stunning: a big, airy tin palace with elaborate props, such as stuffed birds. The restaurant has real cuisine, not just fries. (Dinner and drinks for two, $60.) The clientele dresses very well, with men even in (gasp) suits. The 35–40 crowd is better represented here than in most other clubs. *150 Eglinton Ave. E, not far from Yonge St.; tel. 416/487–9281. No cover.*

Back on Yorkville Avenue is **P.W.D. Dinkel's,** which has been attracting the trendies of the area for many years. The age range is 20–40, and regulars make up much of the crowd. The ratio of men to women is 50/50; the two stand-up bars are where the action is. A black-and-white–tile dance floor has the usual mirrored ball and flashing disco lights nearby. Live bands play Top-40–style, yet original, music. There's finger food and dinner at about $50 for two, with wine. *88 Yorkville Ave., tel. 416/923–9689. Open Mon.–Sun. to 2 AM. Cover charge: about $10 on weekends.*

Pete & Martys is an up-tempo rock-and-roll alternative, a DJ-and-dancing spot, often with pool tables and dining. Of the 13 members of this chain, five are in the Toronto area. All offer dancing on weekends—except the Eaton Centre location. *York Corporate Centre, 125 York Blvd., Richmond Hill, tel. 416/881–0151; 160 Eglinton Ave. E, tel. 416/482–4084; 777 Bay St. at College Park, tel. 416/596–6955; Eaton Centre, tel. 416/593–4660; 14 Duncan St. (near King St. and Spadina Ave.), tel. 416/971–9708.*

RPM, down at Harbourfront, is a psychedelic dance palace with light shows, go-go girls, and more. (Time warp, anyone?) There's a shuttle-bus service from Union Station for the young (19–25), blue-collarish, meat-market crowd. Lots of funk and pop tunes to dance to, and it's very *loud*. On Sunday, there's no alcohol, and it becomes an all-ages dance party. Wednesday is Student Night, with free admission and a complimentary buffet. Thursdays are now retro-disco nights. Upstairs, there's a nice quiet bar with lovely views of Lake Ontario. *132 Queen's Quay E, tel. 416/869–1462. Cover charge.*

A bar/club called **StiLife** recently opened downtown and is very popular. It caters to an older (25–35) crowd and to rapidly aging 40-year-olds. The decor is metallic and modular, with all the furnishings custom-made. The art is aided by sophisticated lighting. No jeans or sneakers. A DJ provides dancing music, and the clientele is Yorkville-ish, with many clothing designers, people who own other restaurants, etc. Check out the bathrooms—you'll find out why. *217 Richmond St. W, tel. 416/593–6116. Closed Sun. Cover charge: $8–$20.*

The most exciting 1950s-type place is **Studebaker's,** in the University Avenue/King Street area. It's bright and colorful, with memorabilia, a jukebox, and a DJ. During the week, it attracts a business crowd, with far more males than females. On weekends, a younger, suburban crowd gathers after 8 or 9; expect a 30-minute wait. No T-shirts. Celebs spotted here include actor Steve Guttenberg, Darryl Hall (the rock star), and G. W. Bailey (of "M*A*S*H"). *150 Pearl St., tel. 416/591–7960.*

Rockit has been described as "the mainstream dance crowd's terrestrial equivalent to rock 'n roll heaven." The pizza is dynamite, the wood-and-brass bar is gorgeous, and upstairs are the college kids in uniform (cool ties and designer jeans), dancing away to the Big Hits. Dancing to DJs on Thursday, Friday, and Saturday nights; Monday nights feature live jazz. *120 Church St., just east of Yonge, tel. 416/947–9555.*

Supper Clubs

Long known as Toronto's "last elegant supper club," the **Imperial Room** of the Royal York Hotel recently dropped its policy of giving this city Tony, Ella, and Lena. Today, it's only dining and dancing to a live band with "a big band sound playing all your requests." The room is still a knockout, and from 8 to 12, Tuesday to Thursday, and 7:30 to 12:30, Friday and Saturday, you can eat ($20–$30 each), dance, and still enjoy one of Toronto's great spaces. *100 Front St. W., opposite Union Station, tel. 416/368–2511.*

Cafés

The **Free Times Cafe** is a showcase for folk music, where singers nightly perform their own original work. The menu is "Kensington Canadian Cuisine," with both vegetarian as well as meat dishes; it's licensed and modestly priced. The decor is white stucco with stained-pine edging; the bar has café chairs with upholstered seats. Every six weeks, the original art changes. *320 College St., near Spadina Ave., on edge of University of Toronto campus; tel. 416/967–1078.*

Lounges

Up on the 51st floor of the ManuLife Centre, **The Aquarius Lounge** is the highest piano lounge in the city, even before you take your first, expensive drink. The busy time in the summer is Thursday–Saturday after 8:30 PM, but there's a high turnover, so the wait is never too long. In the winter, the lines begin as early as 8 PM. This is not a place to meet people, and it is not trendy in the way that most bars in the Yorkville area are. But its romantic atmosphere makes this a marvelous place for a date. No shorts, but jeans are allowed. *55 Bloor St. W, at Bay St.; tel. 416/967–5225.*

In the Brownstone Hotel is **Notes,** an intimate bar/restaurant with a grand piano and a grand bar around it. It's done up in pink-and-beige tones, with black-lacquer furniture and antiques. You'll find no windows here, and the lighting is dim, but it's a good, quiet place to get to know someone. Dinner for two runs about $40–$50, including wine (the fresh sole is fine). A fine pianist plays Tuesday–Saturday. *15 Charles St. E, tel. 416/924–7381.*

In the classy Four Seasons Hotel is **La Serre,** which looks like a library in a mansion: plush and green, with lots of brass and dark wood. It has a stand-up piano bar and a pianist worth standing for. Drinks, coffees, and teas are all expensive, but what can you expect in one of the costliest hotels in the country? Weekdays attract a business crowd, weekends bring out the couples. *Avenue Rd. and Yorkville Ave., tel. 416/964–0411.*

The **Park Plaza Roof Lounge** has been used as a setting in the writings of such Canadian literary luminaries as Margaret Atwood and Mordecai Richler. The decor used to be plush, in an older European style, with chandelier, marble tables, and waiters in red jackets. It remains an important hangout for the upper-middle class, businesspeople, professionals, and, *bien sûr,* literary types. Since 1990, it has been redone, but it's still gorgeous and tasteful. *In Park Plaza Hotel, Avenue Rd. and Bloor St.; tel. 416/924–5471.*

You can't get much handier to downtown Toronto than **The Silver Rail,** standing proudly opposite the Eaton Centre. Let's face it: they no longer put up taverns with 18-foot ceilings and giant mirrors. Welcome to 1947—when this place was built. *225 Yonge St., tel. 416/368–8697.*

At the corner of King and Bathurst streets sits the 143-year-old **Wheat Sheaf Tavern.** You can't get more run-down than this, in spite of its recent face-lift. But if you're in a run-down, century-old mood, it's good, solid fun. *667 King St. W, tel. 416/364–3996.*

Pubs

The best pub in town is **The Madison,** right next door to Ecology House, on the edge of the U of T campus. It has the atmosphere of an English pub, with lots of brass, burlap lampshades, solid oak bars, ceiling fans, exposed brick, and dart boards. Most important, it offers 16 brands of beer on tap, as well as a large selection of imported draft. It serves finger food, and its chicken wings, prepared literally from scratch, are famous. There is nightly piano entertainment at the second-floor bar; the bar in the basement has a fireplace and is dark and cozy. The clientele consists of students, yuppies, and a strong British/Scottish/Irish contingent. The patios are lovely in the summer. *14 Madison Ave., 1 block east of Spadina Ave., just steps north of Bloor St.; tel. 416/927–1722.*

On the edge of Cabbagetown, less than a mile east of the downtown core, is the **Queen's Head Pub.** Very quaint and typically English, it has a good lineup of imported beer and may remind you of the attic on an antique farm: fireplace, oodles of oak, and mahogany. Flowers on the wallpaper, pâté sandwiches on the plate, chandeliers on the ceiling, beer in the belly. And tiny Union Jacks all over the dart boards. It's attached to a pleasant restaurant—Pimblett's. *263 Gerrard St. E, west of Parliament St.; tel. 416/929–9525.*

The Unicorn, in the very hot area of Yonge/Eglinton/Mt. Pleasant, has a friendly, young (20–25) crowd. The atmosphere is very British, with a 6-foot TV screen. It has a nice, homey atmosphere that is missing from too many singles bars. Indeed, that often-unpleasant pressure just doesn't exist here; you can talk to other people without feeling as though you're about to be picked up. On one side, there's a seating area for quiet conversation; on the other, a wine bar and dart board. Both snack food and complete dinners are served. Live guitar or piano Wednesday–Monday nights. *175 Eglinton Ave. E, a few blocks east of Yonge St.; tel. 416/482–0115.*

8 Excursions

Stratford, Ontario

Ever since July 1953, when one of the world's greatest actors, Alec Guinness, joined with probably the world's greatest Shakespearean director, Tyrone Guthrie, beneath a hot, stuffy tent in a backward little town about 90 minutes from Toronto, the Stratford Festival has been one of the most successful, most widely admired theaters of its kind in the world.

The origins of the town of Stratford are modest. After the War of 1812, the British government granted a million acres of land along Lake Huron to the Canada Company, headed by a Scottish businessman. When the surveyors came to a marshy creek surrounded by a thick forest, they named it "Little Thames" and noted that it might make "a good mill-site." It was later christened Stratford, which purportedly means a narrow crossing. The year was 1832, 121 years before the concept of a theater festival would take flight and change Canadian culture forever.

For many years Stratford was considered a backwoods hamlet. Although it had the highest elevation of any town in Ontario—1,150 feet above sea level—it was too swampy to grow anything. In 1871, "Muddy Stratford" was made a division point for a major railway, attracting both industry and population. Though the river was renamed Avon, it was a stump-filled, filthy disaster, bordered by a livery stable, a junkyard, and the city dump.

Then came the first of two saviors of the city, both of them (undoubting) Thomases. In 1904, an insurance broker named Tom Orr transformed Stratford's riverfront into a park. He also built a formal English garden, where every flower mentioned in the plays of Shakespeare—monkshood to sneeze worse, bee balm to bachelor's button—blooms grandly to this day. When Tyrone Guthrie compared an aerial photograph of Stratford's park with a photo of the park in Stratford-upon-Avon, England, he was stunned to find the two nearly identical.

Then came Tom Patterson, a fourth-generation Stratfordian born in 1920, who looked around; saw that the town wards and schools had names like Hamlet, Falstaff, and Romeo; and felt that some kind of drama festival might save his community from becoming a ghost town. (The diesel was coming in, and all the steam-engine repair shops that had kept Stratford alive for generations were soon to close down.)

The story of how he began in 1952 with $125 (a "generous" grant from the Stratford City Council), tracked down the directorial genius Tyrone Guthrie and the inspired stage and screen star Alec Guinness, obtained the services of the brilliant stage designer Tanya Moiseiwitsch, and somehow pasted together a world-class theater festival in a little over one year is almost unbelievable. It is told in its entirety in Patterson's memoirs, *First Stage—The Making of the Stratford Festival*.

The festival is now moving into middle age—1993 marks its 41st season—and it has had its ups and downs. Soon after it opened and wowed critics from around the world with its professionalism, costumes, and daring thrust stage, the air was filled with superlatives that had not been heard in Canada since the Great Blondin walked across Niagara Falls on a tightrope.

The early years also brought giants of world theater to the tiny town of some 20,000: James Mason, Siobhan McKenna, Alan Bates, Christopher Plummer, Jason Robards, Jr., and Maggie Smith. But the years also saw an unevenness in productions, a dreadful tendency to go for flash and glitter over substance, and a focus on costumes and furniture rather than on the ability to speak Shakespeare's words with clarity and intelligence. Many never lost faith in the festival; others, such as Canada's greatest critic, the late Nathan Cohen of the *Toronto Star*, once bemoaned that "Stratford has become Canada's most sacred cow."

Sacred or not, Stratford's offerings are still among the best of their kind in the world, with at least a handful of productions every year that put most other summer arts festivals to shame. The secret, of course, is to try to catch the reviews of the plays, which have their debuts in May, June, July, and August in the festival's three theaters, and then book as early as you can. (*The New York Times* always runs major write-ups, as do newspapers and magazines in many American and Canadian cities.)

In recent years, the famous thrust stage at the Festival Theatre witnessed *Hamlet*, *The Taming of the Shrew*, *The Merchant of Venice*, *Guys and Dolls*, and *Carousel*. Be warned that due to the great fidelity of the stage to its Shakespearean original, it is imperative to have seats that are fairly central in the audience; otherwise, words and even whole speeches can be lost.

There is also a traditional proscenium stage, the **Avon**, where *All's Well That Ends Well*, *Our Town*, *Twelfth Night*, and the musical *Irma La Douce* have recently been presented. Connoisseurs of more daring theater—as well as the budget-conscious—should not miss **The Tom Patterson Theatre** (formerly **The Third Stage**), a more recent space that presents plays in the round and in experimental modes. In the last few years, *Twelfth Night* and *King Lear* were seen here. This is often the most exciting place to see plays, so don't panic if you can't get seats at the two larger theaters.

Arriving and Departing

By Car   "Who's going to drive from Toronto to Stratford to see Shakespeare?" was almost a mantra in the early 1950s, when the festival was struggling to get off the ground; you don't hear it much anymore. The town is only about 90 miles southwest of Toronto, and it takes but 1½ hours to drive there. Take Highway 401 west to interchange 35, then 90 north on Highway 8 and west again on the combined Highways 7/8.

By Train   This is probably the most pleasurable way to go, especially in the fall, when the leaves are doing their quick-change act. **Via Rail** (tel. 416/366–8411 or 800/561–3949) leaves Union Station at least two times a day during Stratford's high season. The trip takes about two hours. **Amtrak** (tel. 800/USA–RAIL) service from Chicago to Toronto stops in Stratford.

By Bus   Two buses leave the Dundas and Bay streets terminal each day, beginning as early as 9:30 AM. The trip can take up to three hours, though, and stops at places you never knew existed. Tel. 416/393–7911.

Guided Tours

Stratford Tours Inc. arranges a variety of tours, including dining and theater. *Box 45, Stratford N5A 6S8, tel. 519/271–8181.*

The Avon Historical Society conducts charming one-hour tours of the city, July 1–Labor Day, daily except Sunday at 9:30 AM. Meet at the tourist information booth at Lakeside Drive and Ontario Street. Tel. 519/271–5140.

Exploring

The Gallery Stratford has regular exhibits of local and Inuit art, as well as design sketches and costumes of the present year's productions. *54 Romeo St., just northeast of Festival Theatre; tel. 519/271–5271. Admission: $3.50 adults, $2.50 senior citizens and students during festival's run, free at other times. Open June–Labor Day, Tues.–Sun. 9 AM–6 PM; Labor Day–Oct., Tues.–Sun. 10 AM–5 PM; Nov.–May, Tues.–Fri. and Sun. 1–5, Sat. 10–5.*

There are many tasteful shops in the downtown area, including antiques stores, arts and crafts studios, galleries, and new and rare bookshops.

The Stratford Festival For tickets and information from late Jan. 1993, phone from Toronto, tel. 416/363–4471; from Detroit, 313/964–4668; from elsewhere 519/273–1600. Or write the Festival Theatre, Stratford, N5A 6V2.

The **Festival Theatre** (55 Queen St.) and the **Avon Theatre** (99 Downie St.) are open from early May to early November. They have evening performances Tuesday–Saturday, with matinees Wednesday, Saturday, and Sunday. Tickets are $25–$50. Rush seats are as little as one half the cost. The **Tom Patterson Theatre** (Lakeshore Drive) has a shorter season, from late May to early September. Prices are less, usually between $25 and $40.

Don't forget that **rush seats** are always available on the day of a performance, either at the **Five Star Tickets booth** in Toronto or at the various box offices, beginning at 9 AM. Tickets can also be ordered by telephone after 10 AM, but they are usually in the lowest price category.

As of 1992 two more money-saving options are available. "Family Experience" entitles adults to purchase up to two children's tickets at $13.50 each (for guests under 18) when purchasing one regular-price ticket in any price category. And The Under Thirty Theatre Club now makes it possible for those under this age to attend Tuesday and Sunday evening performances for half-price. The cost to join is only $25. Bravo!

Wheelchair seating and a mobility bus are available if requested in advance (tel. 519/271–4000). A Phonic Ear F.M. Transmitting System for the hearing impaired is available at the two larger theaters at a nominal fee; book when ordering your tickets.

Meet the Festival is a series of informal discussions with members of the company. *Kiwanis Centre, next to Tom Patterson Theatre. Admission free; no reservations required. July–Aug., Wed. and Fri., 9:30 AM–10:30 AM.*

Thirty-minute **post-performance discussions** take place at the Festival Theatre Tuesday and Thursday nights, late June to early September. *Meet at Aisle 2, Orchestra Level, after the performance. Admission free; no reservations required.*

Backstage tours are offered Sunday morning from mid-June to mid-November. Tours depart from the Festival Theatre every 15 minutes from 9 to 10:30 AM. Admission: $5 adults, $2.50 students and senior citizens. Book in advance through the Festival Box Office, although some tickets are usually available at the door.

Dining

Reviews by Joanne Kates

There is a certain inevitable mania to the Stratford dining experience. Everyone arrives in a great rush at 6 PM, eats rather quickly, and is at the theater for curtain time. We could be, in this instance, the perfect marks for lazy restaurateurs who might enjoy the financial results of quick patron processing. Other theater towns, which shall remain nameless, are guilty of this. But not Stratford. All three of the major players (The Church, sold in the summer of 1988; Rundles; and The Old Prune) tread the fine line between haste and grace, and they do so with enormous generosity of spirit. You could sling overcooked vegetables and precooked entrees our way in that situation, and few of us would have the time or the heart to complain. But these restaurants do not. They succeed at the challenge of a seasonal business that requires that the staff miraculously perform at peak levels, beginning in June, after a winter out of the saddle.

Now if someone would just open a fine hotel in Stratford, all would be well on the creature-comfort front. After a night of magic, who wants a breakfast of coffee and doughnuts in the lobby?

The following credit-card abbreviations are used: AE, American Express; DC, Diners Club; MC, MasterCard; V, Visa. The most highly recommended restaurants are indicated with a star ★.

Category	Cost*
Expensive	over $50
Moderate	$30–$50
Inexpensive	under $30

*for two, not including tax, tip, or drinks

Expensive ★ **Rundles.** It has traditionally played underdog to The Church, but the roles have reversed. It is, of course, a less consequential dining room—smaller, simpler, less formal. The terrace overlooks Lake Victoria, the windows stream with summer light, the napkins, the lamps, and the funny wood mobiles are a cheerful chorus of summer colors. Rundles has splendidly, deliciously matured. There are some who snicker at the trendiness of a menu that features peppers, goat cheese, eggplant, cabbage, and wild mushrooms, all the culinary catchphrases of the '80s. But Rundles is doing it so beautifully that one would be a fool to say no. The roasted red-pepper and eggplant terrine is a stunner, a savory layer cake iced in black-olive puree. Perfectly grilled salmon sits on mustardy *beurre blanc*. Pink roast lamb is scented with rosemary and served with a fine surprise of cabbage and white beans. The cold poached lobster comes with zingy red-pepper sauce; the duck melts in your mouth. *9 Cobourg St., tel. 519/271–6442. Reservations required many*

weeks in advance. Dress: informal. AE, MC, V. No lunch
Tues.; closed Mon.

Moderate **The Old Prune.** This could be considered a junior Rundles—a
little cheaper and a little less mastery in the kitchen. The Old
Prune's vocabulary is like Rundles: goat cheese and peppers,
raw fish, the grill rather than the oven, mustard and garlic
rather than butter and cream. The ideas are fine, but Rundles
does it with more flavor. But this is also a charmer: delightful to
look at, with gray walls and exotic flowered tablecloths, theatrical prints on the walls, and perfect posies scattered on the
Royal Albert teacups. It does well on light meals, quiches,
terrines, pâtés, and salads. *151 Albert St., tel. 519/271–5052.
Reservations recommended weeks in advance. Dress: informal. MC, V. No lunch Tues.; closed Mon.*

Picnics Given the swans and the Avon River, a Stratford picnic is a delightful preamble to the play. You can do well for under $20 for
two by stopping in Toronto at a delicatessen like **Yitz's** (346
Eglinton Ave. W, at Avenue Rd.) or a fine dairy takeout like
United Baker's (Lawrence Ave. W, at Bathurst St.). Or, for
those who like their alfresco exotic, there are picnic boxes of
raw-fish delights from **Taiko-Sushi** (Yonge St. at Wellesley
Ave.). For those whose idea of roughing it is a day with caviar,
picnics ought to be purchased from the **David Wood Food Shop**
(1110 Yonge St., south of St. Clair Ave.). It sells very expensive
salads and pâtés that will please your taste buds. **Chapman's**
(1114 Eglinton Ave. W, 3 blocks west of Bathurst St., tel. 416/
789–7306) can be counted on for delightful party sandwiches,
quality cooked meats and fish, and irresistible salads.

Lodging

Because Stratford is not a hotel city, visitors with the most sav-
vy like to stay at bed-and-breakfasts. Write to **Tourism/Strat-
ford** (City of Stratford, Box 818, 88 Wellington St., Stratford
N5A 6W1, tel. 519/271–5140, fax 519/274–5041) for the superb
Visitors' Guide: Festive Stratford, 1993, which should be out in
early February. Highly recommended hotels are indicated
with a star ★.

Category	Cost*
Very Expensive	over $100
Expensive	$75–$100
Moderate	$50–$75
Inexpensive	under $50

*prices are for doubles, excluding 7% GST (Goods and Services
Tax)*

Expensive **Festival Inn.** An old-English atmosphere has survived modern-
ization and the installation of Jacuzzi water beds in some rooms
here; located on the eastern outskirts of town, it's just a brief
ride to the theater. *1144 Ontario St., Box 811, Stratford, N5A
6W1, tel. 519/273–1150. 151 rooms with bath. Facilities: restaurant, coffee shop, baby-sitting services, tennis, indoor pool,
whirlpool, golf nearby. AE, MC, V.*
Queen's Inn. Built in 1914 to replace an earlier inn that was de-
stroyed by fire, this 30-room inn has been gutted and turned

into an elegant, if still quite small, hotel. The walls are a pleasant two-tone gray and white; the large, curved windows and bright, floral chintz sofas will charm any visitor. The dining room can be quite inventive, and next door stands a "brewpub," where homemade beer is sold only on the premises. *161 Ontario St., Stratford N5A 3H3, tel. 519/271–1400. 30 rooms with bath. Facility: lounge. AE, MC, V.*

★ **Stone Maiden Inn.** This is a beautiful and exotic place near the city center, furnished with antiques and Anglo-Indian arts from the British Raj period. Rooms vary from deluxe with whirlpool to smaller, less expensive rooms. Rates include full English breakfast. *123 Church St., Stratford N5A 2R3, tel. 519/271–7129. 14 rooms with bath. Facilities: guest lounge, outdoor area. No credit cards.*

Moderate–Expensive   **23 Albert Place.** This late-19th-century hotel was completely redecorated several years ago. It is conveniently located in the heart of the downtown shopping area, just a few hundred yards from the Avon Theatre. Suites and minisuites are available, and pets are allowed. *23 Albert St., Stratford N5A 3K2, tel. 519/273–5800. 34 rooms with bath. Facilities: coffee shop, restaurant, baby-sitting services, golf nearby. AE, MC, V.*

Moderate   **Majer's Motel.** This motel sits on landscaped grounds, a good distance from the highway. No pets. *Hwys. 7 and 8, about a mile east of the city, Stratford RR4, N5A 6S5, tel. 519/271–2010. 31 rooms (some small) with bath. Facilities: coffee shop, outdoor pool, golf nearby. MC, V.*

Swan Motel. This motel is in a quiet country setting on generous grounds, just 2 miles south of the Avon Theatre. *959 Downie St. S, RR2, Stratford N5A 6S3, tel. 519/271–6376. 24 rooms with bath. Facilities: outdoor pool, golf nearby. MC, V.*

Inexpensive   **Stratford General Hospital Residence.** Students, or those traveling on a very tight budget, pay less than $20 a night for a single room. It's modern, bright, serviceable. *Housekeeping Supervisor, Stratford General Hospital Residence, 130 Youngs St., Stratford N5A 1J7, tel. 519/271–5084 or 271–2120, ext. 586. Facilities: access to lounges, kitchenettes, laundry facilities, and parking. No credit cards.*

Niagara Falls, Ontario

Cynics have had their field day with Niagara Falls, calling it everything from "water on the rocks" to "the second major disappointment of American married life" (Oscar Wilde).

Others have been more positive. Missionary and explorer Louis Hennepin, whose books were widely read across Europe, first described the falls in 1678 as "an incredible Cataract or Waterfall which has no equal." Nearly two centuries later, novelist Charles Dickens wrote, "I seemed to be lifted from the earth and to be looking into Heaven. Niagara was at once stamped upon my heart, an image of beauty, to remain there changeless and indelible."

Writer Henry James recorded in 1883 how one stands there "gazing your fill at the most beautiful object in the world." And a half-century later, British author Vita Sackville-West wrote to Sir Harold Nicolson, "Niagara is really some waterfall! It falls over like a great noisy beard made of cotton-wool, veiled by spray and spanned by rainbows. The rainbows are the most unexpected part of it. They stand across like bridges between America and Canada, and are reproduced in sections along the boiling foam. The spray rises to the height of a sky-scraper, shot by sudden iridescence high up in the air."

Understandably, all these rave reviews began to bring out the professional daredevils, as well as the self-destructive amateurs. In 1859, the great French tightrope walker Blondin walked across the Niagara Gorge, from the American to the Canadian side, on a 3-inch-thick rope. On his shoulders was his (reluctant, terrified) manager; on both shores stood some 100,000 spectators. "Thank God it is over!" exclaimed the future King Edward VII of England, after the completion of the walk. "Please never attempt it again."

But sadly, others did. From the early 18th century, dozens went over in boats, rubber balls, and those famous barrels. Not a single one survived, until schoolteacher Annie Taylor did in 1901. Emerging from her barrel, she asked the touching question, "Did I go over the Falls yet?" The endless stunts were finally outlawed in 1912, but not before the province of Ontario created the first provincial park in all of Canada—Queen Victoria Park—in 1887.

The Falls alone—with a combined flow of close to 3 million liters per second—are obviously worth the 75-minute drive from Toronto, the 30-minute drive from Buffalo, New York, or whatever time it takes to come from anywhere else. It is, after all, the greatest waterfall in the world, by volume.

Over 10,000 years ago—long before the first "My Parents Visited Niagara Falls and All They Got Me Was This Lousy T-Shirt" T-shirts—the glaciers receded, diverting the waters of Lake Erie northward into Lake Ontario. (Before that time, they had drained south; such are the fickle ways of nature.)

There has been considerable erosion since that time: More than 7 miles in all, as the soft shale and sandstone of the escarpment have been washed away. Wisely, there have been major water diversions for a generating station (in 1954) and other machinations (1954–1963), which have spread the flow more evenly over the entire crestline of the Horseshoe Falls. The erosion is now down to as little as one foot every decade, so you needn't rush your visit.

There's some interesting history to the rest of the area, as well. The War of 1812 had settlers on both sides of the river killing one another, with the greatest battle taking place in Niagara Falls itself, at Lundy's Lane (today, the name of a major street, with a Historical Museum on the site of the battle). Soon after, at the Treaty of Ghent, two modest cities of the same name arose on each side of the river—one in the United States, the other in Canada.

Only some 70,000 people actually live in Niagara Falls, Ontario, and when one considers that close to 15 million visitors come and see the Falls every year, you can get an idea of just how central tourism is to the area. Central? Try its very raison d'être.

It's true: Niagara Falls has something for everyone. For the children, there's Marineland, water slides, wax museums, haunted houses, and more. For newlyweds, there's a Honeymoon Certificate, and free admission for the bride to everything from the giant Imax Theatre to the Elvis Presley Museum.

Sure, many of the motels and attractions are corny, even tacky, but that's really part of the charm. Three towers present their awesome views of the Falls—the **Skylon**, the **Minolta**, and the **Kodak**. The Minolta Tower has a hands-on display of high-tech camera equipment, an aquarium, and a Reptile World display. The Kodak Tower is located in **Maple Leaf Village**, which has over 80 shops, the Elvis Presley Museum, and the world's second largest ferris wheel. **Clifton Hill**, known for its rather wide selection of museums (Tussaud's Wax Museum, the Houdini Hall of Fame, Ripley's Believe It Or Not, the Criminal Hall of Fame, and the Haunted House), that you somehow managed to survive without experiencing until now, had over $1.5 million worth of improvements during 1987, including a widening of sidewalks and planting of trees. A "People Mover" system has recently been introduced, so visitors can leave their cars a good distance away and ride the system all day for a single, nominal fee.

And don't allow a winter visit to the area to put you off. **The Festival of Lights** runs from late December into mid-February. The festival is a real stunner. There are 70 trees illuminated with 34,000 lights in the parklands near the Rainbow Bridge every night from 5:30 to 10:30, plus animated tableaux of various Canadian scenes, and even a Father Frost who welcomes visitors to the Magic of Winter theme park on Buchanan Avenue in Murray Hill. *Falls illuminated nightly Nov.–Feb., 7–9:30; Mar., 7–10; Apr., 8:30–11; May–Aug., approximately 9–midnight; Sept.–Oct., approximately 8–11.*

Arriving and Departing

By Plane   The closest airport to Niagara Falls is **Buffalo International Airport. Niagara Scenic Bus Lines** (tel. 716/648–1500) operates a shuttle service from the airport to both the American and Canadian Niagara Falls. Fares are about $10 one-way.

By Car   Niagara Falls is about 80 miles southwest of Toronto, less than a 90-minute drive. Take the Gardiner Expressway west from downtown, which quickly turns into Queen Elizabeth Way (QEW), heading south around Lake Ontario. Exit at Highway 420, which runs straight into the downtown area.

By Train   **Via Rail** (tel. 416/366–8411; in Niagara Falls 716/357–1644) runs three trains a day from Toronto.

By Bus   **Gray Coach** (tel. 416/393–7911) has three buses leaving the Bay and Dundas streets terminal every morning, and then one each hour from 10 AM to 7 PM. The trip takes about two hours and costs about $40 round-trip.

Important Addresses and Numbers

Tourist Information   Contact the **Niagara Falls, Canada Visitor and Convention Bureau** (4673 Ontario Ave., Niagara Falls L2E 3R1, tel. 416/356–6061).

There is also an **Information Center** at the corner of Highway 420 and Stanley Avenue. You'll see the big TRAVEL ONTARIO sign shortly after you leave Queen Elizabeth Way, heading east into Niagara Falls.

Guided Tours

Double Deck Tours are exactly that: A double-decker bus tours the Falls and environs. During the high season, the buses operate every 30 minutes from 9:30 AM, stopping at many of the major points of interest. Although the complete tour lasts 90 minutes, you may get off at any stop and grab another bus later in the day. *Tel. 416/374–7423. Cost: approximately $16 adults, $9 children 6–12. A more complete tour lasting 5 hours costs twice as much. Meet at the Maid of the Mist bldg.; no reservations required.*

The following all have air-conditioned limos: **Embassy Limousine Service,** 6276 Main St., tel. 416/374–8401; **Honeymoon Tours,** 4943 Clifton Hill St., tel. 416/295–3034; **Niagara Scenic Drive,** 5876 Victoria Ave., tel. 416/374–7511.

Niagara Helicopters (Victoria Ave. at River Rd., tel. 416/357–5672) let you see the Falls at an unforgettable angle. Yes, major credit cards are accepted, so you won't feel the cost for weeks. *Departures Mar.–Nov., 9 AM–sunset.*

Winery Tours takes you on a 90-minute walk through the vineyards, followed by a wine tasting. The tours are free, but the bottles at the recently expanded retail wine shop are most decidedly not. *4887 Dorchester Rd., off Hwy. 420; tel. 416/357–2400. Tours May–Oct., Mon.–Sat. 10:30 AM, 2 PM, and 3:30 PM; Nov.–Apr., 2 PM only. Sun. year-round 2 and 3:30 PM.*

Exploring

Numbers in the margin correspond with points of interest on the Niagara Falls, Ontario, map.

The city of Niagara Falls, Ontario, is quite easy to picture: To the west, running north–south (and eventually east, around Lake Ontario and up to Toronto), is Queen Elizabeth Way. To the east is the Niagara River and the glorious Falls. One of the best ways to get a sense of the layout is to go up the **Skylon Tower.** It's not cheap, but the view is breathtaking. Next to the tower is the **IMAX Theater,** with its giant screen.

Clifton Hill, right near the Falls, and northeast of the Skylon Tower, is the place where most bus and boat tours begin and where many of the better attractions are located: The Oakes Garden Theater; Louis Tussaud's Waxworks; the Rainbow Carillon Tower; the Niagara Falls Museum (which is less vulgar than most); and the Daredevil Hall of Fame. In the same area is **Maple Leaf Village,** with dozens of shops, eateries, and fun-fun-fun, sell-sell-sell. (The word "souvenir" comes from the French, meaning "remember." The big question is, "Do I *really* want to remember my trip to Niagara Falls with this ugly beer glass that has a giant, drenched gorge etched into its side?")

To the north, past Robert Street, is where the Via trains pull in. Here is where you go for the Great Gorge Trip, the Spanish Aero Car, and the helicopter tours.

Just west of the Skylon and the Falls is **Lundy's Lane,** where the rows of motels and hotels look like a Monopoly board run wild. Nearby is the fine **Lundy's Lane Historical Museum.** To the south and east of the Falls is **Marineland.** Along the river is the very beautiful **Queen Victoria Park,** which also has an attractive greenhouse and even a modest-size golf course.

❶ *Maid of the Mist* boats are surely an unforgettable experience; they sail right to the foot of the Falls, and you'll be thankful for the raincoats they give out and for the exciting trip itself. *Boats leave from foot of Clifton Hill St. Tel. 416/358–5781. Cost: approximately $10 adults, $6 children 6–12. Daily mid-May– late-Oct. Late June through Labor Day, trips leave as often as every 15 minutes, 9:45–7:45; off-season boats leave every 30 minutes 9:45 –5:45 on weekends, 4:45 weekdays.*

❷ At **Table Rock Scenic Tunnels,** you don a weatherproof coat and boots, and an elevator takes you down to a fish-eye view of the Canadian Horseshoe Falls and the Niagara River and a walk through three tunnels cut into the rock. *Tours begin at Table Rock House, in Queen Victoria Park. Tel. 416/358–3268. Cost: approximately $6 adults, $5 senior citizens, $3 children 6–12. Open mid-June–Labor Day 9 AM–11 PM; 9–5 rest of year. Closed Christmas.*

❸ **Skylon** overlooks the Falls and is more than just a tower; there are amusements for children, entertainment, and shops. Rising 775 feet above the Falls, it does, indeed, have the best view of both the great Niagara and the entire city. There is also an indoor/outdoor observation deck and a revolving dining room. *Tel. 416/356–2651. Cost: approximately $7 adults, $6 senior citizens, $4 children under 13. Open 8:30 AM–1 AM. Go when Falls are illuminated, especially during Winter Festival of Lights.*

❹ The **Niagara Spanish Aerocar** (the Whirlpool Aerocar) is a cable car that carries you high over the Niagara Gorge—and back, one hopes—on a 1,650-foot-long cable. Far, far below are the river and Whirlpool Basin. *Located on River Rd., about 2 mi north of falls, tel. 416/354–5711. Cost: approximately $6 adults, $4 children 6–12. Ride runs June 1–Labor Day, 9–9; and from then until mid-Oct. when weather permits.*

❺ **Marineland** is, after the Falls themselves, the highest-quality attraction in the area. The 4,000-seat aqua theater has the world's largest troupe of performing sea lions and dolphins, as well as two killer whales, Kandu and Nootka. The "Hot Air Fantasy" consists of various animated, singing characters suspended in balloons above the aquarium. The children will be ecstatic (and so will the adults).

There are rides for all ages as well, including the world's largest steel roller coaster, spread over one mile of track and traveling through 1,000 feet of tunnels, double spirals, and giant loops. The Game Farm is also a delight, with its herd of buffalo, sloth of bears, and over 400 deer to be pet and fed. *Located 1 mi south of Falls; follow Marineland signs along parkway by Falls, or exit QEW at McLeod Rd. (Exit 27) and follow signs; tel. 416/356–9565. Admission: approximately $21 adults, $16 senior citizens and children 4–9. In winter, prices fall to less than half, because rides are closed. Open summers 9–6, off-season 10–4:30.*

❻ **Niagara Falls Museum,** at the Rainbow Bridge, includes everything from shlock to quality. Here you'll find the Daredevil Hall of Fame, dinosaurs, and a solid collection of Egyptian mummies dating from before the Exodus from Egypt. There are also In-

Niagara Falls, Ontario

dian artifacts and zoological and geological exhibits. *5651 River Rd., tel. 416/356–2151. Admission: approximately $6.50 adults, $4.50 students and senior citizens, $3.50 children 5–10. Open June–early Oct. 8:30 AM–midnight; other months, weekdays 10–5, weekends 11–5.*

7 **Lundy's Lane Historical Museum,** dating to 1874, is on the site of a savage battle in the War of 1812. There are displays of the lives of settlers of that era, as well as military artifacts. *5810 Perry St., a little over 1 mi west of Falls, on Hwy. 420; tel. 416/ 358–5082. Admission: about $1. Open May–Nov., 9–4; other months, weekdays noon–4.*

8 The **Minolta Tower-Centre** has its own attractions, beyond its rising some 665 feet above the gorge. There's an indoor observation deck and three more open ones overlooking the Falls, and the aquarium and reptile exhibit will ease the pains of children who might be denied a day at Marineland. There's an Incline Railway that will take you to and from the brink of the Falls, and its Top of the Rainbow dining rooms have won at least four restaurant awards during this decade. *6732 Oakes Dr., tel. 416/356–1501. Admission to exhibits or tower: approximately $6 adults, $4 senior citizens and children 5–18. Combination tickets: $7 adults, $6 children or senior citizens. Tower open summers 9 AM–midnight, other times: 10–10. Aquarium and reptile exhibit open May–Nov., and cost approximately $5 adults, $4 students and senior citizens.*

9 Children, and adults with great patience, will get a kick out of **Clifton Hill** (tel. 416/356–2299), where you can visit the Movieland Wax Museum, The Haunted House, The House of Frankenstein, The Funhouse, The Guinness Museum of World Records, Louis Tussaud's Waxworks, Ripley's Believe It or Not Museum, and the Super Star Recording Studio, where you can make a tape/video of your fabulous voice/face. This is tourism at its most touristy.

10 **Maple Leaf Village** is a 350-foot observation tower with rides, games, shops, shows, and one of the largest Ferris wheels in captivity. This is where you'll find—if you dare—the That's Incredible Museum and The Elvis Presley Museum. *Clifton Hill and Falls Ave., at Canadian terminus of Rainbow Bridge; tel. 416/357–3090. Prices vary for various rides; admission to village itself is free. Attractions are open mid-June–Labor Day 10 AM–midnight. Tower open year-round.*

11 The **Floral Clock** is less than 6 miles north of the Falls, along River Road. Nearly 20,000 plants that bloom from earliest spring to late autumn make up one of the world's biggest, bloomin' clocks. Chimes ring every quarter-hour, and it actually keeps the right time. *Admission free.*

12 **Queen Victoria Park** (tel. 416/356–4699) runs along the Niagara River for 24 miles. The Niagara Parks Greenhouse has four major horticultural displays each year, and there is an outdoor fragrance garden for the visually handicapped.

13 About 4 miles due north of the Falls, along the Niagara Parkway, you can visit the **Niagara Glen Nature Area,** another free and most attractive attraction. You can actually work your way down to the gorge, observing the plant life. And just a bit **14** north, along the parkway, is the **Niagara Parks School of Horticulture,** with 100 acres of free exhibits. *Tel. 416/356– 8554.*

⑮ Whitewater is a water park with everything from minislides and minipools to five giant slides and a wave pool. *7430 Lundy's La. at QEW; tel. 416/357-3380. Open mid-May–mid-September. Special rates after 6 PM.*

Dining

Reviews by Allan Gould

We hope you came here for the Miracle of Nature, not for any taste-bud magic. What Niagara Falls offers is mainly fast foods, faster foods, and fastest foods, with a handful of modest exceptions. You'll find all your old family friends—the King (of the Burger), the Baron (of Beef), Harry (of Char Broil fame), the Colonel (still frying that greasy, finger-lickin' chicken), and Mr. Ronald McDonald, whom we sense needs no introduction whatsoever. Still, there are respectable restaurants at rather moderate prices, considering what a tourist mecca this place is.

Category	Cost*
Expensive	over $25
Moderate	$15–$25
Inexpensive	under $15

**per person, excluding drinks, service, and sales tax*

Moderate **Capri Restaurant.** One of the better Italian restaurants in the area, this place offers ethnic dishes as well as steak and seafood. Its most popular dish is a huge Maritime Platter, piled high with lobster, shrimp, scallops, salmon, and more, at about $60 for two. There are three rooms, and the owner has won the "Restaurateur of the Year Award" several times. *5438 Ferry St. (Hwy. 20), about ½ mi from Falls; tel. 416/354-7519. Reservations not necessary. Dress: informal. AE, MC, V.*

Hungarian Village Restaurant. Family-owned for a half-century, it offers classic Eastern European dishes, as well as traditional Hungarian specialties—and a "famous Gypsy trio from Budapest" entertains in the evenings. There are three rooms, one of them more elegant and formal than the others. *5329 Ferry St. (Hwy. 20); tel. 416/356-2429. Reservations recommended for weekends. Dress: informal. AE, MC, V.*

The Minolta Tower Dining Room. This is on the top of you know what, and the food—veal Oskar and other meaty dishes—is trustworthy. The 26th-floor dining room is in pink and burgundy; the 27th-floor dining room is a more formal white and navy blue. *6732 Oakes Dr., tel. 416/356-1501. Reservations recommended. Dress: informal. AE, DC, MC, V.*

Reese's Country Inn. A real cut above the other restaurants in the area, it is a bit off the beaten track. It offers international cuisine in a country setting, complete with an open patio, fresh flowers, fireplace, and greenhouse. The most popular meal is rack of lamb. *3799 Montrose Rd. (Exit 32B from the QEW, then west about ½ mi on Thorold Stone Rd., and north on Montrose Rd.), tel. 416/357-5640. Reservations requested. Jacket and tie recommended. AE, MC, V. Sunday brunches and dinner.*

Rolf's Continental Dining. The French and German menu features rabbit, fillet of lamb, Dover sole, and Chateaubriand. Meals are served in three small rooms in an old house, with candlelight, fresh flowers, and sparkling china. The full-course "early dinner," served between 5 and 6 PM, costs around $15 a person. *3840 Main St., tel. 416/295–3472. Reservations recommended. Tie and jacket not required. MC, V. No lunch; closed Mon.*

Table Rock Restaurant. Standard American and Canadian fare is served in the pink-and-green dining room. As they love to advertise: "If you were any closer, you'd go over the Falls." It's true. *Located just above Scenic Tunnels; tel. 416/354–3631. Reservations advised. Dress: informal. AE, MC, V.*

Victoria Park Restaurant. Like the Table Rock, it is run by Niagara Parks. Located directly opposite the American Falls, and all done in yellows and earth tones, the eatery offers breakfast, lunch, and dinner on a patio overlooking the crashing waters. It is known for its fresh salmon, prime ribs, and generally good dining—but the view is the best of all. *Corner of River Rd. and Murray St.; tel. 416/356–2217. Reservations not necessary. Dress: informal. AE, MC, V.*

Lodging

There are so many hotels and motels in the area that you can take your pick from almost any price range, services, or facilities. Heart-shaped bathtubs, waterbeds, heated pools, Jacuzzis, baby-sitting services—the choice is yours. Prices fall by as much as 50% between mid-September and mid-May, and less expensive packages for families, honeymooners, and others are usually available.

Category	Cost*
Very Expensive	over $100
Expensive	$75–$100
Moderate	$50–$75
Inexpensive	under $50

All prices are for a standard double room, excluding 15% service charge.

Very Expensive **Michael's Inn.** Located by Rainbow Bridge, there's a view of the Falls from several balconies. *5599 River Rd., Niagara Falls, L2E 3H3, tel. 416/354–2727. 130 rooms with bath. Facilities: wading pool, heated indoor pool, sauna, whirlpool, waterbeds, sexy tubs, theme rooms, restaurant, baby-sitting services, golf and tennis nearby, tours. AE, MC, V.*

Old Stone Inn. Its charm comes from the renovated mill at its heart. Many suites have fireplaces. There is no charge for children under 14. *5425 Robinson St., Niagara Falls, L2G 7L6 (by Skylon Tower), tel. 416/357–1234. 114 rooms with bath. Facilities: restaurant, baby-sitting services, outdoor pool, whirlpool. AE, MC, V.*

Expensive **Lincoln Motor Inn.** A pleasant landscaped courtyard gives this motor inn an intimate feeling. The Falls are within walking distance. Connecting family suites sleep up to a dozen. *6417 Main St., Niagara Falls, L2G 5Y3, tel. 416/356–1748. 57 rooms with bath. Facilities: extra-large heated pool, 102-degree outdoor whirlpool spa, restaurant, baby-sitting services, beach, golf nearby. AE, MC, V.*

Quality Inn Fallsway. Located very near the Falls, the inn is on nicely landscaped grounds complete with patio. Pets are allowed. *4946 Clifton Hill, Box 60, Niagara Falls, L2E 6S8, tel. 416/358–3601. 265 rooms with bath. Facilities: indoor and outdoor pool, lounge, restaurant, baby-sitting services, golf nearby, whirlpool. AE, MC, V.*

Moderate **Canuck Motel.** Located a few blocks from the Falls, this motel has fancy tubs, waterbeds, and yet retains a family atmosphere. Housekeeping units are available. It was recently remodeled and enlarged. *5334 Kitchener St., Niagara Falls, L2G 1B5, tel. 416/358–8221. 79 rooms with bath. Facilities: heated outdoor pool, baby-sitting services, golf nearby. AE, MC, V.*

Vacation Inn. Only 2 blocks from the Minolta Tower, this hotel offers easy access to the bus terminal and highways. Some rooms have waterbeds. *6519 Stanley Ave., Niagara Falls, L2G 7L2, tel. 416/356–1722. 95 rooms with bath, some family-size. Facilities: heated outdoor pool, restaurant. AE, MC, V.*

Inexpensive **Alpine Motel.** This is a disarmingly small place, set back from the road. Rooms have refrigerators, and housekeeping units are available. *7742 Lundy's La., Niagara Falls, L2H 1H3, tel. 416/356–7016. 10 rooms with bath. Facilities: heated outdoor pool, patio, golf nearby. MC, V.*

B&Bs Contact the **Niagara Region Bed & Breakfast Service** (2631 Dorchester Rd., Niagara Falls, L2J 2Y9, tel. 416/358–8988).

Niagara-on-the-Lake

Since 1962, Niagara-on-the-Lake has been considered the southern outpost of fine summer theater in Ontario—the Shaw Festival. But offering far more than Stratford, its older theatrical sister to the north, this city is a jewel of Canadian history, architectural marvels, remarkable beauty, and, of course, quality theater. Though the town of 14,000 is worth a visit at any time of the year, its most attractive period is from late April to mid-October, when both the Shaw Festival and the flowers are in full bloom.

Being located where the Niagara River enters Lake Ontario has both its advantages and disadvantages. Because of its ideal placement, it was settled by Loyalists to the British Crown, who found a haven here when most other Americans opted for independence. Soon after, it was made the capital of Upper Canada by John Graves Simcoe. When the provincial parliament was later moved to York—today's Toronto—it changed its name from Newark to Niagara. But that, too, was wisely changed since it was continually confused with a more spectacular town of the same name, just 19 kilometers (12 miles) to the south.

The downside of its location came in the War of 1812 when the Americans came calling, but not as tourists. They captured nearby Fort George in 1813, occupied the town itself that summer, and burned it to the ground that December. The fort is now open for touring mid-May to October. Like so many other heritage sites in Ontario, it is staffed by people in period uniform, who conduct tours and reenact 19th-century infantry and artillery drills.

Some of Niagara-on-the-Lake's best days were in the 1850s, when it was connected to Toronto by steamer and to Buffalo,

New York, by train. But that era soon passed with the opening
of the Welland Canal and the transfer of the county seat to St.
Catharines. It remained a sleepy town until the last quarter-
century, when the plays of George Bernard Shaw and his contemporaries began to be performed in the Court House. Today,
Niagara-on-the-Lake is one of the best-preserved 19th-century
towns on the continent, with many neoclassical and Georgian
homes still standing proudly—and lived in, too.

The three theaters used by the Shaw Festival do indeed present quality performances—the 10 productions in the summer
of 1990 ranged from epics to murder mysteries, musicals to
comedies, even lunchtime theater—but what's also special is
the abundance of orchards and flower gardens, sailboats, and
the utterly charming town of Niagara-on-the-Lake.

Arriving and Departing

By Car   Take the QEW south and west, around the lake, to St. Catharines. At the first exit past the Garden City Skyway, drive
back north 4 kilometers (2.5 miles) to Highway 55, then turn
right for 11 kilometers (7 miles). It's a 90-minute drive.

By Bus   Most buses require a change in St. Catharines, which can be a
drag. Call **Gray Coach** in Toronto, tel. 416/393–7911.

From Niagara Falls   When you recall that Niagara-on-the-Lake is but 45 minutes
from Buffalo, and less than 20 minutes from Niagara Falls, you
may be wise to consider hooking your trip to this sparkling
town with a visit to the Falls. Contact **Blue Bird Buses** (tel. 416/
356–5462).

By Limo from   **Laskey's Airport Transportation Service of St. Catharines** (tel.
the Airports   416/685–8404 or 800/263–3636) offers door-to-door ground
transportation to and from the Toronto and Buffalo airports,
and from Niagara-on-the-Lake.

Important Addresses and Numbers

Festival schedules, lists of hotels and restaurants, and a Historic Guide are available from The Festival (Box 774, Niagara-
on-the-Lake, Ont., L0S 1J0, tel. 416/468–2153 or from Toronto
361–1544. Also contact the Chamber of Commerce, 153 King
St., Box 1043, L0S 1J0, tel. 416/468–4263).

Guided Tours

The **Niagara Foundation** visits local homes and gardens every
spring. Phone the Chamber of Commerce (tel. 416/468–4263).

Hillebrand Estates Winery (Hwy. 55, Niagara Stone Rd., tel.
416/468–7123) offers free tours, followed by a free sampling of
their award-winning products.

A much larger, more established firm is **Inniskillin Wine**, which
offers tours and has numerous displays that illustrate the wine-
making procedure inside a 19th-century barn. *Off Niagara
River Pkwy., just south of town; tel. 416/468–3554. Tours
June–Oct., daily 10:30 AM and 2:30 PM; Nov.–May, weekends
only, 2:30.*

Exploring

This is a very small town that can easily be explored on foot. Queen Street is the core of the commercial portion of this thriving mini-opolis. Walking east along that single street, with Lake Ontario to your north, you encounter many pleasures.

At **209 Queen Street** is the handsome Richardson-Kiely House, built around 1832 for a member of Parliament, with later additions at the turn of the century. At **187 Queen Street** is an 1822 house, with later Greek Revival improvements. **165 Queen Street** is an 1820 beauty, once lived in by a veteran of the Battle of Lundy's Lane, which took place in Niagara Falls in 1814. **157 Queen Street,** built in 1823, is still occupied by descendants of the Rogers-Harrison family, prominent since the early 19th century in church and town affairs. **McClelland's West End Store** (106 Queen St.) has been in business on this same site since the War of 1812, and with good reason: Its local jams and cheeses are top-notch. The huge "T" sign means "provisioner."

Across the street, but facing Victoria Street, is **Grace United Church,** built as recently as 1852. (It began as a congregation of "Free" Presbyterians, who later sold it to the Methodists.) Also at the corner of Queen and Victoria streets is the **Royal George Theater,** one of the three showcases of the Shaw Festival.

Still going east, you will come across the **Court House,** on the next block, which, until 1969, served as the municipal offices of the town of Niagara; it recently underwent an award-winning restoration. It is another of the three theaters of the Shaw Festival.

Across the street (5 Queen St.) is the **Niagara Apothecary,** built in 1820 and moved here in 1866. The oldest continuing pharmacy in Upper Canada, it was restored in 1971. Note the exquisite walnut fixtures, crystal pieces, and rare collection of apothecary glasses. *Admission free. Open mid-May–Labor Day, daily noon–6.*

Behind the Apothecary is the **Masonic Hall,** also known as the Old Stone Barracks. It went up in 1816, possibly from the rubble of the town after the War of 1812. It still houses the first Masonic Lodge in Upper Canada, and some experts believe that the first meeting of the first Parliament of Upper Canada took place on this site in 1792, when it was used as a church as well.

Continue along Queen Street to Davy Street, and turn right (south) for two blocks. At 43 Castlereagh Street is the **Niagara Historical Society Museum,** one of the oldest and most complete museums of its kind in Ontario, with an extensive collection relating to the often colorful history of the Niagara Peninsula from the earliest Indian times through the 19th century. *Tel. 416/468-3912. Admission: approximately $3.50 adults, $1.50 students, 75¢ children under 12. Open May–Oct., daily 10–5; Jan.–Feb., weekends only, 1–5; March, April, Nov., and Dec., daily 1–5.*

Two blocks east, and a few steps north, is the handsome **Shaw Festival Theatre.** Just beyond it, on a wide stretch of parkland, is **Fort George National Historic Park.** Built in the 1790s to replace Fort Niagara, it was lost to the Yankees during the war of

1812. It was recaptured after the burning of the town in 1813, and largely survived the war, only to fall into ruins by the 1830s. It was reconstructed a century later, and visitors can explore the officers' quarters, barracks rooms of the common soldiers, the kitchen, and more. *Tel. 416/468–4257. Admission: $2.50 adults, $1.50 children 5–16, $6 families, senior citizens free. Open mid-May–late June, 9–5; July 1–Labor Day, 10–6; Labor Day–Nov., 10–5.*

The Shaw Festival. The festival began modestly back in the early 1960s with a single play and an unpromising premise: To perform the plays of George Bernard Shaw and his contemporaries. Fortunately, Shaw lived into his 90s, and his contemporaries included nearly everyone of note for nearly a century.

The Shaw season now runs from April into October and includes close to a dozen plays.

Box office tel. 416/468–2172 or from Toronto 416/361–1544. Tickets in Festival Theatre run from $23 to nearly $50; in Court House and Royal George, from $20 to $40. Lunchtime Theatre, usually a one-act play, costs less than $20 per seat during its July and August run. Half-price tickets available at Five Star Ticket Booth, near Eaton Centre in Toronto, and there are always half-price Rush Seats available on day of performance, on sale at Festival Theatre Box Office. There are performances in all 3 theaters Tues.–Sun. evenings, and matinees occasionally on Wed., Fri., Sat., and Sun.

Dining

Reviews by Allan Gould

The food in Niagara-on-the-Lake is not at the level of the finest dining in Toronto, or even of Stratford. But meals are usually decent, and served in romantic, century-old surroundings.

Category	Cost*
Expensive	over $25
Moderate	$15–$25
Inexpensive	under $15

* *per person, excluding drinks, service, and sales tax*

Expensive **The Luis House—Bella's Great Food.** This family-owned restaurant features seafood and prime ribs. The ambience is homey. *245 King St., tel. 416/468–4038. Reservations recommended. Dress: informal. AE, MC, V.*

The Oban Inn. This is an elegant country inn where you can lunch on the patio and enjoy a superior view of the lake. The fare is standard—steak, beef, duck, and lobster—with a solid Sunday brunch. The fresh poached salmon is popular in the summer. The fresh-cut flowers are from the inn's own gardens. *160 Front St., tel. 416/468–2165. Reservations required. Dress: informal. AE, DC, MC, V.*

The Prince of Wales Hotel. Continental cuisine is served in a handsome Victorian setting. Lamb, fresh Atlantic salmon, and pickerel are the summer specialties. The luncheon buffet and Sunday brunches offer good value. *6 Picton St., tel. 416/468–3246. Reservations required. Dress: informal. AE, MC, V.*

Moderate **Angel Inn.** This is an English dining pub, located in the oldest operating inn in town. Specialties are steak, duck, and seafood, with an emphasis on the latter. Lots of antiques make this a handsome place to dine. *224 Regent St., tel. 416/468–3411. Reservations recommended. Dress: informal. AE, MC, V.*

Buttery Theatre Restaurant. Meals are served on a cozy terrace. On Fridays and Saturdays, there's a 2½-hour feast, "Henry VIII," that will have you looking like him when you finish. *19 Queen St., tel. 416/468–2564. Reservations recommended. Dress: informal, but jacket appropriate at dinner. AE, MC, V.*

Lodging

There are few accommodations in Niagara-on-the-Lake, but the ones that are here have unusual charm.

Category	Cost*
Expensive	over $100
Moderate	$70–$100
Inexpensive	under $70

*for a double room, excluding GST (Goods and Services Tax)

Expensive **Pillar & Post Inn.** This hotel, six long blocks from the heart of town, was built early in the century and restored in 1970. Most rooms have wood-burning fireplaces, hand-crafted pine furniture, and patchwork quilts. Wake up to free coffee and a newspaper. *48 John St., Box 1011, Niagara-on-the-Lake L0S 1J0, tel. 416/468–2123. 91 rooms with bath. Facilities: restaurant, baby-sitting services, hair dryers in rooms, outdoor pool, sauna, whirlpool, tennis, golf nearby. AE, MC, V.*

Prince of Wales Hotel. First built in 1864, this charming Victorian hotel is in the heart of town and has been tastefully restored. Deluxe and superior rooms are worth the extra price. The Prince of Wales Court, adjacent to the main hotel, has many larger, newer rooms at higher prices. *6 Picton St., Niagara-on-the-Lake L0S 1J0, tel. 416/468–3246 or from Toronto 800/263–2452. 104 rooms with bath, some with fireplaces; housekeeping units available. Facilities: restaurant, lounge, coffee shop, heated indoor pool, saunas, whirlpool, health club, tennis courts, baby-sitting services, massage, golf nearby. AE, MC, V.*

Queen's Landing. The Inn at Niagara-on-the-Lake is a remarkable new addition to an old town that has had no new places in many a year. Somehow, the owners—affiliated with the Pillar & Post—have obtained antique furnishings, and given most rooms fireplaces, and even canopy beds (and whirlpool baths, just like Granny used to have). The views are a knockout, since it is located right across from the historic Fort Niagara, at the mouth of the Niagara River. And, unlike the other century-old country inns of this lovely town, Queen's Landing has a superb indoor swimming pool, lap pool, and a fully equipped exercise room. It's a most welcome new/old inn. *Byron St., Box 1180, L0S 1J0, tel. 416/468–2195; from Toronto direct, 847–7666. 137 rooms with bath. Facilities: restaurant, lounge, heated indoor pool, sauna, whirlpool, lap pool, weight room, golf nearby.*

Moderate–Expensive   **The Angel Inn.** Each of the 10 rooms has antiques and beds with canopies. Built in 1823, this English-style inn even claims to have a resident ghost. *224 Regent St., Niagara-on-the-Lake LOS 1J0, tel. 416/468–3411. 12 rooms with bath. Facilities: restaurant, English tavern, golf nearby. AE, MC, V.*

Moffat Inn. This is a charmer, with individually appointed rooms, some with original 1835 fireplaces, outdoor patios, brass beds, and wicker furniture. Enjoy breakfast fritters on the outdoor patio. *60 Picton St., Niagara-on-the-Lake LOS 1J0, tel. 416/468–4116. 22 rooms with bath. Facilities: restaurant, baby-sitting services, golf nearby. AE, MC, V.*

The Oban Inn. Built about 1824 for a sea captain from Oban, Scotland, it was restored in 1963. The charming inn, centrally located, has broad verandas and beautifully manicured gardens. It also enjoys a waterfront view. Pets are allowed. *160 Front St., Box 94, Niagara-on-the-Lake LOS 1J0, tel. 416/468–2165. 23 rooms with bath; housekeeping units and rooms with fireplaces available. Facilities: restaurant, pub, patio bar, babysitting services, golf nearby. AE, MC, V.*

Inexpensive   **Royal Anchorage.** On the river, this is a clean and Spartan place with only 21 rooms. But what other hotel/motel in this lovely town has prices starting at less than $60 a room? *186 Ricardo St., LOS 1J0, tel. 416/468–2141. AE, MC, V.*

Bed-and-Breakfasts

Contact the **Niagara-on-the-Lake Bed & Breakfast Association** (153 King St., Box 1043, LOS 1J0, tel. 416/468–4263). The more than 60 lovely homes range in price from $60 per night up to double that.

Index

Personal Itinerary

Departure *Date*

Time

Transportation

Arrival *Date*   *Time*

Departure *Date*   *Time*

Transportation

Accommodations

Arrival *Date*   *Time*

Departure *Date*   *Time*

Transportation

Accommodations

Arrival *Date*   *Time*

Departure *Date*   *Time*

Transportation

Accommodations

Over 1500 Great Weekend Escapes...

in Six Fabulous Fodor's Guides to Bed & Breakfasts, Country Inns, Cottages, and Other Weekend Pleasures!

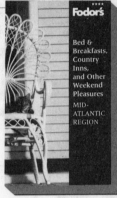

Fodor's ★★★★
Bed & Breakfasts, Country Inns, and Other Weekend Pleasures
MID-ATLANTIC REGION

The Mid-Atlantic Region

Fodor's ★★★★
Bed & Breakfasts, Country Inns, and Other Weekend Pleasures
THE SOUTH

The South

New England

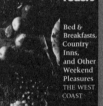

Fodor's ★★★★
Bed & Breakfasts, Country Inns, and Other Weekend Pleasures
THE WEST COAST

The West Coast

Fodor's ★★★★
Bed & Breakfasts and Country Inns
New England
and other weekend pleasures

Fodor's ★★★★
Canada's Great Country Inns
The Best in Food and Lodging
by Anita Stewart

Fodor's ★★★★
Cottages, B&Bs and Country Inns of England and Wales
Staying Off the Beaten Track
by Elizabeth Gundrey

England and Wales

Canada

Fodor's
Where the best memories begin

Fodor's Travel Guides

U.S. Guides

Alaska

Arizona

Boston

California

Cape Cod, Martha's
Vineyard, Nantucket

The Carolinas & the
Georgia Coast

Chicago

Disney World & the
Orlando Area

Florida

Hawaii

Las Vegas, Reno,
Tahoe

Los Angeles

Maine, Vermont,
New Hampshire

Maui

Miami & the Keys

New England

New Orleans

New York City

Pacific North Coast

Philadelphia & the
Pennsylvania Dutch
Country

San Diego

San Francisco

Santa Fe, Taos,
Albuquerque

Seattle & Vancouver

The South

The U.S. & British
Virgin Islands

The Upper Great
Lakes Region

USA

Vacations in New York
State

Vacations on the
Jersey Shore

Virginia & Maryland

Waikiki

Washington, D.C.

Foreign Guides

Acapulco, Ixtapa,
Zihuatanejo

Australia & New
Zealand

Austria

The Bahamas

Baja & Mexico's
Pacific Coast Resorts

Barbados

Berlin

Bermuda

Brazil

Budapest

Budget Europe

Canada

Cancun, Cozumel,
Yucatan Penisula

Caribbean

Central America

China

Costa Rica, Belize,
Guatemala

Czechoslovakia

Eastern Europe

Egypt

Euro Disney

Europe

Europe's Great Cities

France

Germany

Great Britain

Greece

The Himalayan
Countries

Hong Kong

India

Ireland

Israel

Italy

Italy's Great Cities

Japan

Kenya & Tanzania

Korea

London

Madrid & Barcelona

Mexico

Montreal &
Quebec City

Morocco

The Netherlands
Belgium &
Luxembourg

New Zealand

Norway

Nova Scotia, Prince
Edward Island &
New Brunswick

Paris

Portugal

Rome

Russia & the Baltic
Countries

Scandinavia

Scotland

Singapore

South America

Southeast Asia

South Pacific

Spain

Sweden

Switzerland

Thailand

Tokyo

Toronto

Turkey

Vienna & the Danube
Valley

Yugoslavia

Special Series

Fodor's Affordables

Affordable Europe

Affordable France

Affordable Germany

Affordable Great Britain

Affordable Italy

Fodor's Bed & Breakfast and Country Inns Guides

California

Mid-Atlantic Region

New England

The Pacific Northwest

The South

The West Coast

The Upper Great Lakes Region

Canada's Great Country Inns

Cottages, B&Bs and Country Inns of England and Wales

The Berkeley Guides

On the Loose in California

On the Loose in Eastern Europe

On the Loose in Mexico

On the Loose in the Pacific Northwest & Alaska

Fodor's Exploring Guides

Exploring California

Exploring Florida

Exploring France

Exploring Germany

Exploring Paris

Exploring Rome

Exploring Spain

Exploring Thailand

Fodor's Flashmaps

New York

Washington, D.C.

Fodor's Pocket Guides

Pocket Bahamas

Pocket Jamaica

Pocket London

Pocket New York City

Pocket Paris

Pocket Puerto Rico

Pocket San Francisco

Pocket Washington, D.C.

Fodor's Sports

Cycling

Hiking

Running

Sailing

The Insider's Guide to the Best Canadian Skiing

Fodor's Three-In-Ones (guidebook, language cassette, and phrase book)

France

Germany

Italy

Mexico

Spain

Fodor's Special-Interest Guides

Cruises and Ports of Call

Disney World & the Orlando Area

Euro Disney

Healthy Escapes

London Companion

Skiing in the USA & Canada

Sunday in New York

Fodor's Touring Guides

Touring Europe

Touring USA: Eastern Edition

Touring USA: Western Edition

Fodor's Vacation Planners

Great American Vacations

National Parks of the West

The Wall Street Journal Guides to Business Travel

Europe

International Cities

Pacific Rim

USA & Canada

WHEREVER YOU TRAVEL, *H*ELP IS NEVER FAR AWAY.

From planning your trip to providing travel assistance
along the way, American Express® Travel Service
Offices* are always there to help.

Toronto

MARKHAM
101 McNabb St.
416-474-8350

50 Bloor St. West
416-967-3411

157 Yonge St.
416-868-1044

THE BAY STORES:
44 Bloor St. East

Bramalea City Centre
25 Peel Centre Dr., Bramalea

Woodbine Centre
500 Rexdale Blvd. North
Rexdale

Fairview Mall, 1800 Sheppard Ave. E.
Willowdale

Towne and Countrye
6500 Yonge St., Willowdale

Yorkdale Shopping Centre
3401 Dufferin St.

176 Yonge St.

Shoppers World
499 Main St. South, Brampton

Hillcrest Mall
9350 Yonge St., Richmond Hill

Cedabrae Plaza
3847 Lawrence Ave. East, Scarborough

Scarborough Town Centre
300 Borough Drive, Scarborough

Eglinton Square
Eglinton & Victoria Park, Scarborough

Niagara Falls
Matthews Travel International
4685 Queen Street
416-354-5649